Sociological Perspectives on Labor Markets

Also by Bengt Furåker

LABOUR MARKET REGIMES AND PATTERNS OF FLEXIBILITY:
A Canada-Sweden Comparison
(with Axel van den Berg & Leif Johansson)

POST-INDUSTRIAL LABOUR MARKETS: Profiles of North America and Scandinavia
(with Thomas P. Boje)

Sociological Perspectives on Labor Markets

By Bengt Furåker

First published 2005 by
PALGRAVE MACMILLAN
Houndmills, Basingstoke, Hampshire RG21 6XS and
175 Fifth Avenue, New York, N. Y. 10010
Companies and representatives throughout the world

PALGRAVE MACMILLAN is the global academic imprint of the Palgrave Macmillan division of St. Martin's Press, LLC and of Palgrave Macmillan Ltd.
Macmillan® is a registered trademark in the United States, United Kingdom and other countries. Palgrave is a registered trademark in the European Union and other countries.

ISBN-13: 978 1–4039–9151–5
ISBN-10: 1–4039–9151–0

This book is printed on paper suitable for recycling and made from fully managed and sustained forest sources.

A catalogue record for this book is available from the British Library.

Library of Congress Cataloging-in-Publication Data

Furåker, Bengt, 1943–
    Sociological perspectives on labor markets / Bengt Furåker.
        p. cm.
    Includes bibliographical references.
    ISBN 1–4039–9151–0 (cloth)
        1. Labor market. 2. Labor supply. 3. Industrial relations. 4. Labor–Social aspects. 5. Industrial sociology. I. Title.

HD5706.F87 2005
306.3′6′01–dc22   2005051006

10   9   8   7   6   5   4   3   2   1
14   13   12   11   10   09   08   07   06   05

Printed and bound in Great Britain by
Antony Rowe Ltd, Chippenham and Eastbourne

Contents

List of Tables

Preface and Acknowledgments

In the academic year 2002–3 I was allowed a sabbatical leave of five months from the Department of Sociology at Göteborg University, Sweden. Thanks to this leave I could spend four shorter periods at the Department of Sociology and the Center for Comparative Research, Yale University, New Haven, USA. Being away from daily duties in one's own department certainly helps if one wants to concentrate on writing. It was during this visit that my work on this book started and when I finally left New Haven in June 2003 a first draft of the manuscript was done. Ivan Szelényi was my host at Yale and I want to thank him so much for everything that he did for me, in terms of intellectual inspiration as well as in social and practical matters. Not only did I enjoy the necessary stillness but I also had access to excellent libraries, office and computer facilities, and the opportunity of participating in a series of very interesting seminars. I also want to express my gratitude to the Swedish Council for Working Life and Social Research that financed my visit at Yale.

Back in my own department, it was a long time before I could resume work on the book, as many other obligations were waiting, but in April 2004 the manuscript was ready for being discussed in a seminar. Jan Ch. Karlsson from Working Life Science, Department of Business and Economics, Karlstad University, Sweden, was the commentator and I want to thank him for numerous fruitful comments and suggestions, most of which I have tried to consider in the final version. In addition, Dan Jonsson, a colleague at the sociology department in Göteborg, read Chapter 8 carefully and provided many valuable comments that I am also very grateful for. My work has moreover benefited from both specific comments from and general discussions with project co-workers and participants in the seminars that I have organized on the topics in the book. Besides to Jan Ch. Karlsson and Dan Jonsson my thanks go to (in alphabetical order): Mattias Bengtsson, Tomas Berglund, Gunilla Bergström, Paula Berntsson, Marianne Blomsterberg, Jonas Carlsson, Per Gustafson, Lars Hansen, Kristina Håkansson, Tommy Isidorsson, Pal Orban, Bengt Rundblad, Tiiu Soidre, Lennart Svensson, Stefan Schedin, and Rolf Törnqvist.

1
Introduction

Labor markets are crucial institutions in contemporary capitalist countries. It is through them that most people of working age are able to find employment and earn a living. Whatever happens with employment and unemployment is usually considered highly significant news and is accordingly reported on a regular basis in the media. We encounter an incessant stream of information on the creation of new jobs and workplaces as well as on layoffs and plant closures. It is over and over again intensely debated what governments and other actors can and should do to expand employment and to reduce unemployment. Statistical reports on whether the number of jobs and the number of unemployed increases or decreases play a decisive, and often contested, role in the public discussion and the political struggle. A further aspect behind all this attention is that labor markets affect not merely the individuals directly involved in them but all citizens, their financial and social situation, not to mention their whole life.

This book is an attempt to provide conceptual tools and theoretical perspectives that can be put into operation to analyze labor markets sociologically in modern societies and the events and developments that take place there. As the literature on the sociology of labor markets is substantial, my work is very much a matter of discussing and evaluating existing contributions in the field and of selecting among them. Even if this book is not an empirical study, the tools and perspectives that I find useful will also to some extent be applied on concrete phenomena. I try to combine abstract theoretical reasoning with theoretically founded reflections on actual labor market developments. The guiding principle behind this is that theory must be applicable to reality; otherwise there is no point to it.

We should observe that labor markets are not only associated with capitalism, although we have a tendency to think of them in that way. This tendency, I believe, has to do with the fact that countries in which capitalism has a dominant position are often labeled 'market economies'. However, labor markets are also connected with other kinds of socioeconomic structures. In the following chapters, some reference is made to

1

pre-capitalist and state socialist nations and, more importantly, a good proportion of the discussion will be about non-capitalist sectors in capitalist countries. Nevertheless, the analysis mainly deals with advanced capitalism, and my ambition is to elaborate concepts and theoretical perspectives that can be used to account for as much as possible of the variety that modern labor markets show.

Theory and concepts as tools

I am conviced that we need to put more effort into developing sociological theory. This is not an easy task and it seems that all attempts to do so have run into difficulties of one kind or another; no one can successfully claim to have formulated the only right solution. We can recall Talcott Parsons's ambition to build a general, 'grand' theory that on the highest workable level of abstraction would grasp society as a whole. One of the lessons appears to be that very abstract conceptual categories run the risk of being empty, as, among others, C. Wright Mills has so entertainingly demonstrated to us. As a result, the concepts may be of little use when we want to analyze concrete phenomena. It is thus easy to agree with Robert Merton's proposal that we concentrate on 'middle-range' theory, situated on a lower level of abstraction where the specificities of a particular field can be incorporated. However, it should be possible to operate on different levels simultaneously and this was actually also Merton's position.

Another problem is that in all attempts to build conceptual frameworks significant parts of reality are excluded and made invisible; no theoretical categories can give us more than a partial picture of the world. Moreover, seemingly neutral concepts may carry hidden value assumptions; it is difficult or perhaps even impossible to avoid such connotations. We thus find several reasons to be distrustful of theoretical and conceptual endeavors, but the conclusion from this observation is not that theoretical work should be abandoned; theory is a tool that cannot be dispensed with in the production of knowledge. Therefore, instead, we need to examine and discuss with great care the categories proposed and used by researchers. In fact, I occasionally suggest redefinitions of existing concepts in order to neutralize their value load and hence to make them more useful. This is not to say that my text is value-free; with respect to certain issues, I do not want to hold back my value judgments and personal opinions. However, the analytical ambition in my treatise is about something else; it is a matter of creating conceptual tools that are as open and practical as possible.

Basically there are two kinds of tools to be used in scientific work: first, theory, or – to be less pretentious – theoretical concepts, and, second, methods for empirical investigation. Theory deals with concepts and their interrelationships and is aimed at helping us understand and explain how and why things happen in the world. Although the term method is most frequently taken to refer to techniques applied in the collection and processing of empirical data, it can also be employed in connection with theoretical work. In the latter case, it refers to the ways in which concepts are constructed and put together into devices enabling us to see patterns in a seemingly chaotic world and to find meaningful explanations for them. It also refers to meta-theoretical – ontological and epistemological – assumptions. This book is not about empirical investigation but an attempt to develop theoretical concepts and perspectives that can make it possible for us to understand and explain how labor markets work. The method aspect involved has to do with how these tools are elaborated and what meta-theoretical assumptions that are made.

Treating concepts and theories as a kind of tool will hopefully help demystify them, which is important, since an aura of obscurity is sometimes associated with theoretical work. There may be different reasons for this, but one aspect is the lack of clarity that is more common in sociological theorizing than many of us would like to see. Partly, it may be a communication problem; the terminology used by sociologists is generally close to or coincides with ordinary language, which may cause difficulties when concepts are given specific definitions, implying some deviation from their common meaning. It may indeed be confusing that a concept thus can have one signification in a sociological treatise and another, very different signification, in daily conversations. Besides that, the writing style of sociologists is frequently exasperating and although this problem can be a matter of poor handling of the language, there sometimes seems to be more to it. Clarity does not invariably appear to be essential and once in a while one might even suspect that some authors wish to be obscure in order to engage people in interpreting what they actually mean.

Theoretical outlook

In the social sciences, and not least in sociology, we find several, more or less competing theories or theoretical paradigms and it may be asked if this is a sign of poverty or immaturity or, on the contrary, richness. When a discipline rests on a clearly dominant theoretical paradigm, people might interpret this as a manifestation of maturity. However, if we are not convinced that the final truth has been discovered or even that there will ever be a final truth, we may take some comfort in the existence of alternative solutions, which can at least function as correctives to one another.

In the mid-twentieth century, structural-functionalism had a dominant position in sociology or at least in Anglo-American sociology. However, in the 1960s and the 1970s this theoretical perspective came under heavy attack and was soon driven away from the throne. It was a turbulent time and several questions can be raised in relation to the development that took place: Why could not structural-functionalism defend its hegemonic position? Was the assault on it due to its scientific deficiencies or to other factors? Did the theoretical challengers solve the problems that structural-functionalism had been unable to solve? Were their attacks justified on theoretical and empirical grounds and did they come up with more adequate explanations of the world? There were undoubtedly many good reasons to criticize structural-functionalism, for example for its difficulties in dealing with conflict and change, but the criticism was partly based on a caricature of it and was blind to its actual achievements. As a consequence, sometimes everything was rather indiscriminately discarded.

For a while, Marxism may have been a candidate to become the successor of structural-functionalism, but it never got the same dominant position and its hot season did not last long. The main reason for its short peak period was that it did not achieve its status from intra-scientific merits but was based on a wave of political activity. Marxism could provide answers to some, but far from all, of the questions that were raised and its limitations were very much related to the fact that it was theoretically undeveloped or underdeveloped. Sociologists who wanted to apply Marxist theory had to return to the texts of the founding fathers, rely on the stereotyped versions of it provided in the 'really existing' socialist bloc, or try themselves to modernize it. To evaluate, revise and develop the existing arsenal of theoretical tools was an immense task and the attempts to do so occurred in a climate of heated political debates. In view of that, the prospects for failure were considerable and, not very surprisingly, it soon became obvious that Marxism would not become all that successful in accounting for the developments of modern capitalism. Accordingly, it was deserted by many of its celebrated supporters, but despite this it did not entirely leave the arena. By a process of secularization at least some versions or branches of Marxism have survived and become a 'normal' way of analyzing socioeconomic realities, distant from the far-reaching claims and proclamations that were made a few decades ago. In that way, it can continue to play a productive role in the analysis of social and economic structures and processes, although a much more modest role than once expected.

Today no theoretical perspective is clearly dominant in sociology. Many sociologists would probably characterize themselves as working in a Weberian tradition or at least as inspired by Max Weber's work. They generally have a rather humble attitude in relation to other theories, although they can be very sharp in their criticism of varieties of Marxism. One of their merits is their systematic avoidance of mono-causal explanations; their point of departure is instead that social phenomena are generally determined by multiple factors out of which no one can *a priori* be treated as the most significant. Consequently, Weberians do not, for example, endorse the simplified base-superstructure interpretation of society that we find in conventional Marxist accounts. Weberian thinking will probably play a crucial role in most serious attempts to develop sociological theory, but it seems unlikely that it will rise to the same hegemonic position that structural-functionalism once had.

In recent decades, several individual sociologists have tried to build up their own perspectives. Most notably perhaps, during the course of several decades, Pierre Bourdieu elaborated his field theory that has attracted considerable attention. It is an approach with a language of its own and its role in the development of sociological theory remains to be assessed. Until now at least, it does not appear to be on par with structural-functionalism, Marxism, and Weberianism. From the viewpoint of my book, it must also be emphasized that Bourdieu's contribution to the study of labor markets is limited. More recent post-modernist writings neither make much difference in that respect; with few exceptions they have left little direct imprint on labor market studies. For the time being we must conclude that the state of sociology is rather indeterminate and the discipline can therefore be expected to stay multi-paradigmatic for the foreseeable future.

The present work does not line up behind any particular theoretical approach. I have tried to elaborate my own synthesis of what I consider the most relevant and interesting contributions that sociologists and other social scientists have made for the purpose of analyzing labor markets. My thinking has roots in Marxist, Weberian, structural-functionalist as well as other theoretical outlooks. I have not hesitated to draw on work that I consider has something to contribute, whatever theoretical label is attached. This is evidently an eclectic approach and as such open to criticism, although the verdict should not be brought in beforehand but should deal with specific violations of theoretical respectability. Moreover, picking up concepts from one theoretical framework does not require that one has to buy the whole package. Concepts are not theories but can sometimes be made fit in with different theories; then again, I admit and emphasize that there are limits to this.

Innumerable theoretical discussions, over the years, have been devoted to spelling out differences within sociology; sometimes this has been both justified and fruitful, but the gaps between contenders are often exaggerated. In the light of past disputes, I entertain a certain weakness not to mention preference for synthesizers compared to separatists. Despite significant dissimilarities, there are many affinities between, for example, Marxist, Weberian, and structural-functionalist accounts. My inclination is to play down some of the differences that we find in the literature, but hopefully not unreasonably much. Sociologists have made many valuable contributions to our understanding of social life, even if they have had separate theoretical bases as their point of departure. In a way, this book is my homage to sociology or, rather, to those parts of it that have stimulated my thinking.

However, it is appropriate or even necessary for me to take at least one step backward. What has just been said does not at all mean that I consider all sociological theorizing equally good or bad. On the contrary, I do not hesitate to denounce approaches that in my opinion are flawed or ill-founded. The reader will find several examples of this throughout the book; it is not at all free from polemic argumentation. I simply want to keep away from making too much out of differences that might not be as important as we have been accustomed to think. To illustrate my position, a few examples will be provided of how I look at the heritage that Marx and Weber have left.

In the following chapters, several Marxist concepts – such as labor market, labor power, mode of production, relations of production, and productive forces – will appear. However, to some extent I use these concepts in my own way or, perhaps more adequately, in a Weberian way (if that is possible). For example, whereas Marx made a distinction between labor power (people's capacity for work) and labor (work) in order to develop his theory of capitalist exploitation, I keep that distinction because of other reasons. In the Marxist labor theory of value, capitalists hire labor power from workers and pay for their reproduction but not for the surplus that they produce; this is in essence how the mechanisms of capitalist exploitation are accounted for. On grounds to which I briefly return in Chapter 2, I do not adhere to this theory, but I nevertheless find it important to keep some of the conceptual framework. To say that workers hire out their labor power to employers in exchange for money is still the most adequate description of what takes place. (Labor power is inseparable from the human being – which means that in a 'free' labor market the employers hire it only for a limited part of the day – whereas work is an activity that makes use of this specific kind of human capacity.)

Also Weber has provided several useful concepts – for example power, state, social exclusion, and monopolization – and they will show up in the forthcoming chapters, but the perhaps most important components of Weberian sociology are the openness for multifaceted explanations and the anti-determinist approach to history. Marxist historical materialism identifies factors in the economic sphere as crucial for society's development. Reasonable interpretations of historical materialism – to be distinguished from more 'vulgar' interpretations in which the economy mechanically determines everything – admit that ideological and political circumstances also have some role to play. Yet, this role generally appears to be very secondary and it is often difficult to see its concrete implications. Weberians have no attachment to any particular model of how society is structured or to any sterile model of causality and they can therefore allow themselves to be more receptive to the impact of other factors (as, for example, the Protestant ethic).

At the same time, in dealing with labor markets, the centrality of the economy is obvious; labor markets are part of the economic system. To understand what happens with such phenomena as employment and unemployment we must look at the development of the economy. Nevertheless, we need to be open for the possible influence of political, cultural, and other factors and I find no reason to make any *a priori* declarations about how different explanatory factors rank in relation to one another. The simple base-superstructure metaphor is not the most informative guide in our search for explanations of social phenomena and developments. It may be essential as a corrective to naïve idealism to emphasize the importance of economic factors, but the question nevertheless remains what impact cultural, ideological, political, and other non-economic factors really have. How, when, and to what degree do various elements of the so-called superstructure have a significant role to play? To what extent are they independent of or even contradictory to the functioning of the economy?

Another example of how Weber's sociology differs from that of Marx relates to class analysis. Marx's view contains the assumption that the proletariat under capitalism will develop a collective consciousness and collective action, thus forming a social force that will eventually do away with capitalism. The basis for this is that the industrial working class is subordinated to and exploited by capitalists. In contrast, Weber's perspective is that workers' collective consciousness and collective action can be considered only a possibility and nothing to be taken for granted. A given class situation provides the potential for a common way of thinking and acting, but whether or not this potential will unfold depends on a number of different factors. The Weberian position is hence less presupposing and, in my opinion, it represents a preferable way of reasoning.

A few comments should also be made in relation to functionalism, be it of Parsonian, Marxist, or any other brand. Any view of society as an organism in which all phenomena have a function for the totality implies indefensible assumptions. We cannot presuppose that all phenomena are related to the totality in such a way and that they have a positive role in it. Merton has made it clear that such an approach cannot be justified and he has therefore argued in favor of another perspective. The alternative is that we look at the consequences, intended or unintended, manifest or latent, of various elements on the social structures and processes. Actually, this is a common way of analyzing social life and, among other things, it has the advantage of making us see that certain phenomena may have a negative impact upon other phenomena, that is, that they are dysfunctional for them. Despite these merits, the danger still exists that we gear into untenable functionalist assumptions.

Issues concerning the rationality in human action are frequently and intensely debated within sociology. In Weber's typology of social action there is a distinction between instrumentally rational and value-rational action besides two other types, labeled affective and traditional respectively. From Parsons we learn that rationality has to do with the relationship between means and ends and rational behavior signifies choosing the means that are best suited to lead to a desired end. However, we cannot expect actors always to look for the optimal alternative, since they do not have complete information and it would be very costly and impractical for them constantly to try to become perfectly informed. As suggested by Herbert Simon and James March, they can instead be assumed to look for satisfactory alternatives and human action is thus characterized by 'bounded' rationality. This way of formulating the issue still allows us to distinguish between varying degrees of rationality, which must also include irrationality, as actors sometimes select means that are non-functional for the achievement of desired goals. We should also be aware of the difficulties in determining whether people are actually able to know the consequences of choosing various means. On the whole, however, it seems to be a reasonable assumption that human beings generally develop some degree of bounded rationality, but I do not want to make any very strong claims in this respect.

The ontological and epistemological assumptions underlying my work belong to a realist perspective. In my view, what people see in the world is dependent upon what they are looking at, although it is also very much colored by their conceptual 'glasses'. I thus assume that the world has an objective existence outside the observer. Strictly speaking, this statement may be impossible to prove, but the alternative solution is unworkable, as it would simply mean that we reduce everything to the subjectivity of the observer. Such a position is nothing but solipsism that ultimately makes us incapable of claiming any common knowledge at all. It is necessary to treat reality as both objective and subjective and, contrary to what some theorists want to accomplish, I do not aim at overcoming this distinction. The reason is that I find it useful or even indispensable for our orientation in the world.

To my mind, there is an outside, objective world and it is possible to acquire knowledge about it, although we have no way to guarantee that our knowledge is accurate. What we have is no more than certain rules to guide our scientific efforts. In empirical sociological work there are guidelines to follow concerning, for example, how to treat historical sources, how to draw representative samples, how to phrase questions in questionnaires and interviews, how to process quantitative and qualitative data, and what conclusions various kinds of data allow. With respect to theoretical work, our rules have to do with logic and conceptual clarity. Concepts should be defined and interrelated in a systematic, stringent, and logically coherent way. The categories used in a classification are required to be mutually exclusive and to cover all relevant phenomena. Hypotheses should be derived logically from theory and they should be consistent with one another.

Still, no guarantees can be given; we know a lot about this world, but knowledge that seems accurate today may have to be modified tomorrow or even completely deserted. New theoretical insights, perspectives, and concepts may overrun well-established ways of thinking. The most crucial part of the scientific endeavor, however, lies in the confrontation of theory with empirical observations and in this respect I think we need to take in the spirit of Karl Popper. Although empirical data are not independent of the observer's world view and conceptual tools, when treated scientifically they provide some basis to judge whether general theoretical reasoning or specific hypotheses hold or do not hold. To obtain reliable knowledge is the ultimate goal of science, and the mechanisms of verification and falsification are the principal ways in which this is done.

In this book, I outline several theoretical perspectives that can be applied to labor markets, above all in advanced capitalist societies. My ambition is to formulate concepts, relate them to one another, and develop the tools in our analytical arsenal. This endeavor involves clarification of concepts and of their interconnectedness and the outcome will hopefully be a set of theoretical devices and a theoretical framework, which can be used for the purpose of understanding and explaining labor market developments as well as for generating hypotheses to be tested in empirical studies.

The structure of the book

In concluding this introduction, I wish to give an overview of the structure of the book. The next three chapters are intended to present the fundamental theoretical structure of my approach. Chapter 2 deals with the basic concepts, first and foremost the concept of labor market but also several closely related concepts such as labor power, employment contract, job, occupation, capitalist versus other labor markets, mode of production, marketness, commodification and decommodification. In this account and discussion I turn both to classical sociology and to more recent theories. Concepts frequently have a variety of meanings in the literature and I try to trace the most useful alternatives, although even these may sometimes need to be elaborated or redefined.

When the fundamental conceptual building-blocks have been put in place, we must move beyond the most abstract concept of labor market, because in the real world we easily discover numerous ways of identifying submarkets. The overriding motive behind Chapter 3 is to describe some basic structural features of our object of study and this endeavor starts out from the assumption that jobs tend to cluster along certain lines. There are several factors that cut up the labor market into different slices; for example, we find divisions in terms of geographic location, occupation, sector, class, gender, and ethnicity. These divisions also provide a basis for studying individuals' mobility, that is, their movements between places, occupations, social classes, etc.

The next step in my analysis is to turn to the principal actors in the labor market and their interaction. Chapter 4 distinguishes five main categories of actors: jobseekers/workers, employers, employees' organizations, employers' organizations, and the state. It starts by analyzing recruitment and separation processes and brings up such concepts as selection, discrimination and matching. Once individuals have been recruited to jobs, they interact with employers regarding the various conditions under which their work tasks are to be carried out. There are many issues involved, related to work organization, workers' motivation and performance, work control and the reactions to it, and so on. The interplay between employers and employees partly takes place through their respective collective organizations and some attention will be paid to these organizations and certain problems associated with them, particularly on the side of the workers. Finally, the role of the state in relation to the labor market is discussed.

Chapter 5 takes a closer look at how the commodity status of labor power is affected by diverse social and economic factors. Many individuals are under strong pressure to offer their labor power for hire in the market to earn a living, whereas others have alternative ways of supporting themselves. However, even if people are in a position to refrain from paid work, they may be attracted by the material and immaterial remunerations offered. There are accordingly – to use the language that I suggest – mechanisms of both commodification and decommodification. The aim of this chapter is to investigate some of the forces and mechanisms in operation; I concentrate on processes within the economy, the family, and the state, bringing up such questions as the wearing out of workers' capacities for work, the opportunities of self-employment, the family as a reproductive unit and supplier of labor, and the intervention of the welfare state in the labor market.

The next four chapters all concentrate on specific developments in the labor market and on how different theorists interpret them. Chapter 6 brings up the issue of what comes after the industrial epoch or, rather, after the period when industrial employment reached its height. Post-industrial theory, taken in a broad meaning, represents a main approach in accounting for what has happened and what is going on, and different authors – from Daniel Bell and onward – put more or less emphasis on the expansion of services, information, and knowledge. More recently, attention has been focused on processes of globalization and internationalization. There is a good deal of debate as regards how modern societies are changing and I spell out some of the dividing lines and try to draw certain conclusion for my own part. The chapter ends by taking up some of the possible consequences for labor markets.

Chapter 7 is devoted to a discussion of the individual–collective character of the employment relationship and the tendencies toward de-collectivization and individualization. Among other things, there has been a considerable decline in unionization and union influence in many advanced capitalist countries. The literature in the field provides a range of explanations for this development and other processes of de-collectivization and some of it is touched upon. Authors such as Ulrich Beck and Elisabeth Beck-Gernsheim have put forward a strong thesis of individualization that is presented and scrutinized in the chapter. I also contrast the individualization thesis with what I see as enduring collective features in working life, for example that work continues to have a markedly social character and that people tend to compare themselves with their workmates. Furthermore, it is argued that the trend toward professionalization means that a new mixture of individualism and collectivism is growing.

Next I turn to the issue of labor market flexibility, which has been intensely debated over the last few decades. In Chapter 8, besides the concept of flexibility, I also take the concept of stability into consideration as well as the antonyms of the two categories: inflexibility and instability. It is, moreover, important that we identify the units of analysis, for example individuals, organizations, and the labor market as a whole, as this will help us see the possible conflicts involved: between workers and employers or between different categories on the two sides. In addition, the chapter presents a typology of flexibility that is used in a subsequent discussion of several topics and it will then become clear that flexibility types can be functional alternatives to one another. If one kind of adjustment cannot be accomplished, the same goal may be obtained, more or less, through some other arrangement. It is suggested that actual solutions often consist of what I refer to as flexibility mixes.

In Chapter 9, my focus is on certain arguments regarding the fact that large numbers of people are left outside of working life, even though they want and would be able to take a job. Unemployment, marginalization, and exclusion can no doubt be considered some of the most serious problems of contemporary capitalist labor markets and must indeed be taken seriously. First, however, these concepts need to be defined and I spend some energy on that. Next I pay attention to the diagnoses by some authors that modern capitalist countries tend to develop into 'two-third societies' or undergo a process of 'Brazilianization'. There are also those who claim that 'work-based society' is heading toward its end – or even that it should come to a halt – and therefore advocate a basic income for all citizens. This picture of the development of modern capitalist labor markets is examined and discussed.

The final chapter (10) returns to some of the concepts and analyses in the book, but besides that it concentrates on the overall issue whether labor markets are undergoing dramatic change or whether they tend to keep their fundamental characteristics. In my opinion, the literature and the public debate today often put too much emphasis on change. The recent discussion on labor market developments is full of 'end-of' theses: end of industrialism, the nation-state, government regulation, class, unionism, collectivism in general, standard employment, wage-work, or even work society itself. Although I do not at all deny that significant changes have taken place, I wish to emphasize that labor markets in many respects remain the same as before. The reason is of course that employment relations are to a large extent part and parcel of the capitalist mode of production and capitalism at present sits more firmly in the saddle than it has in a very long time. All the same, it is important to take both continuity and change into consideration or – to phrase it differently – to study which phenomena undergo change and which do not.

2
Some Concepts with Which to Start

This chapter is aimed at presenting and discussing certain key concepts that will appear throughout the book. First, of course, there is a need to define the main institution under scrutiny: the labor market. People use the words labor market in their daily conversations and probably have no difficulties at all to convey what they mean or to understand what others mean by it. When pursuing theoretical work, however, we should make our concepts as distinct as possible, avoiding the kind of vagueness that often accompanies daily language. We must therefore take a closer look at the notion of labor market and the purpose is to provide a definition that can be of use both in the treatment of various theoretical issues and in empirical analysis. In this elaboration I also run into several related concepts – such as labor power, job, occupation, and employment contract – and they all need to be specified.

After the first rather lengthy section, I consider how labor markets are connected to the capitalist sector as well as to other parts of the socioeconomic system in modern societies. It is sometimes supposed that capitalism – where it is the dominant mode of production – is overpowering everything else. In my opinion this is not a satisfactory assumption, because it simplifies too much a complex reality. Societies in which capitalism has a dominant role are not completely ruled by it, even if other sectors have a subordinate position; what I am suggesting also applies to labor markets and we should thus distinguish between different segments of them. At the same time, I utilize the concept of 'marketness' that will be presented and developed below. Its main advantage is that it provides us with an instrument to see how much market there is in a given market.

Finally, I introduce the concepts of commodification and decommodification. They do not frequently appear in the public debate – probably because they are clumsy and not very well established among observers and commentators – but I nevertheless believe that they can be valuable devices in the analysis of labor market issues. The two concepts are applicable, for example when we want to deal with the relationship between the welfare

13

state and the labor market. However, as clarified toward the end of the chapter, there are reasons to raise some questions regarding how they are usually conceived; we need to eliminate some of their value load and I therefore to some extent modify the definitions to which we have become accustomed in the last few decades.

The labor market: hiring labor power

As the labor market is a subtype of the overall market, an appropriate start-ing point is to say something about the general concept. It has been dis-cussed by, among others, Neil Fligstein (2002: 30) and in his analysis markets are treated as 'fields', taken to signify 'social arenas that exist for the production and sale of some good or service'. Moreover, they are char-acterized by 'structured exchange', which means that the activities in ques-tion are expected to occur repeatedly and hence to require a set of guiding rules and organizing devices. In other words, unstructured or 'haphazard' exchange – of which history is full – does not seem to fall under the market concept. However, this is not the full story, because there is actually some further specification provided. Fligstein (2002: 30–1) suggests that a given market may become 'a "stable market" (i.e., a field) when the product being exchanged has legitimacy with customers' and when the dominant suppli-ers of goods or services 'are able to reproduce themselves on a period-to-period basis'. It thus appears that the author wants to distinguish between markets and 'stable' markets; only the latter category can be treated as a field.

There are certain merits with Fligstein's definition, but I prefer not to include production in the market concept; the two phenomena should be kept analytically distinct from one another. Fligstein justifies his solution by saying that buyers and sellers cannot exist without products and that someone has to produce them. No doubt, he puts the finger on an impor-tant aspect, but it is obviously possible to sell or hire out non-products such as fishing and hunting rights. Moreover, production can result in goods and services that are not taken to any market; most of what people in modern societies produce in their homes are never offered for sale. The conclusion is that production should not be included in the market concept, but as the two are in general closely interrelated they will both have a central role throughout my exposition.

Furthermore, it seems unnecessary to confine the market concept, as Fligstein does, to structured exchange. At least as a beginning, we should develop a more abstract and thus simpler definition. Karl Polanyi (1957: 56, 72) has defined market as 'a meeting place for the purpose of barter or buying and selling' and, empirically, 'as actual contacts between buyers and sellers'. For reasons that will soon be spelled out, however, it must be underlined that the concept also covers hiring activities and, accordingly,

I take markets to stand for arenas in which objects are exchanged between buyers and sellers or are hired and hired out. The objects in these transactions can be almost anything, for example goods, services, land, stocks, patents, currencies, and – as is much discussed in this chapter and this book – labor power. In addition, money or other kinds of payment are involved in the exchange and it should also be emphasized that certain rules and organizing devices are indispensable.

Labor power, the object for the transactions in the labor market, refers to people's capacity to carry out work or, to use Karl Marx's words in the first volume of *Capital* (1996: 177), 'the aggregate of those mental and physical capabilities existing in a human being, which he exercises whenever he produces a use value of any description'. Generally we refer to the objects that people exchange as commodities, although – as suggested above – they do not have to be things. Human labor power is not a physical thing such as a table or a chair, but it may nevertheless appear as a commodity in the labor market; its price is referred to as wage or salary.

Three aspects of labor power

People's capacities to carry out work, their labor power, can be analyzed along different dimensions. An essential aspect is the biological capacities of individuals: their physical strength, speed, endurance, concentration, etc. For some kinds of work, also in contemporary technologically advanced societies, it is indeed important to have good physique and strong muscles. It goes without saying that things have changed substantially over the decades; muscles used to be an essentially more vital asset earlier in history, before modern technology made the majority of work tasks much less bodily demanding. Nevertheless, we must emphasize that a minimum of physical capability is necessary in all sorts of work. To lecture in sociology may above all be considered an intellectual task, but it cannot be done without some physical strength. Those teachers who have tried to lecture while, for example, suffering from flu, are likely to know exactly to what I am referring.

Qualifications represent another aspect of labor power. They include all types of skills and knowledge applied in the production of goods and services. The term 'unskilled' worker most of all seems misleading, because even the most menial jobs require some qualification. In addition, both theoretical knowledge and practical skills are relevant; the two aspects appear side by side, although the ways in which they are combined vary from one job to another. Workers generally acquire their qualifications partly through the educational system and partly through the workplace. Whether on-the-job training is more important than formal education, or vice versa, is a question to be answered through empirical investigation and the answer can be expected to differ from one case to another.

Over the last decades, a great deal of attention has been paid to the changes regarding skills and qualifications in modern economies (see, e.g., Kerr *et al.* 1960; Blauner 1964; Braverman 1974; Gallie *et al.* 1998: Ch. 2; Kern and Schumann 1990; Piore and Sabel 1984). Some argue that most jobs now demand much more qualified workers than ever before; upgrading is for them the major trend and, among other things, they refer to the fact that people stay longer in the school system. Others have drawn the opposite conclusion that jobs have generally become less demanding in terms of qualifications; degrading is thus the dominant feature in the development of labor markets. That people now on average spend more years in education is seen as related to mechanisms of competition and selection. Although far from all jobs really require advanced qualifications, employers are assumed to have a preference for better-educated employees and jobseekers consequently need to have trustworthy credentials to be competitive. Yet other analysts suggest that polarization is the main trend, that is, the gap between the top and the bottom of the job hierarchy has become wider.

To be all-inclusive, the concept of labor power qualifications has to cover social competence as well. The latter concept, including the more or less synonymous terms cultural and emotional competence, is frequently used in other contexts, for example in connection with the psychological development of children, the treatment of psychiatric patients, and the adjustment of immigrants to their new country. Turning to working life issues, we can quote C. Wright Mills (1956: 182) from his book *White Collar*, where he points out that with 'the great shift from manual skills to the art of "handling", selling, and servicing people, personal or even intimate traits of the employee are drawn into the sphere of exchange and become of commercial relevance, become commodities in the labor market'. This quotation is part of an analysis of 'The Great Salesroom' – the expanding consumer markets in mid-twentieth century United States – but the formulation is valid too for other fields. A related concept is that of emotional labor; it can be exemplified by flight attendants who obviously perform some physical work, but who are also, in relation to passengers, supposed to bring about 'the sense of being cared for in a convivial and safe place', requiring 'a coordination of mind and feeling' (Hochschild 1983: 7). The modern labor market has numerous jobs – within hotels and restaurants, healthcare, childcare, education, and so on – in which such or similar abilities are required. I prefer to use the concept of social competence (or social skills) and, regarding jobs, it can be defined as people's capability of maintaining, looking after, and improving social relations that are important to their work tasks. This matters in principle in every job but appears to be especially salient in certain parts of the service sector.

Social competence or social skills play a significant role with respect to relationships both inside and outside of the workplace. Jobs usually presuppose interaction among colleagues at the workplace – be it in organized work teams or in a more general sense – and it is important for the performance of an organization how this collaboration is handled. Today teamworking is rather common and in order to be successful the members involved must be able to function together. Moreover, many employees have a lot to do with people coming from outside: customers, deliverers, patients, students, clients, and other categories. It is often essential that employees can manage such contacts in a skillful way; the expansion of services in society has made sensitive job relationships a reality for an increasingly larger workforce.

A third dimension of labor power has to do with motivation or willingness to work, an aspect dealt with in numerous research publications (see, e.g., Gellerman 1963, 1998; Kleinbeck *et al.* 1990; Maslow 1970; McGregor 1985; Vroom 1964). Workers' motivation is a matter of commitment, either to the work itself or to the employing organization (see, e.g., Lincoln and Kalleberg 1990: 22–4). It does not matter how excellent credentials or qualifications an individual has; if he/she is unwilling to carry out the tasks connected with a job, there is little reason for the employer to hire him/her. From the employer's point of view, it may then be much better to recruit another individual who is less qualified but who is willing to do his/her best and who sooner or later will be able to make up for his/her lacking qualifications.

Motivation is connected with the remuneration that is provided in a given job and remuneration is of different kinds; it does not only refer to payment but also to such factors in people's situation as stimulating and challenging work contents, sufficient autonomy in work activities, reasonable participation in workplace decisions, learning possibilities, career opportunities, and social contacts related to the job. In addition, there are also negative sanctions – various kinds of punishment – that may affect motivation. Employees' willingness to work hard and to be loyal with their employer is thus dependent on the use of both stick and carrot.

The commodity status of labor power

In the perspective outlined here, the labor market is a system for hiring labor power. I prefer the terms 'hiring' and 'hiring out' instead of 'buying' and 'selling', simply because I find the former more adequate to describe the characteristics of modern labor markets. A table or a chair can be bought and sold once and for all, which means that these objects cease to belong to their previous owner. Labor power is, however, different in this respect; it is not turned over to the employer but only for a limited period of time. As noticed by both Marx (1996: 177–86) and Polanyi (1957: 72–3), it is inseparable from its bearer; the individual and his/her labor power are so to speak part and parcel.

For Polyani (1957: 72), labor is a 'fictitious' commodity, because com-modities are, in his view, 'objects produced for sale on the market'. Like land and money, it is not produced for that purpose and the conclusion is therefore that all three have a 'fictitious' character. Although hence not being genuine commodities, they are nevertheless 'actually bought and sold on the market' (Polyani 1957: 72). As I see it, there is no need to include any original purpose in the definition of the commodity concept. It frequently happens in a market economy that objects are transformed into saleable objects without having been originally produced for sale. Another point is that training and education are examples of how people aim at improving the marketability of their capacities for work. It can thus be con-tended that labor power is to some extent 'produced' to be hired out in the labor market.

Linking up with the analysis by Polanyi, Claus Offe (1985: 56–7) has argued that labor power must be considered a 'fictive' commodity, because in contrast to conventional commodities it is characterized by a 'marked variability and plasticity'. These characteristics are connected with the fact that employment contracts are commonly indeterminate with respect to work tasks, work intensity, and the like. However, thinking of variability and plasticity as prerequisites for people to undergo training and educa-tion, we can just repeat what was said above, that is, that the human capac-ities for work can actually be prepared to become a commodity. Furthermore, Offe (1985: 57) suggests that labor power is fictive, also because it is not 'clearly separable from its owner'. Strictly speaking, however, it can be separated from its owner but not from its bearer and the two should not be confused. Slavery is an illustration of this; the capacity for work that slaves have is actually owned by their masters who can sell it (including the bearer), once and for all, in the market (see further below).

To 'hire' and 'hire out' labor power are the two verbs that I prefer to use to describe the main transactions in the labor market, but with respect to suitable, corresponding nouns we run into difficulties. It has already been pointed out that I am not satisfied with the terms 'buyers' and 'sellers' of labor power, which are the most common expressions in the literature, par-ticularly in Marxist analyses. They do not capture what it is really all about, namely that employers have workers' labor power at their disposal for a given period of time. Instead the terms 'employers' and 'employees' or 'workers' will be utilized, although they have no direct link to the verbs 'hire' and 'hire out'.

If, in the labor market, labor power is not the property of its bearer, slavery is the proper notion. Marx (1933: 19–20; 1996: 178) expresses this very clearly by contrasting the modern free labor market with the slave market. Through a straightforward and vivid comparison he demonstrates the crucial differences between the two systems. The slave owner controls both the labor power and its bearer and can sell the whole package to any prospective buyer. Accordingly, the slave is not free and cannot offer his capacities for work to an employer any more than an ox can do it to a peasant: 'He *himself* is a commodity, but his labour-power is not *his* commodity' (Marx 1933: 20).

In a modern labor market, however, the individual is free to market his/her capacities to anyone who wants to make use of them. A prerequisite is that labor power is made available for the owner of money only temporarily, for a limited period of time; otherwise the worker will be converted 'from a free man into a slave, from an owner of a commodity into a commodity' (Marx 1996: 178). Still, there is a limit to the freedom of the 'free' labor market; the individual has to be available unless he/she can support himself/herself in some other way, for example through ownership of a fortune or through family relationships. Underlying many of the transactions in the labor market, we discover an element of economic necessity or coercion and, in this context, two important remarks need to be made. First, the economic necessity in the affluent capitalist world usually goes beyond securing the mere survival of the individual; the adequate expression should rather be survival at a 'normal' standard of living. Second, the labor market provides opportunities at least for some employees to earn (much) more money than required for 'normal' consumption; it is then not an economic necessity but the attraction of higher purchasing power – an incentive mechanism – that explains why people are recruited to jobs.

To sum up some of what has just been said, a free labor market requires that the bearers of labor power treat their capacities for work as their own property; otherwise slavery is the appropriate label. Employers do not become owners of other people's working capacities but obtain the right to make use of them for a limited number of hours per day, per week, or whatever time unit agreed upon, as it is only an affair of hiring labor power. Compared, for example, to the market through which apartments are rented, we find certain parallels but also obvious differences and one such difference is that apartments are normally available for the tenants all day and night, whereas the use of individuals' labor power is limited in time.

In the free labor market, above all associated with capitalism, jobseekers can approach employers willing to hire people. They can take a job offered to them or turn it down, but they have to find employment, unless they have other sources for support such as their family, a private fortune, or the welfare state. It is a basic predicament of all societies that at least some segments of the population have to work if people are to survive. Although the modern welfare state does not normally allow its citizens to starve to death, those able to work are under more or less strong pressure to take available jobs and refusal to do so implies a risk of suffering substantial financial losses. However, if individuals can be supported in some other, legitimate way, they will usually not be subject to this kind of pressure.

People who offer their labor power in the market but cannot find someone willing to hire it are to be considered unemployed. This is the most abstract and accordingly the simplest definition of unemployment: offered but not hired labor power. However, for the purpose of making use of it empirically we need to add a number of qualifications and, although my analysis is not an empirical study, I return to these issues later in the book, primarily in Chapter 9.

The term labor market is sometimes used synonymously with working life in general, but we should be careful to keep the two analytically distinct. With the approach suggested here, the labor market is a system or arena for hiring labor power, whereas working life stands for all activities covered by the notion of gainful employment, including those of the self-employed without employees. There is a crucial difference between the situation of the self-employed and that of employers and workers; the former do not hire out their labor power and nor do they hire this capacity from others. They work on their own account, producing goods and services for the market but are not involved in employment relationships and thus remain outside of the labor market. Undoubtedly, the distinction between, for example, a self-employed consultant to a company and an employee with similar tasks is not always clear. Nonetheless, even if the substitution of an employment contract for another kind of contract is all that happens, an essential difference is introduced. By the way, the social sciences constantly encounter borderline cases and this should not lead us to give up making distinctions.

Jobs and occupations

In everyday conversations, people talk about jobs and occupations and – as was pointed out above in connection with the discussion of the term labor market – they probably have no difficulty in conveying what they mean or in communicating their opinions about various issues related to these terms. In accordance with the general purpose of this book, I examine the concepts of job and occupation somewhat more closely and try to specify them for use in a sociological context.

Demand for labor power means that employers need people to carry out certain work tasks. These tasks cluster into 'jobs' that in turn normally can be classified as belonging to different occupations and in the literature we find more or less clarifying definitions of these categories. The American labor economist Herbert Parnes (1954: 25) observes that in most empirical studies on labor mobility a job is usually considered 'a continuous period of service with a single employer'. He also notes that this solution is not satisfactory, since it excludes all changes of work assignments within a workplace. People can switch to other positions at the workplace and the work tasks that an incumbent of a given job actually performs may vary from time to time.

Some have formulated rather elaborate definitions of the concepts dealt with here. Chris and Charles Tilly (1998: 25–6) define a job as 'the set of rights and obligations that connects a given worker with other members of the same firm' and occupations are for them 'sets of jobs in different firms that employers and government officials consider equivalent, building them into organizational rosters, censuses, labor market interventions, and vocational education'. It is important, in order to classify two people as having the 'same' occupation 'that their employers have equivalent claims on them, not that they perform their work in the same manner or maintain the same relations with their fellow workers and people outside their firm' (Tilly and Tilly 1998: 26).

There are some merits in the two authors' arguments – above all that jobs and occupations are socially defined – but the definitions above seem a little bit overworked. The British labor market and social policy analyst Guy Standing (1999: 21) has remarked that, in comparison with occupation, job must be considered 'a much humbler word', sometimes even with 'a pejorative meaning attached to it'. For him it stands for a set of work tasks that can perhaps be classified into an occupation and this is a move in the right direction, but in the next step more determinants than necessary are added. Occupation is then taken to mean 'as a set of related activities learned or refined through a *career*', with the addenda that 'the set of work tasks may be small' and that 'the learning process may be short or long' (Standing 1999: 21; emphasis in original). Although the career dimension is often relevant, its inclusion in the definition itself is not needed, particularly as it is assumed that the learning process may be short. The fundamental aspect of an occupation is its specialization in terms of work tasks and this is admittedly implicit also in Standing's definition. Max Weber (1978: 140) has come rather close to what I am seeking by proposing that the concept of occupation signifies 'the mode of specialization, specification, and combination of the functions of an individual so far as it constitutes for him the basis of a continuous opportunity for income or earnings'.

One Swedish sociologist has suggested an even simpler definition along similar lines, saying that an occupation is just 'a bundle of work tasks' (Karlsson 1983: 168–70; my translation). This makes it very simple, but if we also add that such 'bundles' are socially defined and that they are clustered into occupational families, we have a good starting point. We can then specify the relationship between the actors in the labor market somewhat further. Employers have a demand for workers whom they want to allocate to different jobs – sets of work tasks – usually classified into different occupations. Those who offer their labor power for hire are, in everyday language, looking for jobs, and if they have specialized experience, skills, and knowledge they may focus on a given occupation or a broader occupational category.

It should be added that some occupations are commonly classified as professions. Even though it is contested how the concept of profession is to be defined, many analysts would come rather close to the characterization given by Talcott Parsons (1964: 372). He claims that incumbents of such positions must have qualifications based on theoretical knowledge and skills, acquired from long-lasting education. Because of this they are recognized by the environment as the experts in a given field and are thus entrusted to enact their occupational role on their own discretion. Only those with the proper training are regarded as qualified for practising the profession. A main criticism against Parsons' view concerns his faith in the altruism of professionals or, rather, in the ability of the norms and mechanisms surrounding them to secure altruistic behavior. Others, of both Marxist and Weberian leanings, have been more inclined to see cynical power and self-interest behind the ideology of professionalism (see,e.g., Freidson 1986, 1994, 2001; Larson 1977; MacDonald 1995; Witz 1992). Besides the generally accepted professions such as those of medical doctors and lawyers, several other occupational categories strive for professional recognition and in these struggles they usually try to obtain some kind of authorization from the government or some other body.

A job is basically a set of work tasks and the same can be said about an occupation, although in the latter case there is some further specification of what the incumbents are supposed to do. For the most part, a job can be given an occupational label, but there are exceptions to this; some positions are simply not possible to classify in such terms but fall outside of existing categories. We should additionally be aware that even very specialized jobholders usually carry out a combination of tasks and obligations. Bus drivers are expected to drive buses and teachers are expected to teach, but this is normally not all they have to do in their jobs; for example, they may also have to handle certain administrative tasks.

One further comment has to be made. Jobs should not be treated as given once and for all and nor should occupations. Employers generally define the work tasks for which they need workers, but the set of positions they organize can be recast in many different ways. Hence, jobs are not always that well defined, especially not from the beginning, and they may sometimes even be created to fit in with an incumbent (Granovetter 1995: 14–15). An employer may find a certain individual so valuable that if no position is available for him/her, it is created. Workers also modify existing jobs according to their own abilities and preferences. This is the normal pattern, because people tend perform their work or occupational roles in different ways, thus giving them at least some personal imprint; social phenomena are often less structured in advance than we tend to think.

The employment contract

Those who hire and those who hire out labor power normally agree on some kind of employment contract that can be formal (written), informal (oral), or tacit. No matter what form it takes, it is undoubtedly crucial for the relationship between the two parties, although its contents – unsurprisingly – can vary a great deal. Treating the concept of contract more generally, Parsons and his co-author Neil Smelser (1956: 105) conclude that it refers to 'the institutional basis of market structure' and, in their perspective, contracts can be analyzed in two different ways. The first is to study them as a process of bargaining in which each party tries to get the most advantageous outcome. With respect to employment, the primary *quid pro quo* is the workers' performance for the organization and the organization's provision of payment for that effort. The second way to deal with contracts is to focus on their conditioning rules that are 'socially prescribed and sanctioned', existing, among other things, to guarantee 'the interest of third parties' and to put 'restrictions on fraud and coercion' (Parsons and Smelser 1965: 105). In other words, this has to do with what Émile Durkheim (1964: 200–29) called the 'non-contractual' elements of contract. Durkheim's notion, as well as the observations made by Parsons and Smelser, helps us become aware of how the labor market is embedded in a wider social and normative framework.

Besides the *quid pro quo* dimension of the employment contract, there are other important aspects of it such as its duration and the conditions under which it can be ended. In particular, if the contract does not have a time limit but is open, both parties are likely to be interested in having the conditions of separation specified. There are then several questions that need to be answered, for example how long the notice period will be, whether this period is the same for both the employer and the employee, whether or to what extent workers are entitled to severance pay, and under what circumstances the employment contract can be ended before it is up. In modern labor markets, the answers to these questions are often, at least to some degree, given through labor legislation.

In juridical terms, the contract appears as an agreement between two equal parties, but as Marx (1996: 177–86) has underlined this is not the whole truth. Behind the idea that capitalists and workers voluntarily and on equal terms exchange money for the use of labor power, he sees an asymmetric relationship. Workers are free to offer their labor power to any capitalist of their own choice, but in order to survive they are forced to find someone willing to hire it and in that sense they belong to 'the whole class of buyers, i.e., the capitalist class' (Marx 1933: 20; italics removed). In other words, there is an economic necessity concealed behind workers' freedom in the market; this coercive mechanism has certainly been mitigated by the rising standards of living and the development of the welfare state, but it has not disappeared completely. Individuals who take their labor power to the market but find no one willing to hire it will generally suffer income losses, even if the welfare state provides unemployment benefits and other kinds of support.

Evidently, it is also necessary for capitalists to find workers, as capitalism is inconceivable without workers. The system is oriented toward producing goods and services for profitable sale and without production and producers there will be no profits to reap. In other words, the two main parties in the economic system are dependent upon one another. However, 'at the most basic level' a capitalist employer can 'survive longer without labour than the employee can survive without work' (Blyton and Turnbull 2004: 34; see also Western 1998: 226). In that sense the relationship can be characterized as asymmetric.

Many recent studies of labor markets lay emphasis on the distinction between standard and non-standard (or 'atypical') employment contracts. Standard contracts usually refer to full-time and permanent jobs, whereas non-standard contracts mean part-time and temporary jobs as well as self-employment (e.g., Felstead and Jewson 1999b; Blyton and Turnbull 2004: 10). It is common among analysts to claim that the latter type is on the increase in contemporary labor markets and there is undeniably empirical evidence in support of this statement, although all available facts do not point in the same direction.

To take the analysis one step further, we can ask what happens after an employment contract is agreed upon. There are normally many aspects of an employment relationship that are not or even cannot be covered in the original agreement. One explanation is that contracts are partly tacit and implicit, which may lead to different interpretations, but another reason is that many conditions cannot be decided in advance. It is simply difficult or impossible to know what will happen in a few years' time with the goods and services that are produced at the workplace, the technical equipment used, the structure of work tasks, the organization, and so on. The same can be said about the individual workers, their health, skills, family situation, etc. Nobody is able to foresee all the different things that may occur, but a contract can of course specify the terms for re-negotiation when conditions are changing.

More importantly perhaps, the asymmetric character of the employment relationship becomes more visible once the contract is settled. This is a main theme in Marx's analysis of the capitalist rule in the factory, but it is also recognized by Weber (1978: 729–30):

'The formal right of a worker to enter into any contract whatsoever with any employer whatsoever does not in practice represent for the employment seeker even the slightest freedom in the determination of his own conditions of work, and it does not guarantee him any influence on this process. It rather means, at least primarily, that the more powerful party in the market, i.e., normally the employer, has the possibility to set the terms, to offer the job "take it or leave it", and, given the normally more pressing economic need of the worker, to impose his terms upon him.'

Weber's conclusion is that contractual freedom makes it possible for actors with property assets to exercise power over others. Accordingly, the legal order of contractual freedom is a highly significant institution for them. State intervention in the labor market since Weber's time has modified the conditions of employment relationships, but in essence these relationships are very much the same even today.

The two parties may have agreed upon the tasks that the worker is to carry out, but with the development of new technology and due to many other changing circumstances job contents must be modified or altered altogether. Normally it is the employer – as the one who organizes the work process – who takes the initiative to carry out such changes. As a result, workers may feel overrun and conclude that the contract the two parties once agreed upon has been broken; under such circumstances we can expect their discontent to build up. In any case, in most employment relationships some significant degree of indeterminacy is likely to prevail; I come back to these questions in Chapter 4.

Capitalist and non-capitalist labor markets

Markets are indeed a crucial element in capitalism that is often even labeled 'market economy'. However, they can also exist outside a capitalist structure, as we can see, for example, by looking back in history. Trade was indeed an important feature in the Roman Empire as well as in Medieval Europe. Although a labor market in the modern sense of the word did not exist until the nineteenth century, it should be observed that slavery comprised a kind of market for labor power. As we have seen, this system meant that the human capacity for work was bought and sold among slave owners. The state socialist countries in eastern Europe, Asia, and elsewhere supply other examples of non-capitalist markets. Despite their more or less planned economies, these countries to some extent relied on markets, including arenas for hiring labor power (see, e.g., Oxenstierna 1990), and those that remain state socialist still do.

The purpose of this section is to spell out how labor markets are related to the socioeconomic structure in society. In the case of modern societies, more than anything else, the overriding structure equals capitalism. The market is the main mechanism for the exchange of products, services and other objects, among them labor power, in the capitalist economic system. Firms that need workers for their profit-making endeavor hire people who have to or want to support themselves from wage-work. However, the hiring of labor power goes beyond its capitalist connection; it is also related to the public sector and other non-capitalist activities. In the following, I present this picture somewhat more in detail, but first I develop some arguments with regard to the 'marketness' of labor markets. This is a concept that can help us see how different sectors of the general labor market differ from one another.

The 'marketness' of labor markets

It can be argued that the transactions in the capitalist labor market are characterized by more 'marketness' – to borrow a concept from Fred Block (1990: 51–73) – than the transactions in other labor markets. The idea is that a continuum can be constructed to depict the role of price mechanisms and other factors. Accordingly, we can take 'high' marketness to mean 'that there is nothing to interfere with the dominance of price considerations, but as one moves down the continuum to lower levels of marketness, nonprice considerations take on greater importance' (Block 1990: 51). Prices are not irrelevant at this lower end, but they have to compete with other factors in determining consumer choices.

Block has a good point and I want to expand the concept by adding that marketness also has to do with markets' connections with and dependence on other markets. By comparing capitalist enterprises with public sector institutions, we can illustrate this. Capitalist firms have to sell their products to customers – individuals, other firms, and other organizations – and are dependent on success in that respect. If they are unable to sell at prices that exceed production costs, they will sooner or later end up going out of business. These conditions make a great difference compared to those of non-profit public sector institutions (profit-oriented government firms such as railway and water supply companies are another story). For example, a public hospital provides healthcare services to fulfill certain needs among the population no matter whether people can (fully) pay for them or not; it is not dependent on a market. The main incomes are usually derived from taxes, although patients may pay certain, often highly subsidized, fees. Whether a non-profit public institution is successful or not is rather a matter of goal attainment and user satisfaction with services.

Yet, public sector institutions are involved in the labor market; they need to recruit employees to jobs and to some degree they do so in competition with other employers. In that respect the price mechanism can be as important for them as for any other competitor. The relationship between wage levels in different spheres will have an impact on which employers will be able to recruit the most attractive personnel, since various arenas are simply communicating vessels. Moreover, public sector institutions are connected with other markets too, because they buy numerous goods and services from private firms and because they may be involved in financial transactions with private banks. What happens in these other markets will also affect public sector budgets and activities.

In the way I use it, the concept of marketness stands for dependence on the price mechanism and on other (networks of) markets. It is a gradational concept; there can be more or less of marketness. Owing to this perspective, we do not have to bother about whether the public sector has a real labor market in the same sense as capitalism. It is enough to say that the former is generally characterized by less marketness, although, at the same time, we must also be observant of differences in this respect within both the public and the private sector, most of all perhaps among public sector institutions.

Capitalist labor markets

The capitalist labor market can perhaps be characterized as the prototype of the general concept of labor market. By constructing an ideal type we can isolate and identify the distinguishing features of a phenomenon, but we should keep in mind that reality may deviate considerably from the model. The constituent characteristics of the labor market related to capitalism can briefly be described in the following way: Capitalism means that workers produce goods and services as use values, but at the same time their work must be profitable for the capitalists; otherwise the latter will lose interest in employing them. Firms compete with one another in the markets and are therefore under pressure to increase sales and to rationalize production and reduce costs in general. Jobs are simply dependent on a profitability criterion and will have difficulties in surviving – at least not in the long run – if not supposed to be helpful in the process of generating profits.

Thus, if a capitalist firm does not make profit or, rather, enough profit compared to competitors or according to expectations, it will be restructured, moved to another country, or closed down; it does not matter how important the goods and services may be. Naturally, if certain goods or services are strongly demanded by many, it is also rather likely that the firms producing them make profits. However, the individuals who want the goods and services may not have the money to pay for them, because they are too poor or because prices are extraordinarily high (as in the case of heart transplantations and the like) or both. We hence need to make a distinction between want and demand, a distinction that can help us understand the mechanisms in operation. Wants are subjectively defined needs (I prefer to avoid the concept of objective needs, although we might raise a good case for it, at least regarding aspects such as nutrition). Demand, however, can be defined as wants backed up by money, that is, what Weber (1978: 108) has called 'effective demand'. When some segments of the population do not have enough purchasing power, their needs may not affect the market or even be known by its actors.

Workers in capitalist firms are thus dependent on the firm's profitability no matter what use values they produce. When those who need the goods and services are not able to pay for them, demand will decline and jobs become threatened. This is perhaps the best explanation as to why non-capitalist activities exist at all. The lack of purchasing power is remedied in different ways, among other things through public sector production of services, which is a major example of how human needs are fulfilled regardless of what financial resources people have.

Modes, relations, and forces of production

Capitalism can be described as a mode of production. Generally, this Marxist concept refers to the ways in which goods and services are produced; it implies raising questions about who owns the means of production (machinery, raw materials, etc.), who does what in the division of labor, what technology, machinery, and other equipment are being used, who coordinates and controls the production process, who makes the decisions and who executes them, and who gets what out of the return. Throughout history several different modes of production have appeared, for example the feudal, the capitalist, the petty bourgeois, and the (state) socialist mode of production. The concept is related to two other concepts: relations of production and productive forces.

There has been a great deal of discussion about how the concepts mode of production, relations of production, and forces of production are to be defined (see, e.g., Cohen 2000; Therborn 1976: 353–86; Wright 1994: 117–20). Marx and Engels did not write about these matters in a consistent way and nor did they provide an unambiguously most authoritative statement on the issue, although some texts have been interpreted that way (see, above all, perhaps, Marx 1971: 20–1). I have no intention to engage in any exegetic analysis of what different connotations the two authors brought into play or what they really meant or might have meant. For my purpose, it is enough to make some comments on how I want to use to the concepts.

The societies at focus in this book are all dominated by the capitalist mode of production. One aspect of the social relations of production characterizing capitalism is that labor power is attributed commodity status. Social relations have to do with ownership and control and with the division of labor. People who own, or lease, means of production (machinery, other equipment and facilities, raw materials) hire labor power from workers and organize production of goods and services for sale. This in turn requires that consumers – individuals but also organizations, including firms and government institutions – are willing and able to buy the output. The overriding purpose is not to satisfy needs but to make profit; in other words, the incomes from sales must exceed the costs for labor,

Mile End Library
Queen Mary, University of London
Easter Vacation and Revision Week
2nd April - 2nd May

Extended Vacation Loans
Ordinary Loans borrowed or renewed
from Saturday 5th March
will be due back on Friday 6th May

One Week Loans borrowed or renewed
from Saturday 26th March
will be due back on Wednesday 4th May

Borrowed Items 23/03/2011 13:48
XXXXXX9896

Item Title	Due Date
* Market society : markets a	30/03/2011
* Sociological perspectives c	06/05/2011

* Indicates items borrowed today
PLEASE NOTE
If you still have overdue books on loan
you may have more fines to pay

raw materials, machinery and other material means of production, and capital (loans).

Within a given society several modes of production may coexist, although one is likely to be dominant. For example, in all advanced capitalist countries, and more or less integrated with capitalism, we also find petty bourgeois (or simple commodity) production. The latter type signifies a system in which small entrepreneurs themselves, without employing others, produce goods or services for the market; they may have assisting family members but in principle no employees. Accordingly, the petty bourgeois mode of production has no connection with the labor market and is therefore outside most of the discussions in this book. Its relevance primarily lies in the fact that, for some segments of the population, self-employment is a possible alternative to wage-work as the basis for making a living.

The concept of productive forces has to do with the capacity to produce, which is of course to a large extent determined by the development of technology. With the arrival of the industrial epoch, great progress was made compared to agrarian society in terms of technical equipment and energy sources, and – as I shall return to later in the book – the emergence of the new information technology has meant further big steps forward. However, the concept of productive forces does not only refer to the physical means of production but also to the organization of work and to labor power. Organization is a set of social relations that are part of the productive forces as well. By finding new ways of organizing its system of production, a firm may increase its output without introducing any new machinery or energy sources. Moreover, the productive forces are dependent upon individuals' capacities to work and all the three previously discussed dimensions of labor power are essential in this respect. For example, if workers become physically stronger and healthier, they have the potential to produce more and to do a better job. More and better training and education can likewise be supposed to increase their productive capacity, if individuals learn things that fit in with their present or future work tasks. Finally, motivation is another vital dimension; in the event that it is raised, the possibility is at hand that workers increase their output and improve its quality.

Mode of production can be considered a concept to capture the different mechanisms through which exploitation takes place. In the Marxist analysis of capitalism, exploitation is synonymous with the generation of surplus value. Marx's labor theory of value rests on the assumption that only workers produce value and that they produce more than needed to reproduce the workforce at any given standard of living (that in advanced capitalism by far exceeds the mere means of subsistence). Due to their ownership and control of the means of production, capitalists are able to appropriate the surplus that workers create. One problem with this theory is its assumption that only labor produces value; this statement is either simply normative or just a postulation about working life. A normative statement does not have any analytical value and a postulation of the kind mentioned is impossible to defend, as production requires the interplay of many factors. Moreover, the theory is unable to clarify the relationship between theoretically determined values and empirically observable prices in the market. It thus does not provide any useful tool for research and must therefore be left aside.

Nevertheless, we should not argue the other way around that capitalism – or for that matter other economic systems – does not or even cannot involve exploitation. The concept of exploitation can be interpreted in many different ways (Nielsen and Ware 1997a). It can be normatively neutral or non-neutral; a common dictionary interpretation is that it can refer to 'use' as well as to 'selfish or unfair use' (Nielsen and Ware 1997b: x). At least the word 'unfair', but perhaps also the word 'selfish', implies a value-based point of departure. We must not, however, exclude the possibility that the concept can be applied in a non-normative way to signify unequal exchange based on some kind of coercion or some already existing privilege. Exploitation would then mean that one actor in a social relationship – due to such mechanisms – gets more out of it than she contributes. The problem is still how to define the categories through which it can be established empirically that exploitation takes place and in that respect we have no good answer.

In general, Marxists tend to focus on relations of production, while forces of production are paid less attention. Although we find exceptions to this (e.g., Cohen 2000), it generally seems that the distributive rather than the productive aspect is at the center of their interest. The development of the forces of production is often taken as more or less given and is rarely subject to any deeper examination. Yet, both concepts are available and it does not have to hurt the conceptual framework to shift the emphasis to some degree. Among economists of neoclassical orientation, however, we find a greater interest in productive capacities and their realization than in the distribution of what has been produced. A common argument is that if output can be increased, everybody will benefit or, to put it the other way around, 'any insistence on carving the pie into equal slices would shrink the size of the pie', that is, there is an assumption of a 'tradeoff between economic equality and economic efficiency' (Okun 1975: 48). No one can possibly deny that perfect equality in terms of remunerations would create difficulties for production, as there would be no individual incentives at all, but it is a contested issue how, more exactly, to specify the relationship between equality and efficiency (for an overview of discussions, see, e.g., Kenworthy 2004).

Dealing with Marxist theory, we run into the idea of a tension between the forces and the relations of production. In a frequently quoted paragraph, Marx (1971: 21) asserts that 'at a certain stage of their development, the material productive forces of society come into conflict with the existing relations of production', as the latter from having been 'forms of development of the productive forces' have turned into 'fetters'. There may be a point in this, but we cannot take it as a general law for economic development; it implies too much of unsustainable functionalist thinking. Yet, relations of production and productive forces stick together and research will have a lot to benefit from considering both dimensions. The interplay between the two, or between productive capacities and distributive patterns, needs to be dealt with in a sensitive way so that we avoid drawing too rushed conclusions on the multifaceted efficiency and equity issues.

Public sector employment

The main organizer of non-capitalist production in advanced capitalist societies is the state, including its regional and local branches and it is very much a matter of service production such as healthcare, education, childcare, and care for the elderly. These services are provided no matter whether people are able (fully) to pay for them or not. They are financed through taxes and sometimes, at least partly, through user fees, but no profit-making is involved. Workers of different occupations such as doctors, nurses, and teachers – educated and skilled to carry out the necessary tasks in the production of various services – are recruited in the labor market. In other words, public sector employees are not part of the labor market, but they are outside the direct mechanisms of capitalist profit-making.

We find a large public sector in all advanced capitalist countries, but its relative size varies substantially between them (see Alestalo, Bislev and Furåker 1991; Furåker and Lindqvist 2003; Furåker 2003: 257–60). In terms of employment, the cross-national variation very much depends on the volume of social services, but on the whole the nation-states in the rich capitalist world are rather far from the concept or ideal of the 'minimal' state (cf. Nozick 1974). This ideal stands for a model in which the reach of government is very limited and essentially a matter of defense, lawmaking, law enforcement, and little else. The really existing advanced capitalism is, however, commonly associated with a rather large welfare state and, among others, the Scandinavian countries are known for having developed a huge social service sector.

The issue of a state mode of production

In another context, I have suggested that we employ the label state mode of production to refer to public sector activities such as the production of welfare services (Furåker 1987). Alternatively, we might talk about a public sector (or even socialist) mode of production. Whatever label is chosen, this would be a way of recognizing these activities in their own right. The reason for my original proposal was dissatisfaction with neo-Marxist analyses in the 1960s and the 1970s, because they either did not bother about the public sector at all or, in case they did, largely came up with unsustainable answers. Specifically and most strikingly, many accounts showed a tendency to reduce state activities to the fulfillment of certain functions for the capitalist system (for some further discussion, see Chapter 4).

The assumption that state activities mainly exist because they are needed to reproduce capitalism cannot possibly explain the large variation in the size of the public sector across countries. An even greater difficulty with that point of departure is to explain the eagerness of business interests and pro-business political parties/organizations to cut down on welfare state benefits and services and the concomitant, although not always consistent, working-class support for maintaining or expanding these transfers and activities. Far from surprisingly, therefore, this neo-Marxist approach had essentially nothing to say concerning the trends toward privatization and downsizing of the public sector in many capitalist countries during the 1980s and the 1990s.

Another area that suffered from the inability to deal with the public sector in a reasonable way was class analysis. In this context, the crucial question is how public employees are to be taken into account and what status they are assigned in the class structure. For example, what does it mean that these categories are not (directly) subject to capitalist control and profit demands but placed under the political-administrative system? In many neo-Marxist accounts such questions have simply been avoided, probably due to the absence of any thought-out idea of how to deal with the public sector. At the same time, it should be emphasized that other types of class or social stratification analysis, often inspired by a Weberian perspective, have rarely made any difference for the better.

Public sector production is the most 'socialist' part of the provision of goods and services in contemporary capitalist societies. It is concentrated to services, but we also find some usually smaller segments of goods production, owned and managed by the government. The organization of public services has a number of characteristics that are not capitalist but fit in with what is referred to as statism or state socialism (cf. Wright 1985: 78–82). In particular, the means of production are public property, production is carried out not for the sake of profit but for the use values that it creates, activities are organized through a system of planning, and the system is placed under political control. A decisive difference between the really existing state socialism and the public sector in advanced capitalism is that the latter is governed through a system of political democracy.

This difference should not make us reluctant to use the concepts such as statism, state socialism or state mode of production to describe public sector production (because also capitalism appears in combination with political dictatorship), but there are certain other characteristics that may do so. The public sector is mainly financed through taxation and governments do not have much else on which to base its resources than the legislative power to put taxes on wages, profits, property, and sales. Although users of services to some extent pay fees, these normally make up only a small proportion of the total resources. If fees were set to cover all the costs for the production of services, it would mean a higher degree of marketness and the system should then be labeled state capitalism. A general pattern is, however, that public sector activities are directly dependent upon the functioning of the capitalist system to become financed. The profit-oriented firms and their workers are the major sources from which taxes are collected. Accordingly, in order for public services to be produced it is essential that capitalism thrives. There are also many other, rather strong ties between the public sector and the capitalist markets; for example, public hospitals, childcare centers, homes for the elderly, schools, etc., enter the market to buy goods of consumption, in basically the same way as private firms and other private organizations.

My general answer to the conceptual issues discussed here is that we can very well talk about a state (public sector or socialist) mode of production. We should perhaps also add words such as 'dependent' or 'subordinate' to emphasize the position that public sector production has in relation to capitalism. There are at least two obvious advantages with my proposal. First, it represents a step out of a situation in which the role of the public sector has been largely neglected or under-theorized in sociological and especially Marxist accounts. Second, it also has an advantage compared to alternative approaches such as the idea of the 'mixed' economy (see, e.g., Rees 1973), because it gives us a theoretical framework for clarifying what the 'mix' is all about. With respect to the issues dealt with in this book, the concept of a state/public sector mode of production opens our eyes to a subdivision of the labor market that is different from the capitalist mode. Undoubtedly the capitalist and the public sector show many important similarities, but the underlying mechanisms are quite different and this is to some extent reflected in employment contracts and employment conditions. The differences are above all a matter of the role of profits and markets; I pay some further attention to this in Chapter 3.

Other non-capitalist sectors

There are also other labor markets outside of the capitalist sphere, but they are generally of a considerably smaller size than those connected with the capitalist and the public sectors. I am thinking about two types of labor market; one is related to voluntary and non-profit organizations and the other to services for which individuals and families pay but that are still not profit-oriented. In principle, I cannot see any reason why the concept of mode of production could not be used in these cases as well, although they are minor and subordinate phenomena relative to the whole system of goods and service provision in society.

In pursuing their various goals, unions, political parties, environmental organizations, charity societies, and other voluntary organizations also appear as employers in the labor market. Although many individuals work voluntarily for them – in other words without being involved in an employment relationship – these organizations often hire people to take care of certain tasks. Unions and political parties are set up to look after members' interests and to achieve certain political goals and their employees are paid by way of membership fees and other possible sources of income. The like of it holds for many other voluntary organizations, such as educational associations and literary clubs that have been established to cultivate and further common interests. At least in some respects, charity organizations do similar things as government agencies, although they often focus only on categories with particularly great problems (the poor, the homeless, the handicapped, and so on) and do not collect money through taxation but mainly through donations and membership fees.

Voluntary organizations can have salaried presidents, managers, secretaries, and other staff and they employ various technical and judicial experts. These employees are often recruited among volunteers – more or less on the basis of ideological or political criteria and merits – and the level of marketness is accordingly low. The selection of individuals to jobs can be part of an internal labor market (for some further discussion on this concept, see Chapter 3), but it may still be possible for outsiders to get a job in such organizations. People without any previous connection to the organizations are sometimes let in, due to the need for specific skills. This type of labor market is hence in many respects different from others, although it is included in the total 'hiring fair', to use the expression suggested by Ralph Fevre (1992: 10). Again, employment in independent and voluntary organizations is not a matter of producing profit, but of providing services for members, or other groups, or of advancing certain goals.

Another type of non-capitalist labor market can be illustrated by the example of a family hiring an individual to clean its house, occasionally or on a regular basis. It is a market relationship but not capitalist in nature; to express it in Marxist terminology, revenue is exchanged for a service. There is no profit-making purpose involved; the work is carried out only for the use value (cleaner house) for which it is set up. This sector used to be rather large back in the history of modern societies, but even today it amounts to a considerable size in many places. Not least, we should observe that large numbers women leave poorer regions of the world and come to the affluent countries to carry out domestic work (e.g., Momsen 1999; Parreñas 2001; Stalker 1994: 106–10). As they are sometimes also illegal immigrants, their social position is often exceptionally vulnerable.

Table 2.1 Some characteristics of labor market sectors

	Profit orientation	Main sources of income
Capitalist firms	Yes	Sales Subsidies
Public sector institutions	No	Taxes Fees
Independent and voluntary organizations	No	Membership fees Donations Subsidies
Households	No	Personal assets

Table 2.1 gives a summary description on two essential dimensions for all four sectors treated here. As a first dimension the table takes up whether profit-making is an overriding goal or not and the answer is yes only for capitalist firms. None of the other employers hire workers to make profit but do it simply for the use values that workers are expected to produce. The second dimension describes the main sources of income that employers have and that enable them to hire people in the labor market. By far the most important source of income for capitalist firms is sales, but it happens that they receive government subsidies. Public sector institutions mainly rely on taxes, although fees may play a significant role for them. The activities of independent and voluntary organizations are above all based on membership fees and donations, but they can also be subsidized by governments. With respect to the final category, families and individuals or households, the resources to pay for employing workers derive from personal assets, which in turn consist of income from both paid work and private property.

To sum up, labor markets in contemporary advanced societies are to a large extent connected with capitalist production of goods and services, but this is not the whole story. Some parts of the labor market are tied to activities that are non-capitalist in nature. The employers in these cases are not capitalist firms, but public sector institutions, voluntary organizations, or households. This is a fundamental labor market division, although often neglected; it means that some people are directly under pressure to produce profits and subjected to market forces or price mechanisms, whereas other kinds of work are organized simply for the purpose of providing certain use values. Although the degree of marketness thus varies between these different sectors, they are all part of the same wider system.

Commodification and decommodification

In the literature dealing with labor power as a commodity in the market, we sometimes run into the concepts of commodification and decommodification (cf. Offe 1984, 1985; Esping-Andersen 1985, 1990, 1999; Furåker and Lindqvist 2003). These concepts can be used to analyze diverse phenomena in society, but in this context – needless to say – we can restrict ourselves to the labor market. Commodification and decommodification are given somewhat different meanings by different authors, although the most common interpretation is that they have to do with market dependence. There is an important point in this definition, but I nevertheless want to suggest some modifications. My proposal and the arguments behind will be presented after taking a look at some of the literature.

Following Gøsta Esping-Andersen (1990: 37), labor market decommodification is not a matter of completely eliminating the commodity status of labor power but rather of reducing the degree to which individuals and families are forced to rely on the labor market for upholding a reasonable standard of living. Through various kinds of support from the welfare state, work does not have to be a matter of necessity but more of a free choice. Guy Standing (2002: 14–16) has even concretized 'labor decommodification' in terms of the ratio between social incomes and wages, the idea being that the larger the proportion of social incomes, the higher the degree of decommodification. This seems to be a simplistic solution and, as seen in Chapter 5, the question of the decommodifying role of the welfare state is more complicated than suggested by Standing.

In the reverse, Esping-Andersen's argument, as well as that of Standing, also applies to commodification. The latter concept is thus taken to signify a process through which individuals become more dependent on the market. We should note that neither of these authors pays very much attention to the concept of commodification. In their perspective, the focus is on decommodification, probably because this aspect is seen as most relevant for the analysis of the welfare state. According to Esping-Andersen (1990: 41–7) decommodification represents the political approach of socialism, whereas liberalism is associated with the view that the market is emancipatory and with efforts to strengthen the commodity status of labor power, that is, with politics of commodification. It must be added and emphasized that socialist policies have often simultaneously been strongly oriented toward putting people into work, which implies that individuals obtain commodity status in the labor market.

There is no doubt that market dependence is a crucial element in any discussion of commodification and decommodification. For Esping-Andersen and Standing, mechanisms that reduce this dependence are worth aiming at and it follows that those increasing the dependence on the market are less desirable. I wish to step back from that discussion and make the concepts more open. My suggestion is that commodification in the labor market first should be taken to refer to processes through which labor power is transformed into and sustained as a commodity in the market, regardless of how we look at causes and consequences involved. To illustrate my line of reasoning, if a woman who has spent most of her time doing unpaid housework enters into paid employment, we could call that step commodification. In addition, we should include processes in which there is an expansion in the commodity role of labor power; hence, if another, part-time-working woman increases her working hours, this can be referred to as commodification as well. The concept of decommodification in the labor market can be applied just inversely; it thus captures processes through which labor power ceases to be a commodity or is sustained in a non-commodity status. Also in this case we should include gradual changes; a decrease in working hours can thus be treated as a step of decommodification.

Market dependence and independence are important mechanisms behind the processes outlined, but they do not constitute the processes themselves and should therefore not be part of the definitions. Although I agree with the view that most people carry out paid work in order to provide for themselves, as they lack other means of subsistence, we should not focus on the elements of necessity and coercion only. There are also other mechanisms in operation; for example, an individual with a fairly high income – that gives her a decent standard of living – may nevertheless be thinking of taking on some extra engagement in order to earn more. This may then have nothing to do with economic necessities (although it happens that even affluent people are trapped by mortgage payments or other financial obligations) but rather with a desire for more purchasing power to be spent on general consumption or on some specific object such as an apartment or a car.

In this context, we can recall the observations made by Weber (1930: 58–60) on the contrast between 'traditionalism' and the 'spirit of capitalism'. He recognized that increases in the piece-rates in agriculture did not always, as we might expect, lead to increased efforts but to shorter working time. When, under modern capitalism, attempts have been made to raise productivity, pre-capitalist attitudes have often been obstacles. In Weber's example, a farm worker was offered a higher rate per acre for mowing, but, instead of working more or at least earning more money by doing the same as before, he chose to earn the same by mowing less land. In other words, this worker had not adopted the attitude of striving for as much as possible; he just did what was required to satisfy his traditional needs. Today, people sometimes have similar attitudes, but many also work more than necessary just in order to increase their standard of living further or to save money for the future or for their children. Without going deeper into the issue of how people actually behave in situations such as that described, we should be aware of the tradeoff between leisure and income. Up to some limit, people may want to work more and thus earn more, but they may also find it reasonable, if they can manage on less, to lower their working-time, for example to get more leisure or time for children.

Motivation is consequently an aspect that must be attributed a crucial part. There is of course variation across social categories, but, generally speaking, the whole culture in our societies seems to be geared into a norm that people should engage in gainful employment and work a great deal, unless they have some legitimate excuse for doing otherwise. Several studies in different countries have shown that it is important for people, not least the unemployed, to have a job (see, e.g., Gallie and Alm 2000; Nordenmark 1999; Russel and Barbieri 2000). The reason why the unemployed are likely to feel a strong desire for paid work is probably that they have actually experienced the hardships and the stigmatizing mechanisms associated with joblessness. Besides, the old gender differences in employment commitment seem to be on their way out, as in many countries the traditional gender roles are being transformed.

We should also consider the pros and cons of the options that people have. For example, for a housewife who does not have to take paid work, since the husband's income is enough for the family and no demand is put upon her to enter the labor market, it can still be something very desirable to get a job. Apart from the wage or the salary, gainful employment often involves several other kinds of rewards: learning new things, doing something valuable for others, doing something particularly interesting, getting social recognition, establishing wider social contacts, and so on. Paid work has many possible advantages that can make it very attractive compared to alternative activities; it may, among other things, imply liberation from family obligations, that is, 'defamilialization' to use a concept suggested as parallel to that of decommodification (see, e.g., Lister 1994: 37, 2003:172).

Individuals' decisions to enter or to leave the labor market, or to increase or decrease their labor market input in terms of working hours, are thus affected by both 'push' and 'pull' factors, by both the stick and the carrot. To some considerable extent, people are driven into paid work out of necessity; they have to support themselves and lacking other means of subsistence they have little choice but to take a job. In the advanced capitalist world, it is not a matter of mere survival but of survival at a considerably higher normal standard of living. This economic necessity is a crucial mechanism for the labor market; if it did not exist employers would certainly have difficulty in recruiting people to jobs and it therefore has a commodifying impact. However, people already provided for are also to some degree attracted by the possibility of earning (more) money as well as by the non-material – social and other – remunerations provided in jobs. Accordingly, they engage in paid employment, although they would be able to survive with a reasonable standard of living without doing it. We can thus also identify an incentive mechanism that may lead to commodification of labor power, that is, to making people offer their work capacities for hire.

3
Labor Market Divisions

The most abstract concept of labor markets is helpful to depict the general features of the transactions between those who hire or want to hire labor power and those who offer it in exchange for money. As has been observed many times, however, in the real world there is not just one single labor market but several submarkets, more or less separated from one another (see, e.g., Althauser and Kalleberg 1981; Kalleberg and Sørensen 1979). Submarkets can be distinguished along several dimensions and we find quite a few such attempts in the literature. Jobs are usually the point of departure, as it is their characteristics that make up the major dividing lines. This chapter concentrates on a number of significant labor market divisions and the assumption is that they provide fundamental structures for actors to adapt to or try to transgress or transform. By identifying submarkets, we also establish a basis for analyzing individuals' mobility.

To begin, I call attention to the spatial dimension of labor markets. It refers to their geographic location and extension, due to the distribution of jobs. A common pattern is that vacancies are filled by individuals living in the area in which the workplace is located or within some suitable commuting distance from it. Nevertheless, for many jobs, prospective incumbents are searched for and recruited from outside the local community or region. The geographic dimension is, as a consequence, directly associated with the two mobility phenomena of commuting and migration.

Labor markets are also divided along other lines. As pointed out in Chapter 2, jobs can be classified in terms of bundles of work tasks that are the constituent elements in occupations. This dimension expresses the division of labor in society, that is, how far the processes of differentiation and specialization have gone. An important aspect is that occupations – or families of them – are more or less exclusively reserved for people with certain skills or credentials. Even without such very sharp mechanisms, however, the occupational dividing lines in labor markets make up obstacles to the mobility of individuals between jobs.

Sectors represent another type of division in the labor market. We have previously run into the distinction between four categories: the capitalist, the government, the voluntary, and the household sector respectively. I make a few further remarks on this divide here, but before that another dimension will be discussed, namely the division into three familiar spheres: agriculture, industry, and services. This three-sector model is normally understood as a descriptive classification, but in post-industrial thinking it has to some extent been given a place within a theoretical framework. Sociologists and economists have suggested yet another sector categorization, a division into a primary and a secondary labor market. There is a rather extensive literature on the labor market's 'dual' or 'split' character, its 'segmentation' or 'balkanization'. Bifurcation is a common denominator in many of these accounts, but when it is assumed that there are more than two categories we usually run into the concepts of segment and segmentation. This kind of approach has played a significant role particularly in many American labor market studies and is commented upon below.

Occupational divisions are, in addition, related to class divisions, although the two are analytically distinct. The concept of occupation generally refers to the technical division of labor, whereas class is a matter of social relations. This does not exclude, however, that the two dimensions are correlated; for example probably without exception, assembly line workers are categorized as belonging to what we call the industrial proletariat. In contrast, to take two other examples, carpenters as well as lawyers can be (small) capitalists hiring others to work for them, self-employed without workers (petty bourgeoisie), or employees. The concept of class thus goes beyond the technical division of labor and focuses on aspects of hierarchy, power, and, sometimes, exploitation. For a long time, there have been extensive discussions among sociologists on how to depict the character and development of the class structure in modern societies. This chapter is primarily concentrated upon two approaches that I consider the most important among more recent accounts.

Finally, there are divisions along gender, age, ethnic, and similar lines in the labor market. I will above all pay attention to gender, but the same or corresponding ways of reasoning can be applied to other dimensions. Certain jobs are more or less earmarked for men and for women respectively, which in turn is associated with a strongly uneven gender distribution. In this context, it is not the biased composition *per se* that is important but rather how jobs are constructed to fit in with supposed male or female characteristics.

Spatial divisions

The reason why spatial divisions of labor markets deserve attention is that jobs tend to cluster geographically and that jobholders tend to do the same. Due to the size and composition of existing industries, local labor markets differ substantially from one another in terms of employment opportunities. Metropolitan areas do not only have an abundance of jobs but also a great diversity of them, attracting people with various skills and educational backgrounds. In contrast, other labor markets, such as those located in remote regions and based on the extraction of natural resources, are much more limited and one-sided and they often provide jobs that require very specific qualifications.

Sometimes vacancies can be filled with jobseekers from the local area, but it happens that labor power has to be furnished from outside. The recruitment base varies from one job to another and for certain highly specialized jobs, incumbents must be picked from a thin stratum of workers. Employers may thus have to search in very specific environments, perhaps in different countries, to find the individuals in whom they are interested. In some cases, it is even a requirement that candidates are sought, more or less, all over the world; for example, due to political considerations and agreements, quite a few leading positions in the United Nations must be filled with individuals from different countries. These assignments are of course exceptional, but among the large and growing number of international organizations there are other examples.

In regard to mobility, geography implies that there are certain obstacles to be overcome. Employers' prospects of recruiting people from outside of the local area are related to individuals' willingness and capability to commute or move. Another option is to move jobs to places where suitable employees are available. 'Suitable' labor sometimes translates into 'cheap' labor, but – as Manuel Castells (1996: 93) has pointed out – it may also be a matter of workers who have proper skills or who are easily controlled. When employers make decisions on allocation of production and other activities, the potential supply of workers can be a crucial factor, although there are also many other important circumstances to consider. Among other things, the discussion on globalization focuses on how jobs are located and relocated with respect to countries, regions, cities, etc. (see, e.g., Castells 1996: Ch. 2). One essential development in recent decades, the deindustrialization of the advanced Western economies, has been accompanied by a considerable expansion of industrial employment in some other countries. Guy Standing (1999: 64) has suggested that globalization must not lead to increasing labor mobility, since multinational firms can rather easily redistribute their jobs. This may be true in many cases, but there can be severe obstacles to such redistributions. Decisions on employment allocation usually involve a complex set of factors besides the supply of suitable labor: distance from raw materials, from consumer markets, and from business partners, the hosting country's infrastructure and political stability, etc.

Employers have most frequently been considered the main actors, and sometimes the only significant actors, in shaping the economic geography of capitalism. In contrast, Andrew Herod (2001) has argued that workers and organized labor should also be attributed a decisive role in spatial change. According to his view, the working class is active in several ways, directly or indirectly and consciously or unconsciously, in determining the location of capitalist economic activities. Herod wants to see what he calls a 'labor geography' instead of the 'geography of labor' that is common among analysts in the field. There is a good point in this argument; spatial developments obviously derive from the interaction of different social forces, although large capitalist employers often have an upper hand or even the ultimate power in making such decisions.

Once the location of a workplace is determined, we can distinguish at least three important geographic aspects concerning recruitment of people to jobs. The first has reference to the possibilities of commuting. In the course of a few decades, it has become much easier for people to commute long distances and today many have their jobs quite far from their homes. There is also the option of weekly or other periodic commuting, staying in the workplace neighborhood during work periods and returning home in between. Second, it may be possible for employees to work from a distance – which may mean from home – thanks to computers and other communication facilities. Despite still being a much more limited alternative than some had expected, there is a potential for at least part-time arrangements of that kind – to an extent that was unthinkable just a few decades ago. One implication is that commuting does not have to be such a heavy burden, as it would otherwise be. Third, if individuals are to be recruited from a long distance, they may simply have to move from one place to another; this includes migration both inside and across national borders.

Modern means of transportation and communication have made it easier to recruit people from a spatially wider area than ever before, but far from everything can be done with these means. It takes energy to commute long distances and something, either the job or the individual's life outside of work, will have to pay a price; this 'something' can be working pace, quality of work performance, health, time for family and children, recreational activities, and perhaps other aspects as well. Working at home is impossible in many jobs, because incumbents' presence is required at the workplace. In other words, it is easy to understand why, to a large extent, both employers and jobseekers look for one another in the area where they are located. Even though they have generally widened in recent decades, the geographic boundaries of labor markets are still rather narrow.

An important aspect is that employment and life outside of work interact. Many families have a complex daily puzzle to solve to make everything fit together with two income-earners' jobs, housework, children's schools or daycare, other social responsibilities, leisure time activities, and so on (see, e.g. Crompton 1999; Drew, Emerek and Mahon 1998; OECD 2001: Ch. 4). There are numerous factors that must be taken into consideration when in the search for ways of reconciling paid work and family life. For one thing, it may be very important to have flexible arrangements, not least in terms of working time. Once satisfactory solutions to the work-family puzzle have been obtained, people have strong incentives to stay in their jobs and they become less likely to look for employment far away; the local labor market is thus simply the only realistic arena for many who want to have paid work.

We must also consider other obstacles for those who want to move. It is costly to move geographically and, depending on the distance, there is a risk for relocated individuals that their social ties – to relatives and friends – become weakened or broken off. This must then be weighed against the benefits of getting to know new people and gaining new experiences. Another aspect is that when people move across national borders they may run into visa and work-permit problems, although it does not always seem to make much difference if such obstacles are eliminated. We can, for example, note that citizens within the European Union have the legal right to move to and settle down anywhere in the member states, but that so far very few have made use of this right (European Commission 2002: 28). Numerous restraining factors, such as language difficulties and the social and psychological costs of becoming an immigrant, are in operation. In my view, one of the most underestimated of these costs is that immigration frequently leads to social degradation.

Nevertheless, there are many who move geographically (see, e.g., Castles and Miller 2003; Faist 2000; Stalker 1994). The long-distance migrants consist of heterogeneous categories and one such category is that of professionals who are rather strongly inclined to look for the kind of job they want in other regions or countries instead of taking something else closer at hand. In discussing globalization, Castells (1996: 93) asks whether it is reasonable to talk about a global labor force and his answer is basically no, although with some qualifications. The argument behind the negative answer is that we do not yet have a unified global economy, but there is, in Castells's view, one exception: the small but increasing segment of professionals and scientists; for these groups, geographic obstacles are relatively unimportant.

Another category of migrants is made up of workers who are willing to go to wherever they have a chance to find a decent life. Many of these individuals suffer from political and other kinds of repression, but their motives may also be primarily economic in character. Large numbers of people move from poverty in countries where they may have great difficulties in finding employment at all and where no unemployment benefit and other social benefits are available. A crucial aspect for geographic mobility is hence the differences in pay and working and living conditions across countries and across regions. For an immigrant from the Third World, it may entail a huge increase of income and living standard to take even a low-paid job in the affluent world. At the same time, the economically developed nations put up various obstacles – visa requirements and the like – to prevent too large inflows of poor immigrants.

Occupations, sectors and segments

The following section deals with labor market divisions in terms of occupations, sectors, and segments. Although these categories are often not very clearly defined, they all play a significant role in our conceptions of how labor markets are divided. I start with occupation that represents the smallest and most basic unit of the three categories.

Occupational divisions

A most essential divider in labor markets is occupational specialization. As pointed out in the previous chapter, different work tasks are combined into jobs that in turn tend to cluster into occupations or professions. Some jobs, however, have no clear identity of that kind, as incumbents are not very specialized but do more or less anything at their workplace. Still, this is exceptional and most jobs can actually be assigned an occupational label. The existing occupational categories and divisions in the labor market have evolved out of a complex historic process, including negotiations between various actors such as employers, workers, employers' associations, trade unions, educational institutions, and politicians.

In some occupations the available jobs are few and they are geographically scattered or concentrated in a few places, whereas in other cases jobs can easily be found almost everywhere. A main characteristic of occupations, and particularly of professions, is that they are more or less closed to people without the required skills, education, or experience. It is then simply necessary to have the right background to find employment and the number of potential jobseekers is consequently limited, typically by credentials requirements. Unless an individual wants to try something different, having a specialized occupation means being restricted to rather few job openings. Both employers and jobseekers may be interested in keeping it that way; the former need people with certain skills and expertise and those who have the proper qualifications do not want unqualified jobseekers to take 'their' jobs.

However, even if, for example, an engineer and a lawyer have very different education and skills and normally look for very different kinds of jobs, it may happen that they become applicants for the same vacancy. For certain higher positions in society it does not seem to matter very much what specific occupational background a candidate has – if engineer or lawyer does not make much difference – but then, obviously, we are not talking about jobs that require specific knowledge in engineering or law. Instead, the decisive aspect appears to have something to do with the candidates' general educational level; although incumbents of the two occupations mentioned usually appear in very separate parts of the labor market, they have academic degrees with about the same standing.

Jobs and occupations are the basic categories for those who do research on social mobility. They represent origins and destinations of movements within the labor market (of course, origin and destination may also refer to people's status as unemployed or as being outside of the labor force). There are many reasons why studies on job mobility and, to take the viewpoint of the organization, labor turnover are interesting; these phenomena are related to individual and workplace characteristics as well as to business cycles (see, e.g., Hedberg 1967; Holmlund 1984). For example, youths are generally more inclined than middle-age and older people to switch jobs. A workplace with low wages and bad working conditions can be expected to have high turnover rates relative to those where wages are higher and conditions better. Recessions tend to slow down mobility, as people then have fewer vacancies for which to look but cling to what they have.

Studies of job mobility frequently focus on individuals' changes of employer. This was noted in the previous chapter and declared not to be all that satisfactory, because it excludes moves between jobs within the workplace (cf. Parnes 1954: 25–6). At the same time, however, we must be aware of other limitations in studying internal job mobility; it is often difficult to distinguish job switches at the workplace from simple modifications in work assignments. A crucial question is also which and how many occupational categories are distinguished. The choices made in these respects will directly affect how much mobility we discover. It is common in empirical studies to distinguish rather broad categories – everything else would be impracticable – but the more detailed occupational schemes we use, the more mobility we find.

The significance of sector

Although, or because, the term sector is frequently applied to designate various labor market divisions, it appears to have a rather trivial, descriptive meaning. This nevertheless means that it can be incorporated into theoretical constructs. A common sector distinction is that between agriculture, industry, and services, three categories that we can find, for example, in the Organization for Economic Cooperation and Development (OECD) publications and statistics on employment. This three-sector model gives us some idea of broad economic developments, although the dividing lines are somewhat arbitrarily drawn. To give just one illustration, if a manufacturing company has a staff of its own to clean its factory and office buildings, these workers will be classified as employed in industry. However, in the event that this work has been outsourced to a cleaning company, the people doing the work will be counted as service sector employees.

Leaving these empirical problems aside, I will briefly call attention to post-industrial theory and its treatment of the notion of sector. To be more precise, I intend to make a few remarks in relation to the perspective put forward by Daniel Bell, probably the most well-known theorist in the field, in the second edition of his *The Coming of Post-Industrial Society* (1976). This edition has a freshly written preface that is crucial for my discussion, because it is an effort to develop the theoretical concepts in the book and it provides a number of significant observations. For comparative purposes, Bell (1976: xii, 116–19) separates the industrial and pre-industrial forerunners to post-industrial society. The economy of the pre-industrial world was based upon such activities as agriculture, fishing, and forestry and can be characterized as extractive. Industrial society above all means production of goods by utilization of energy and machines. Post-industrialism, in contrast, is primarily 'processing' of knowledge and information in service production. Whereas the specific designs of pre-industrial and industrial society are characterized as a 'game against nature' and a 'game against fabricated nature' respectively, post-industrialism represents a 'game between persons'.

The advent of post-industrialism implies that production of services becomes the dominant economic activity in society. However, services also exist in the pre-industrial and industrial world, but they are then of another kind (Bell 1976: 15). In pre-industrial society, they were mainly a matter of work in private households; those who could afford it hired people to help with the tasks of daily life. With the rise of industrialism there was an expansion of services related to the production of goods: transportation, communication, financing, etc. Goods must be transported, marketed, and sold, and the need for improvement of the financial system developed. Post-industrialism, finally, means the growth of other types of services such as education, healthcare, and similar professional activities. A vital assumption in the theory is, however, that post-industrial society does not replace industrial society totally any more than the latter replaced pre-industrialism (Bell 1976: xii, xvi). Instead, it is suggested that the three types of productive activities will continue to coexist. Strictly speaking, therefore, we should talk about a pre-industrial, industrial and post-industrial *sector* rather than society. One problem in Bell's analysis is that he does not provide any definition of the service concept, but I raise this question in Chapter 6, where post-industrial theory will be subject to a more detailed discussion.

One sector distinction with a clearly theoretical connotation is that between capitalist and non-capitalist labor markets (the latter including, on the employing side, the public sector, voluntary non-profit organizations, and households). This issue has already been dealt with in Chapter 2, where the ambition was to spell out some of the main differences between the four categories. I just want to add a few things and my comments will be limited to a comparison between the capitalist and the public sector labor markets. In this connection, the concept of 'marketness' – as outlined in Chapter 2 – will be ascribed a crucial role. Employment in capitalist firms is subject to profitability demands and thus to firms' success or lack of success in markets. Workers' jobs are dependent on the condition that their firm makes enough profit for its owners, which in turn presupposes that customers buy enough quantities of their goods and services and do so to prices that exceed costs. In contrast, in producing educational, healthcare, childcare, or other services, public sector employees do not have to bother about profitability but only about the work itself and the use values aimed at. Also capitalist firms are oriented toward producing use values – in that sense there is no difference – but the overriding purpose is profit.

We may ask whether the profit/non-profit difference between the capitalist and the public sector has any significant impact upon work cultures. Although this is a highly relevant question as regards how organizations in the two sectors function, it is not much studied. It can possibly be argued that the strivings for profit make capitalist firms particularly sensitive to consumers' needs; otherwise they will be unable to sell as large quantities of their produce as required and they must therefore adjust themselves to consumers' desires. A complication with the argument is that many firms use deceiving measures – such as manipulative television and radio commercials – to increase sales; this calls for at least some modification of the idea of consumer sovereignty. However, the lower degree of marketness in the public sector may imply too weak incentives for taking people's wishes into consideration; instead politicians, bureaucrats, and professionals have an upper hand in determining what will be produced and how it is to be done.

The absence of a profitability criterion in many public sector activities is important, among other things because jobs are not eliminated due to insufficient profits. Principally there are two different ways in which public sector jobs disappear. One is that the services produced are not needed any longer or to the same extent as before; for example, a school may have to reduce its teaching-staff, because the number of children of school age is going down. The other explanation as to why jobs are done away with in the non-profit public sector is that the budget does not hold. Expenditures may not be met by sufficient incomes from taxation and fees and the possibility of taking loans may be exhausted. Deficits are likely to be tolerated for some period of time – if loans can be provided – but there are both political and financial limits to this.

Job security has traditionally been lower in the capitalist sector than in the public sector, but with large cutbacks of government expenditures and employment certain exceptions to that pattern can be found (OECD 1997: 132–3; Furåker 2000). Still, the difference in terms of profitability demands is reflected in how downsizing is handled. In capitalist firms, managers are normally required to execute layoffs rather quickly, although the process may be slowed down due to employee resistance and because employment protection legislation and agreements have to be considered. Layoffs in the public sector usually involve a political process, which means that non-market factors are allowed a greater part. This is likely to make the whole process protracted and the end result more open.

There is also variation in wage-setting practices that has to do with the degree of marketness. Whereas capitalist firms can outbid each other in order to recruit the workers they demand, public authorities and institutions are not that likely to do the same, at least not very openly. The mainly tax-based financial resources in the public sector are allocated to various activities through political decisions and politicians will hardly accept that the agencies receiving the money use it for competition among themselves. The possibilities of competing with capitalist employers are also limited, because large tax incomes require that capitalist firms make enough profit. If workers on the same skill level would be paid clearly more in the public than in the capitalist sector, detrimental consequences can be expected to follow in the latter, which in turn would affect tax collection negatively; in other words, there is a risk for a negative spiral to appear. The hierarchical order described explains why we usually find a wage gap between workers with similar education and skills to the advantage to those employed in private profit-oriented firms.

Labor market segments

In the next few pages, I pay attention to another 'sector' division that has often been discussed, mainly among American researchers but to some extent also among European researchers. Different labels are used in the literature, but several of them have one thing in common; they suggest that the labor market is specifically divided. For example, the labor market is considered to be 'segmented', 'dual', 'split', 'balkanized', or broken up into a 'primary 'and a 'secondary' sector (see, e.g., Kerr 1977; Doeringer and Piore 1971; Gordon 1972; Edwards, Reich and Gordon 1975; Gordon, Edwards and Reich 1982). Some researchers stick to a bifurcation thesis, but others argue that three or more segments should be distinguished. One variant has been to divide the primary sector into two sub-segments or tiers (Edwards 1979: 165–77; Piore 1975: 126–8).

A basic ingredient in this literature is the distinction between primary and secondary labor markets. In the primary sector, jobs are highly qualified, secure, well paid, and part of career ladders, whereas in the secondary labor market, in glaring contrast, jobs do not require much education, they are insecure, badly paid, and associated with little opportunity for promotion. Mobility between the two segments is supposed to be if not zero at least very low. We should note that the meaning of the words 'primary' and 'secondary' is not unambiguous (Doeringer and Piore 1971:

166–7; Althauser and Kalleberg 1981: 124). Sometimes reference is made to the demand side (jobs or firms) and sometimes to the supply side (the workforce).

Surveying how the supposed segmentation of labor markets is to be explained, Michael Piore (1980: 24–6) has discovered four principal explanations in the literature. The first is that employers tend to give particularly favorable treatment to workers in whose training they have invested; these workers can be considered a 'quasi-fixed' production factor or 'quasi capital'. A second explanation is that employers concede to the demands by certain groups of employees – exerted through union or other kinds of collective activity – to have job security. Third, a similar idea is that duality has its origin in national contracts between employers and employees, also presupposing differences among various categories of workers. The final explanation, suggested by Marxists and radical economists, is that employers try to divide the workforce, thus making it less likely that workers form a united class. Something might be learnt from this classification, but we should keep in mind that the theories on segmentation have not had the ambition to present a general analytical framework for the study of labor markets. They once developed out of research done on poverty and employment problems in the United States and have not really supplied more than 'a "time specific" set of hypotheses', to use a phrase by David Gordon (1972: 43). Yet, it does not follow that there are no general conclusions to draw from this work.

The distinction between primary and secondary labor markets is rather close to that between a 'core' and a 'peripheral' workforce, formulated by, among others, John Atkinson (e.g., 1984, 1987; Atkinson and Meager 1986). This is a European brand with a roughly similar content but with another background; it is intended to spell out the consequences of increasing domestic and international competition. The idea is that because capitalist firms are subject to intensified competition in the market they have to become more flexible, which makes them divide the workforce into a core and a periphery. Atkinson thus takes the firm and not the labor market as a whole as his point of departure. In the core, above all we find well-educated and well-paid workers with full-time and permanent jobs, while the periphery is mainly populated with workers with low education, low pay, temporary and often part-time jobs. However, the periphery also includes highly educated consultants and similar categories, who are contracted on a time-limited basis; this is another special feature of Atkinson's approach.

A key concept in the discussion of segmented labor markets is that of the internal labor market. It can refer either to an employing organization or to an occupation (Doeringer and Piore 1971: 2–4; Althauser and Kalleberg 1981: 121-3). The implication of the formation of an internal labor market is that those who are outside can only be recruited through specific 'ports of entry'; the remaining jobs are available only for those who are already employed by the organization. There has been a good deal of discussion as to why there are internal labor markets and the above-mentioned classification by Piore can perhaps supply some lead. He has also co-authored another text, in which three factors are suggested to be important: specificity of skills, on-the-job-training, and custom (Doeringer and Piore 1971: 13–27).

Apparently, the first two of these factors are closely connected with one another. Some skills are specific to a particular job or workplace – and to some degree they may have been acquired through on-the-job training – whereas others are more universal. If employees leave their workplace they will take both types of skill with them, although it is only the general skills that have a value in the labor market (in practice, the distinction between the two categories is not all that clear). Since it is costly to replace people, employers are interested in reducing quits, especially when large investments have been done in on-the-job training or other kinds of education. They have every reason to find mechanisms that can tie their best personnel to the organization for a longer period. One way of doing this is to offer positive wage or salary developments and good career opportunities; to make this plausible, competition from outside needs to be kept under control and an internal labor market is thus established.

The third factor, custom, is 'an unwritten set of rules based largely upon past practice or precedent' (Doeringer and Piore 1971: 23). What happens in a workplace, above all in a long-term perspective, is that workers interact with one another and develop common norms and rules for the various activities in which they take part. Custom is a consequence of employment stability and provides principles for wage determination and other allocations. It thus represents some kind of rigidity in relation to dynamic economic forces. However, management – particularly at lower levels – is also part of the environment and may find alternative norms discomforting or even wrong. Besides, it may come to the conclusion that 'the cost of the inefficient practice' is 'less than the cost of change' (Doeringer and Piore 1971: 25).

Internal labor markets are thus valuable to part of the workforce, as they imply employment stability and other advantages. These arrangements are also important for employers, because they reduce the costs of labor turnover, including costs for recruitment and training of new recruits who need to acquire job-specific skills. There is a further significant aspect to consider and it is related to internal recruitment. Taking people from outside usually involves a great deal of uncertainty about the actual capacities and motivation of candidates, since credentials do not always convey that much reliable information on such dimensions. Selecting people from inside is different in that respect; if an individual has been at the workplace for a long time, it is likely that her potential qualifications for a job are well known among managers and colleagues.

No matter what term is being used – dual labor market, primary and secondary labor markets, core and periphery, or whatever – the literature referred to presents rather similar ways of viewing the labor market. As pointed out above, much of the research has been done in the 1960s and the 1970s in the United States with its specific situation regarding ethnic minorities in the big cities, but there are also some European studies using, more or less critically, a similar point of departure (see, e.g., Carroll and Mayer 1986; Sengenberger 1978, 1987; Wilkinson 1981). The question is whether segmentation theory gives us a good description of the labor markets studied and, if so, to what extent it can be generalized. I share the doubts of Mark Granovetter (1981: 21) as to why the economy should 'be cut up in some small number of separate markets... that are semi-impermeable and have little mutual influence'. It has also been said that dual or segmented labor market theory 'oversimplifies reality by incorporating many conflicting dimensions of inequality in a single dichotomy' (Jacobs and Breiger 1994: 45). A crucial criterion of segmentation is that mobility between the segments identified should be very limited, but this has actually not been verified empirically (cf. Cain 1976; Granovetter 1981: 20; Jacobs 1983; Jacobs and Breiger 1994).

What we need to know, in order to adopt the theory of labor market segmentation, is whether the division of workers into one category with a favorable 'core' position and another with a disadvantaged 'peripheral' status is relatively permanent or not. This question involves two dimensions. First, there is the mobility issue, that is, to what extent individuals belonging to the secondary workforce will remain in their position without ever having a chance to get a job in the primary sector or the core. If we discover that it is rather easy for them to find such a job, it also means that the merit of segmentation theory has to be questioned. Second, we must ask whether the advantages that the primary sector has over the secondary sector – in terms of payment, employment protection, and working conditions – are stable over time. It may happen that – due to market forces – conditions become if not equalized at least more even. Without going further into the problems with the segmentation approach, we must note that researchers' interest in it seems to have faded away, which is probably a sign of its limited usefulness.

It is unclear whether intensified competition tends to lead to a core-periphery division, but I think this distinction can be used in a slightly different way, for a more general description of certain workplace phenomena. All work organizations need to recruit personnel from time to time, partly because employees incessantly quit their jobs for different reasons. Moreover, many organizations do not have a stable need for workers; it may fluctuate from day to day, from week to week, across seasons, or from one year to another. Sometimes extensive changes take place in a short period of time, whereas during other periods there is little change. Any organization of some size is likely to have a mixture of personnel – some with longer and others with shorter job tenure (although it happens that one cohort of employees is clearly dominant) – and to have a continuous need for fresh recruitment. New employees will have to fit in with the organization and whether this will work out positively is difficult to know in advance. Therefore, employers are somewhat wary of newcomers at the workplace and they want to have the freedom to act and react in accordance with changing circumstances.

In a market economy, rapid adjustments due to external pressures are relentlessly needed; nevertheless core workers have a crucial role, as they represent continuity and are the best suited to handle various troublesome tasks at the workplace or in relation to customers, suppliers, and others. From an employer perspective it is essential to find a reasonable balance between change and continuity. With too much and too rapid change, the core may simply become too much impaired to the detriment of the firm's activities. Employers instead need to develop stable, long-term employment relationships with some of their personnel and to do this they may have to give in to certain worker demands. However, it is also vital for them to have a reservoir of peripheral workers who eventually can be transferred into the core; peripheral workers must therefore at least be given the hope of becoming a core member. This is then consequently a fundamental argument against too strong divisions of the workforce.

Class divisions

Among sociologists the concept of social class, or social stratification, is one of the most intensely debated topics. One field in which class plays a crucial role is the study of people's life chances, connected with the discussion on equal opportunity for individuals regardless of what social background they have. Despite increasing standards of living and numerous reforms with respect to education, healthcare, housing, etc., inequality persists in the advanced capitalist countries and it is associated with people's socioeconomic status and heritage. One kind of approach to the issue of life chances is the research on mobility between social classes or strata (see, e.g., Erikson and Goldthorpe 1993; Ganzeboom, Treiman and Ultee 1991; Lipset and Bendix 1959). It is then asked what happens to people during their life course and to what extent the principle of equal opportunity is overrun by social origin. The aim is to examine the permeability of the class structure, that is, to determine whether or to what degree members of different classes or strata are able to transcend the social divisions already established. Mobility can refer to both vertical and horizontal movements, up and down a hierarchy of positions or between locations on the same hierarchical level. Obviously, in the first case, the class structure must be conceived as hierarchical, which is not self-evident. Moreover, social mobility may be studied from an intra- or an inter-generational perspective, related either to early positions in the individual's own career or to family background.

The concept of class is furthermore crucial within another framework, referring to whether individuals with similar positions in the social division of labor tend to develop similar interpretations of their situation and to act concertedly. This approach, which has a prominent place in Marxist but also in other perspectives, departs from the assumption that people's values and norms are somehow correlated with their socioeconomic position. The possibilities for collective action – on the basis of a common socioeconomic situation – are then the focus of the analysis. Linking up with the issue of individuals' life chances, we can say that this approach has to do with collective life chances and it is connected with other concepts such as class conflict and class struggle.

There is a huge sociological literature on class and stratification. Sometimes prestige is taken to be a decisive underlying factor. In *The Social System,* Talcott Parsons (1951: 172) argues that class refers to 'an aggregate of kinship units of approximately equal status in the system of stratification' and this system is supposed to be based on prestige. In other words, the essence of the concept belongs to a subjective dimension. Although Parsons (1964: 328–9, 426–7) also emphasizes that prestige is mainly founded on occupation, he simplifies the issue too much and it is not surprising that class is a very secondary component in his perspective. Concepts can surely be defined in any way we like, at least as long as it is done in a clear and logically consistent way, but we must always look for the best tools possible for the analysis of given phenomena. In this case, the approach suggested by Parsons and his followers does not meet that requirement; for example, the emergence of class-related organizations such as unions can hardly be satisfactorily dealt with in terms of prestige hierarchies.

Occupational prestige scales and status rankings have been a significant element above all in American sociology. One example is the series of studies in *Yankee City*, starting in the 1930s, by Lloyd Warner (1963) and another is the work on occupational rating scales in the mid-twentieth century by Cecil North and Paul Hatt (1949; Hatt 1950; see also, e.g., Reiss 1961). There are several theoretical and empirical problems with the attempts to establish a status order (see, e.g., Gordon 1963: 173–93). One of the key issues is whether a status continuum makes it meaningful to distinguish separate classes at all (cf. Brown 1965: 113–20). Gradations may be of interest, in particular if they include objective factors such as ownership, power, income, and education, but what it all comes down to is, as usual, what we want to study.

For the purpose of analyzing labor markets, a gradational approach has obvious limitations and in order to formulate a more fruitful class concept we need to consider relational aspects (cf. Crompton 1998: 15; Ossowski

1963). My next step is to turn to Karl Marx and Max Weber who both provided relational approaches, although the presence of gradational dimensions is evident in both authors' work. Thereafter I continue to two more recent attempts to adjust the classical perspectives to the developments in contemporary societies.

The classics

It has been repeated many times that Marx never systematically spelled out the concept of class in his writings, although there is a fragment of such an outline in the unfinished last chapter of *Capital* (Marx 1998: 870–1). Nevertheless, class plays an important role throughout his work and, generally, it has references to people with a similar relationship to the means of production. Ownership and non-ownership of such means are thus crucial; to see this more clearly, we need to go back to the concept of mode of production that provides an analytical point of departure. Each mode of production is characterized by a set of social relationships and by uncovering them we can find out how the system works, that is, the *differentia specifica* of the systems of feudalism, capitalism, socialism, etc. These make up the basis for class divisions and they have to do with ownership and control of the productive resources, the division of labor, and the mechanisms for distributing the outcome of production.

The first dividing line in a capitalist system then goes between those who are owners of means of production and those who are not; in order to earn a living the latter have to offer the former their labor power for hire. Accordingly, there are two main categories: wage or salaried workers who hire out labor power in the market and capitalists who hire it. However, the basis of class relations for Marx is how production is organized; according to his view, the secret of profit-making is nowhere else but in the sphere of production. The fundamental aspect is what happens when the owner of money and the bearer of labor power leave the 'noisy' market place and enter the factory (Marx 1996: 186). Even so, it all begins when workers and owners of capital meet in the market.

A complication is that both capitalists and workers are very heterogeneous categories. Among the former we find small entrepreneurs with a few employees as well as large business owners with a staff of thousands and among the latter there are several divisions with respect to skills, authority, type of work, etc. Marx was not consistent in his treatment of workforce divisions, but a crucial distinction is that between 'productive' and 'unproductive' workers. Individuals are considered to be productive if they produce 'surplus value' for the capitalist, regardless of whether their work is a matter of producing goods or services:

'If we may take an example from outside the sphere of production of material objects, a schoolmaster is a productive laborer, when, in addition to belabouring the heads of his scholars, he works like a horse to enrich the school proprietor. That the latter has laid out his capital in a teaching factory, instead of in a sausage factory, does not alter the rela-tion' (Marx 1996: 510).

Those who produce surplus value are exploited and thus have an antago-nistic relationship to capital. It all boils down to the assumptions behind the labor theory of value; I have already dismissed that theory and I can see no feasible method to determine who is 'productive' and who is not.

In other words, the differentiation of employees is an unsolved problem in Marx's analysis. Since his days, certain issues related to that unsolved problem have become increasingly more urgent for class analysis: the growth in the proportion of white-collar workers, the enlargement of the service sector, the expansion of public sector employment, or, to phrase it in another way, the rise of the 'new middle-class'. Marx's theoretical frame-work is not sufficient to deal with these issues in a satisfactory manner. A large number of neo-Marxists have tried to fill the gap, most often without very successful results, and I will shortly pay attention to the most thought-out and interesting of these attempts, but let us first take a look at Weber's notion of class.

It should be noted that Weber was very brief in his treatment of the class concept. There are not that many pages on the topic in *Economy and Society* and they are neither systematic nor overwhelmingly illuminating. These pages present an approach to the subject of class that is partly different from that of Marx, although some striking similarities also appear. For Weber, relationship to the means of production is an important aspect, but in his view the main factor seems to be the market situation that affects life chances. We should keep in mind that Weber's – like Marx's – handling of the concept of class is not all that consistent.

Weber (1978: 927) considers the class concept relevant 'when (1) a number of people have in common a specific causal component of their life chances, insofar as (2) this component is represented exclusively by economic interests in the possession of goods and opportunities for income, and (3) is represented under the conditions of the commodity or labor markets'. In other words, class has something to do with economic opportunities, ownership is important, and so are market chances. Most notably, perhaps, the author also says that 'property' and 'lack of property' are 'the basic categories of all class situations' and that those who are prop-ertyless have 'nothing to offer but their labor or the resulting products' (Weber 1978: 927). This is surely very much in line with Marx's way of rea-soning. Weber continues by pointing out that the two main categories are further differentiated due to the kind of property employed to obtain returns and to the kinds of services taken to the market. Ownership can refer to very different objects and a large number of examples are given, such as dwellings, workshops, stores, 'agriculturally usable land in large or small holdings', mines, cattle, 'men (slaves)', 'capital goods of all sorts, especially money or objects that can easily be exchanged for money', and 'products of one's own labor or of others' labor' (Weber 1978: 928).

Those who have nothing but their 'services' to offer are also differentiated. Weber (1978: 928) maintains that this differentiation is just as much related to the kind of services as to the way in which they are used. Yet, we are here left with a rather cryptic statement that does not help us very much, since no example is provided. Instead, Weber (1978: 928) comes back to what he considers to be the fundamental determinant of class, namely the chances that people have in the market: 'Class situation is … ultimately market situation'. This sounds like a contradiction to the quotation on ownership above, but the two statements can be interpreted as compatible insofar as property can be bought and sold. At this point there is a bridge between Weber and Marx, although the two differ in respect of the emphasis placed on markets and production respectively.

In a later text, Weber seems to attribute less prominence to the market aspect. He then argues that class has to do with 'the relative control over goods and skills' and 'their income-producing uses *within a given economic order*', that is, he does not suggest that there must be a market involved (Weber 1978: 302; emphasis added). On the same page, we find the following statement: 'In principle, the various controls over consumer goods, means of production, assets, resources and skills each constitute a *particular* class situation' (Weber 1978: 302; emphasis in original). These quotations do not exclude that the market has the key role, but the focus is placed on the concept of economic order, which in itself does not presuppose the existence of a market.

One other important difference between Marx and Weber – mentioned in Chapter 1 – should be emphasized and it has to do with collective action. In *The Communist Manifesto*, Marx and Engels (1998: 34) write that the history (insofar as it is written) 'of all hitherto existing society is the history of class struggles'. These struggles are simply considered to be a more or less automatic consequence of class-divided society and Marx and Engels express optimism about the development of collective action among the proletariat that they see as the bearer of a new social order: socialism and eventually communism. Weber (1978: 927) takes a cautious position arguing that classes are not 'communities' but 'possible, and frequent, bases for social action'. However, he has a much more skeptical attitude; although admitting the possibility of collective action, he soon adds that 'the emergence of an association or even of mere social action from a common class situation is by no means a universal phenomenon' (Weber 1978: 929). I return to these questions in the next chapter.

Two recent accounts

Social scientists of neo-Marxist orientation have struggled with the issue of how to develop the Marxian class categories in order to make them useful for the analysis of contemporary capitalist societies. In particular they have been concerned with the differentiation among employees and the rise of the so-called new middle class, although the question of public employees has frequently been left out. With regard to the position and development of the new middle class, very different solutions have been suggested (see, e.g., Gouldner 1979; Poulantzas 1978; Walker 1979; Wright 1978, 1985, 1997). Since the 1970s, there is one researcher who more than anyone else has been continuously struggling with the issues of class in contemporary capitalism, namely Erik Olin Wright, and I take a somewhat closer look at his contribution.

In his early work, Wright (1978) makes a simple distinction between economic ownership and possession that are both concepts related to control. Economic ownership means command over investments and the process of accumulation. Possession in turn refers to two different dimensions of control, on the one hand, over the physical means of production and, on the other hand, over other people's labor power. Ideal-typically, the main classes in capitalist society are each other's opposite in these respects; whereas the bourgeoisie has control along all three dimensions (investments, physical means of production, and labor power), the proletariat has no control in any of them. The most innovative element in Wright's (1978: 61–83) first analysis is the concept of 'contradictory class locations'. These positions can be found within a given mode of production or between two such modes. Wright suggests that it may be reasonable to characterize all class locations as contradictory, since they all are – as he sees it – antagonistic. However, in his view some positions are so in a double sense, because they are located between the basic contradictory class relations in society; these are referred to as 'contradictory class locations'.

Several years later, in a second scheme, Wright (1985: Ch. 3) comes up with another solution, intended to be more in line with Marx's theory of exploitation and inspired by the work of John Roemer. The latter had some years earlier developed a game theoretical approach to exploitation, basically arguing that an individual in a social relationship is exploited if she would be better off not being in that relationship (Roemer 1982). Wright's approach is above all a theory of how certain resources are distributed in a population and the consequences of this distribution. Because they have particular assets at their disposal, exploiting classes get a larger share than average of the total production in society.

The analysis focuses on four assets: labor power, means of production, organization, and skills. A given class may control more than one of these assets, but in each mode of production one of them is crucial. Wright also assumes that state socialism (statism) and even socialism (not yet at hand) can be conceived as exploitative systems. To be very brief, the scheme is as follows (Wright 1985: 82–6). In feudal society (serfdom), serfs' capacities for work make up a decisive asset for landlords – although the latter also have other assets – and command over labor power is the distinctive feature of feudalism, allowing landlords to exploit serfs. In contrast, capitalism is primarily characterized by unequal distribution of means of production; ownership of capital is the main asset for exploitation. The labor market is 'free', that is, labor power is equally distributed in the sense that the bearer of it is also its owner. In statism, private ownership of the means of production has been done away with, but organizational assets instead become particularly important and those who control the main state apparatuses are thus able to exploit the work of others. Finally, in socialism, the only remaining differences are to be found in the distribution of skill assets; by having certain selected skills, some individuals get more than average out of society's collected produce.

There are many problems with this theoretical scheme, in particular perhaps the definition of organizational assets and the treatment of how skilled workers exploit other workers and Wright has later discussed many of these problems himself. One of his main concerns is the analysis of the middle class and he comments upon 'the Weberian temptation'; although a Weberian perspective might help us avoid some of the Marxist 'conceptual knots', it implies lower theoretical ambitions and more ad-hoc solutions (Wright 1989: 313–23). Among other things, such an approach allows us to give up the attempt to link class analysis to modes of production, which would be to take a step backward. There is a point in this, but, if the crucial dimension of class relations is to be exploitation – which Wright (1989: 316) appears to suppose – the problem may lie in how the notion of mode of production is interpreted. Although the latter is not a Weberian concept, it might benefit from being developed in such a direction. I believe that if we are to use the mode of production concept it must be done in an open and non-presupposing way, in the spirit of Weber as a social scientist.

In response to various problems, Wright (1989: 347) introduced new concepts: secondary exploitation, mediated location, and temporal trajectories. Secondary exploitation is used to argue that organizational and skill exploitation should not be treated as bases for class divisions but for strata within classes. Mediated locations mean that some locations are simply best understood if viewed in terms of some other class relationship. The example given is the situation for married women whose class position may be assumed to be largely defined by that of their husbands. Temporal locations are those locations that people have for a shorter period of time. We can, for example, think of the jobs that students sometimes have during their studies; these jobs are commonly very different from what the education is expected to lead up to.

A further issue is that of the class location of state employees. Wright (1989: 342) is somewhat open to using the concept of a state mode of production. As he sees it, this might then imply that there is a dominant class, politically directing 'the appropriation and allocation of the surplus acquired by the state', and a dominated class, producing use values, with managers and bureaucrats in contradictory locations in between. However, probably because Wright is so preoccupied with the dominance of capitalism and cannot take the concept of mode of production simply to refer to the ways in which the production of goods and services are organized, he must look for another solution. He then argues that 'so long as state employment occurs within a society in which the capitalist mode of production is dominant, one cannot define the class locations of state employees exclusively in terms of their locations within state production relations'; rather they 'occupy a kind of dualistic class location' (Wright 1989: 345). To my mind, this does not very much clarify the issues at stake.

In yet another book, *Class Counts*, exploitation based on organizational and skill assets is no longer applied as a way of describing the class position of the new middle class (Wright 1997: 19–20 n.25). The latter is simply differentiated in terms of authority and skills without any reference to exploitation. Whereas capitalists own the means of production, hire workers and dominate them within production, managers and supervisor are employees themselves but have delegated power to control other workers and, consequently, they are in a contradictory class location. To make sure that they are effective and responsible, owners provide them with a 'loyalty rent'. People with skills and expertise represent a parallel case; they are difficult to control due to their knowledge of things of which others are ignorant and they thus also have significant power or authority. Employers must have the means to ensure their cooperation, effort, and loyalty, and there is accordingly a basis for a 'skill rent'.

Another highly influential account of the class structure in modern societies is that worked out by John Goldthorpe and his associates (1987, 2000: Ch. 10; Goldthorpe and Hope 1974; Erikson and Goldthorpe 1993). It has sometimes been considered 'Weberian', but Erikson and Goldthorpe (1993: 37) point out that they draw on the work of both Marx and Weber, although the ideas of these classic analysts have had to be adjusted to modern developed societies. Moreover, they maintain, quite accurately I believe, 'that the opposition between Marxian and Weberian conceptions of class that is by now enshrined in sociology textbooks is in many ways exaggerated, and especially in view of the fact that the work of neither author can be regarded as providing a canonical statement of his position' (Erikson and Goldthorpe 1993: 37 n.10).

The first Goldthorpe scheme was a scale based on occupational grading, in line with a common way of dealing with these issues during the first decades after World War II (Goldthorpe and Hope 1974). There is some continuity between this occupational grading scale and the later classifications, but we can immediately turn to *Social Mobility and Class Structure in Britain*, first published in 1980 and in a second edition in 1987. The point of departure in this book is the grouping of people as to whether they have, on the one hand, a similar market situation, referring to 'sources and levels of income and other employment conditions', 'degree of economic security and ... chances of economic advancement', and, on the other hand, a similar work situation referring to 'location within the systems of authority and control governing the processes of production in which they are engaged' (Goldthorpe 1987: 40). This is then the basis for a class scheme that includes seven categories aggregated from a collapsed version of the Goldthorpe-Hope occupational scale (Goldthorpe 1987: 40–3). Later we find different versions of the scheme, with several subcategories or collapsed into five categories (white-collar workers, petty bourgeoisie, farm workers, skilled workers, and non-skilled workers) as well as into three (non-manual workers, farm workers, and manual workers) (Erikson and Goldthorpe 1993: 38–9).

Employment relations have become more important over time for Goldthorpe and his collaborators. Although also in the first edition of *Social Mobility*, employment status (that is, in this case, the distinction between employers, self-employed and employees) was treated as an important dimension, it has eventually been emphasized more strongly (cf. Marshall, Swift and Roberts 1997: 23–4). This is, for example, reflected in the later division of the self-employed into 'small proprietors with employees, small proprietors without employees, and farmers and smallholders' (Marshall, Swift and Roberts 1997: 23). We should observe that Erikson and Goldthorpe (1993: 29–35) emphasize that their approach is 'class-structural' and their class concept refers to social positions defined in terms of relationships in the labor market or workplaces; it is thus relational and not hierarchical or gradational.

A specific innovation that Goldthorpe (see, e.g., Goldthorpe 1982; Erikson and Goldthorpe 1993: 37–47; Goldthorpe 2000: Ch. 10) has introduced is that employment relations can be based on 'service' or 'labor' contracts respectively. The starting point is that employment relations – and not work tasks *per se* – make up the decisive elements for the class concept (Erikson and Goldthorpe 1993: 42 n.14, 43 n.16, 236). While labor contracts 'entail a relatively short-term and specific exchange of money for effort', service contracts are arranged for employees who 'exercise delegated authority or specialized knowledge and expertise in the interest of the employing organisation' (Erikson and Goldthorpe 1993: 41–2; emphasis removed). Most significantly, a service contract also implies prospects of future rewards: salary increases, social benefits, career opportunities, etc. This type of arrangement requires that the employing organization is prepared to put great reliance upon people. Goldthorpe (2000: 217–21) later developed his arguments as to why employers are willing to trust employees in the service class and provide them with large rewards. To be brief, the answer is that the kind of work these employees do is difficult to monitor and therefore employers must try to tie them to the goals and values of the organization by means of high salaries, profit-related bonuses, stock options, and the like. Compared to public sector and other non-profit organizations, it is much easier for private sector firms to do this.

One critical point in Erikson and Goldthorpe's scheme is that it does not distinguish a separate capitalist class; the service class concept has thus been said to be too broad or to represent too much of a mixture of categories (cf. Marshall, Swift and Roberts 1997: 25). In an answer to that argument, Erikson and Goldthorpe (1993: 40–1) maintain that the capitalist class is simply too small to be meaningfully treated as a category of its own in a study of social mobility. Given the type of study the two have done, we can hardly have any objections to their solution, but there may be a need for other dividing lines in the event that we want to do other kinds of research.

A further criticism is that the family is taken as the basic unit of analysis. However, it is reasonable to do so when the aim is to study intergenerational mobility or educational attainment. There should then be no doubt that family background is the most relevant factor. Erikson and Goldthorpe (1993: 232–9) prefer to let the individual, no matter whether male or female, who has the 'dominant' position, determine a family's class status. This is one step away from the traditional 'male breadwinner' approach, but the two authors do not go as far as to adopt the 'individual' or the 'joint classification' model. A crucial drawback with the individual approach is its inability to account for the different class situations of, for example, two women with lower-level service jobs but married to a manager and a blue-collar worker respectively. 'Joint classification' means that the employment status of both the husband and the wife is considered, which may seem an attractive solution, but it is despised as unpractical in empirical research. If we were to redefine the family's class position every time there is change in one of the family members' employment status, it would lead to rather unstable categories. We should note that Goldthorpe previously used a definition that just took the husband's class position as the point of departure, which not surprisingly initiated criticism and intense debate (cf. Crompton 1998: 65–6). How to deal with cross-class couples is a problematic issue and it is difficult to come up with any general recommendations.

Where does this take us?

There is no question that issues of social class are controversial and this observation seems to indicate two things. On the one hand, analysts have not been able to find solutions that are satisfactory or – to express it more adequately perhaps – that many or most sociologists could agree upon. On the other hand, it appears that the issue still matters, as so many bother about it, despite the fact that class has been declared dead over and over again. There are actually many different attitudes and positions that appear in the debate.

First, for some analysts class does not matter any more; class is simply a dead (Pakulski and Waters 1996) or a 'living dead', 'zombie' category (Beck and Beck-Gernsheim (2002: xxiv, 203–9). This position must be rejected as simply wrong; we have numerous studies – from different countries – showing a continuing relevance of class for people's incomes, health, living conditions, attitudes, political opinions, and collective action (cf., e.g., Wright 1985, 1997; Marshall 1997: 55–61; Svallfors 2004). For the present discussion there is nothing to add to this overwhelming evidence.

A second position is that class still matters but not so much any more or not as much as other factors such as gender and ethnicity (see, e.g., Crompton *et al.* 2000). As I see it, this does not amount to the argument that we should stop doing class analysis; it is not a big deal if other dimensions – depending on the object of a given study – turn out to be just as weighty or even weightier. Besides, the most urgent business is not to have a contest on which sociological dimension or factor is generally most important. It might at first seem challenging to elaborate an overall score for that purpose, but such an endeavor would entail great difficulties in attempting to avoid arbitrariness. Sociological analysis is hopefully something else than to make top-ten lists of popular music. At any rate, as long as class is one of the relevant factors, we should use it in empirical research and therefore also work with it theoretically.

Third, it is often argued that the concept of class needs to be reworked or renewed (see, e.g., Hall 1997; Crompton *et al.* 2000; Savage 2000; Devine *et al.* 2005). Actually, this is what happens all the time and we could not find better examples of this than in the works by Goldthorpe and Wright. The question is, though, what the reworking of the class concept means; one might hope that some new insights would be gained each time, but we cannot take that for granted. Moreover, some of those who most eagerly argue that class must be re-conceptualized are probably not very interested in the kind of changes that Goldthorpe and Wright have carried out. They often want to bring in lifestyle and cultural issues and this may very well be justified, but I still believe that class should primarily be related to the social division of labor and to economic orders.

The main conclusion I want to draw for the study of labor markets is that the foundation of class divisions lies in the ways in which the production of goods and services are organized. Class is best conceived of as linked to modes of production, but the latter concept should be interpreted in a less presupposing way than is frequently the case in Marxist accounts. Above all, it does not have to be based on assumptions about exploitation. A given society is normally a mixture of different modes of production, although one is leading. In contemporary affluent societies, capitalism is dominant, but we can distinguish other subordinate systems for producing goods and services, such as those with the epithets 'petty bourgeois' and 'state' or 'public sector' respectively. When we are focusing on the labor market, the petty bourgeois mode of production can be excluded, as its role incumbents are self-employed entrepreneurs who do not hire or hire out labor power. The capitalist and the public sectors are the two principal systems, but we should not forget the minor sectors of voluntary organizations and household services. Actors tied to these four systems make up the two main categories in the labor market: employers and workers/jobseekers.

Accordingly, employers consist of capitalist firms as well as public sector agencies, voluntary organizations, and households. Among them we find only one distinct class, capitalist owners, with a stratum of managerial employees closely tied to them. In analyzing power relations in the economy, we must furthermore take into account how property structures are affected by pension funds and other similar institutions appearing as owners and partners. Also certain public sector firms are profit-oriented and operate in the market; they are owned collectively and are thus not controlled by a specific ownership class but by salaried managers. I suggest that we use the concept of state capitalism in that case. Public sector, non-profit institutions are a different story; employed bureaucrats are found in the employer role and the crucial decisions as regards various activities are made by politicians and bureaucrats. These social categories may have certain privileges, but the public sector is owned collectively and controlled (more or less strongly) through the political system, which is democratic in advanced capitalist countries.

With respect to other employers without a profit goal, such as voluntary organizations and households, only a few observations will be made. Voluntary organizations represent a very special category, partly located outside the money-related production of goods and services. They often do not easily fit in with the general class patterns in society, which means that we must take into consideration for what they are set up and what they are doing. For example, unions are organizations established to look after workers' interests, a fact that characterizes their relationship to employers, but, at the same time, they may also hire people and thus be employers themselves. Employers' associations, however, do not have this kind of double-edged position. Concerning families and individuals who hire people to assist them with such things as childcare, cleaning, and gardening, I want to make another remark. These categories are frequently employed themselves and their class position is mainly determined by this other employment.

On the labor power side in the labor market, we find a broad range of categories. Some have much authority or power at the workplace, whereas others have almost nothing of that; some are highly educated with expert knowledge, while others are low-skilled, etc. Goldthorpe's service class concept may be useful and so does Wright's analysis of authority and skills; the two approaches are actually not so far from one another. At this point it also seems relevant to incorporate a gradational dimension into the analysis; delegated authority and skills respectively can be graded. I doubt, however, that much can be gained by making a great many subtle distinctions, although they may be needed in concrete empirical research due to the specific object of study. Generally, the concept of class just refers to people with roughly the same position in the social division of labor; we should take a pragmatic position and avoid getting stuck at details.

Gender and other divisions

In all modern societies, individuals of different gender, age, ethnicity, etc. are unevenly distributed across jobs. Although some variation exists across countries, there is everywhere a substantial amount of segregation in the labor market due to factors such as those mentioned. This seems to reflect some kind of interrelation between jobs and various social categories.

For the following brief discussion, I take gender as an example. As we all know, many occupations have very unequal proportions of men and women and the gender bias exists both horizontally and vertically in the occupational structure (e.g., Hakim 1996; Rubery, Smith and Fagan 1999). Women are over-represented, for example, in caring and secretarial jobs and often at lower hierarchical levels of work organizations, while male over-representation is found in technical occupations and in jobs higher up in the hierarchies. Full-time contracts are relatively more common among men, whereas it is the other way around with part-time contracts. There is also a gender gap in terms of pay, to the advantage of men, and more so in some countries than in others (see, e.g., Rubery *et al.* 1998). Certain patterns seem to be very lasting, but there have been some important changes over the last decades; we thus find a somewhat mixed picture with both continuity and change.

One conclusion is thus that labor markets are partly divided along gender lines, as some but not all jobs show a bias in this respect. In order to throw more light on the unequal and equal gender distributions we need, among other things, to look at the distinctive features of jobs. Positions that mainly recruit men seem to fit in with certain qualities that men are supposed to have and the same applies when women make up the vast majority. Some research has been done on themes of this kind, for example on women's allegedly exceptional ability to provide care and perform secretarial tasks (see, e.g., Ferguson 1984; Pringle 1989). To pinpoint the problem of gender-specific job characteristics, the notion of sex typing may be useful (see, e.g., Bradley 1989; Vogler 1994; Lovering 1994). The question is also how we account for the existing conceptions of how men and women are.

There are also other factors to consider, such as work cultures that go beyond the characteristics of the single job; it may thus be the whole environment that is gendered. A 'gendered work environment' means that men and women respectively 'develop their own highly specific and mutually excluding cultures' (Bradley 1989: 69). This can be seen in workplace decorations, conversations, and rituals that are often strongly imprinted by traditional gender roles. Catherine Hakim (1996: 165) has suggested that it is quite often 'the work culture that defines an occupation as male or female rather than the work task itself', including bolstering of physical strength, masculinity, and patriarchal attitudes. Of course, both the atmosphere at the workplace and single jobs may very well be gendered at the same time.

As mentioned above, it is to a very large extent women who are part-timers (see, e.g., Hakim 1996: 60–74; OECD 1999: 18–39, 2001: Ch. 4; Rubery, Horrell and Burchell 1994; Rubery, Smith and Fagan 1999: Ch. 7). A major explanation seems to be that, due to expectations connected with existing gender roles, women often have family obligations that men do not have. They can hardly avoid these obligations but must try to combine them with a job, in case they are to be employed at all. In that sense, shorter working hours is a consequence of the specific situation that women have in society and many part-time jobs are established to make it possible for their potential, female, incumbents to hold them. No doubt, employers sometimes have an interest in hiring people on a less than full-time basis, because it might fit in with work schedules and workload variations. There is, though, one particular reason why this cannot be the whole truth; if part-time work were nothing but an employer interest, we would expect men and women to be evenly distributed across both part-time and full-time jobs. In other words, the existence of part-time work also reflects women's situations, implying that they are the main caretakers of family duties.

Regarding the interaction between employers and jobseekers a few things need to be emphasized. There are two processes of screening – to use the terminology suggested by Ralph Fevre (1992: 11–12) – through which individuals searching for a job single out certain employers and employers searching for workers opt for certain individuals. If men and women generally look for very different jobs, we can expect to find a lack of gender balance among jobholders and in order to avoid this it is preferable to have a rather equal gender composition among jobseekers to begin with. A simple inspection of how children or their parents (or possibly children

together with their parents) choose educational programs in school immediately reveals a very strong bias already at this stage. For example, boys are
over-represented in data and technology classes and girls are over-represented in courses oriented toward caring and the like (see, e.g., Arnot 2002;
Dryler 1998; Jonsson 1999). Boys and girls are therefore likely to end up in
different occupations later on; in other words, the process of (self-)selection
starts early and, consequently, a gender-biased distribution across jobs
cannot be regarded as merely a labor market phenomenon.

Another possibility is that jobseekers are treated in such a way that
women or men do not get certain jobs, even if they have adequate
qualifications, because employers – as a result of prejudice, 'taste', or whatever – want to reserve these positions exclusively for one of the sexes.
Undeniably, such discrimination exists, but at the occasion of recruitment
it may be a secondary issue, when the composition of jobseekers is greatly
biased already. Even though the employer would not hesitate to exercise
'unfair' discriminatory practices, the outcome is perhaps more or less determined in advance by other circumstances.

Similar arguments as those that I have brought up regarding gender may
also apply to age, ethnic background, sexual orientation, etc., but every
dimension has its own specific features. For one reason or another, it is
rather common that people with certain characteristics cluster in certain
jobs and occupations. However, the explanation does not have to be that
jobs are earmarked for specific categories, but it can involve other aspects.
For example, youth are generally under-represented on higher hierarchical
levels in work organizations, simply because, as a rule, individuals are
required to have a fairly long work experience to be promoted to higher
positions.

4
Actors and Interactions

The basic actors encountering one another in the labor market are employers with demand for labor power and individuals who supply their work capacities. As pointed out before, in advanced capitalist societies those who hire labor power make up a very heterogeneous category; they consist of capitalist firms of different size, public sector agencies, voluntary organizations, and households. Anyone can – at least theoretically – employ another individual to carry out work. To become a small employer does not require much else than the resources to pay for the wages, the equipment to be used, and other expenditures that may be involved (it is another thing to become successful). Actors who hire out or want to hire out their labor power are in principle individuals, the bearers of the capacity for work. Still, in contemporary societies we find phenomena that appear to be exceptions to this rule such as temporary work agencies. These organizations supply workers to employers, but – and this is crucial – they do not own the labor supplied. At the bottom of the chain of transactions there is always an individual on an employment contract with the temporary work agency that has in turn established a contract with another employer. Sports teams represent one more case to consider; a soccer team can sell a player to another team and sometimes this happens without the player having much to say.

In the first part of this chapter, the interaction between employers and jobseekers is brought into focus. Employers with vacant positions are searching for workers and jobseekers are looking for a job. The interplay between the two parties involves a complex process of selection to be examined and, among other things, I discuss the concept of discrimination. Another section of the chapter concentrates on the interaction between employers and workers once recruitment has taken place. Labor power is hired because employers want to carry out certain tasks, which in turn requires some kind of organization. Workers are expected to fit in with the organization, but they join in with different attitudes to their specific jobs and to having a job in general. Regardless of whether the workplace is

67

part of the capitalist economy or not, there is a need for work control, although – as we shall see – the variation in this respect is huge. This diversity is partly due to the indeterminacy of work tasks and to the fact that employees sometimes have a considerable knowledge advantage over the employer.

Besides the two main actors in the labor market, Herbert Parnes (1968: 481) has identified three other categories: unions/professional organizations, employers' associations, and the government or the state. All of these organizations may hire labor power, but I will not deal with that aspect here; my focus is instead on their part in determining the conditions for the exchange between employers and workers. In this connection, I bring up certain issues regarding the potential for collective organization.

Employers and jobseekers

I start by considering the interaction in the labor market when employers and jobseekers are searching for one another. This interaction involves several steps and in relation to it many questions can be raised. If employers do not succeed in their attempts to find suitable people to recruit, they are left with the problem of having a shortage of workers and if jobseekers fail in their efforts they qualify as unemployed. I briefly touch upon these issues and then turn to another aspect, namely, the processes of selection in the labor market, including recruitment, separation, matching as well as discrimination.

Needless to say, employers with vacant jobs primarily want to hire workers with skills and qualifications suited for these vacancies. Appropriate training and experience within the occupation or some similar background are thus significant recruitment criteria. Sometimes there are vacancy chains at the workplace; when a position goes to an individual from the same organization, another position becomes vacant, producing a need for a second recruitment, and so on. If the number of workers is to remain the same, in the end of course some outsider must be appointed. Correspondingly, there may be queues of candidates for jobs (Thurow 1975: 91–7). In that case, when a position becomes vacant, one or several individuals are already waiting for it. I want to call attention to one important difference between job queues and other queues. An individual who stands in line to buy a hamburger will have to wait for her turn but will eventually reach the counter. Job queues do not always function that way; a qualified latecomer may immediately surpass other individuals. The reason for this is that the other actor concerned, the employer, has the ultimate power over the employment decision and does not have to bother very much about customary queue norms. In other words, it is possible to be in a job queue for a long time without finding employment or even getting closer to it; during a recession chances may even decrease with time.

A main concern for employers in the labor market is the risk that they do not find the workers wanted, which explains why they sometimes advertise more vacancies than they actually have (cf. Ehrenreich 2002: 15). Nevertheless, positions may remain vacant and employers can then be expected to search for alternative solutions. One option is that they raise wages or increase the attractiveness of the jobs in some other ways. A very different strategy is to rely on those already employed to increase their input of working hours, but there is also the possibility of finding ways of restructuring the labor process in order to reduce the number of employees. However, if the one or the other of these alternative solutions cannot be implemented with satisfactory results, employers may even have to give up certain activities.

Some jobseekers are employed while looking for something else, but others have no job and their problem corresponds to that of employers having labor shortage. With no employer willing to hire their labor power, they become unemployed. This is the basic definition of unemployment; it refers to individuals whose labor power is being offered in the market but does not become hired. People may enter into unemployment from different backgrounds: from outside the labor force or from a previous job from which they have been laid off or quit voluntarily. Whether an individual will stay jobless for a longer or shorter period of time is very much a matter of her use value or employability in the market. As pointed out above, there is often no turn to wait for, because in the end employers decide who will get a job and who will not.

Clearing of the labor market means that jobseekers and employers find each other, vacancies are filled, and jobseekers become jobholders. This can be described as a process of selection in which both parties – as well as competitors on both sides – make their choices. We shall next take a somewhat closer look at recruitment as well as at the other side of the coin, that is, voluntary and involuntary separations of individuals from their jobs. Both recruitments and separations are to be treated as selection processes in the labor market.

Processes of selection

Whenever vacancies are to be filled, and particularly when there are more candidates than openings, selection must take place. Employers want to have individuals with suitable qualifications and skills and they want to get a certain amount of work out of them. They also expect their workers to have some motivation to carry out the tasks associated with the job; otherwise there is no point in employing them. The ambition of employers is, generally speaking, to find the 'right' people to the existing positions, and they are not likely to pay more than necessary for this, neither in terms of search costs nor in terms of wages or salaries. Because they also compete among themselves for workers, it happens that the outcome will be higher pay and more favorable working conditions than originally intended. It goes without saying that the likelihood for such higher bids is larger during periods of economic boom, when there are plenty of vacancies and greater difficulties than normal to fill them.

Selection also takes place among jobseekers; although they compete with one another for the jobs available, some of them have more vacancies to choose between than others and some have the option of not taking a job at all. Again, it should be stressed that the process is two-sided; selection occurs in interaction with employers. For jobseekers, the wage or salary is commonly of vital interest, but several other aspects are also likely to play a significant role. Jobs should ideally fit their physical condition, health, interests, skills, education, and experience as well as other factors such as family obligations and available transportation arrangements. It is also essential for people to find work tasks that they like, which is something from which employers for their part may benefit. At the same time, we must stress that the possibilities of being choosy are limited; particularly when the labor market is tight and unemployment is high, many jobseekers will be satisfied with whatever employment they can get.

Some employers find suitable workers and some jobseekers find suitable jobs, but all actors on the two sides do not get what they want. Selection to jobs is a combination of different steps taken by the actors involved. To describe these steps we may use the categories – or some modified version of them – suggested by Ralph Fevre (1992: 10–13). He has identified five main processes in the labor market that he calls the 'hiring fair'. They are all two-sided (i.e., they involve both employers and jobseekers) and refer to informing employers, informing workers, screening employers, screening workers, and the offer to 'buy and sell labor'. In each of these steps there is an element of selection and the end result is that one individual rather than another is recruited and that by accepting the offer the new employee leaves other job chances behind.

However, Fevre (1992: 72) has a somewhat peculiar concept of selection, formulated in contrast to discrimination and matching, and it means 'that employers are getting the best people for different types of work'. This is how the labor market is assumed to function when universalistic principles of merit and competence are dominant. According to Fevre, the proposed concept of selection derives from structural-functionalist theory, but his long quotation from Parsons (not reproduced here) does not even mention the word. Anyhow, the author points out that it is 'just as easy to get carried away by the idea of selection as it is by the idea of discrimination ... Just as partisan opponents of discrimination can find the thing they dislike throughout the labour market, so those sociologists who see selection as a good thing tend to see it as characteristic of the way labour markets work' (Fevre 1992: 73).

Before making these programmatic statements, Fevre (1992: 71–2) has described the concept of discrimination as the 'bad' functioning of the labor market, which means that ethnic minorities, women, etc., do not get what they would have got had they been treated in the same way as others. Again, it should be emphasized that the author does not himself believe that the labor market transactions are generally discriminatory in this sense; he is careful not to present that kind of simplified view. Fevre has yet another concept, namely matching, and the idea is then that market values make up the basis for recruitment. This is supposed to be different from both discrimination and selection, because 'the market matches workers to jobs and vice versa' (Fevre 1992: 75). The distinctions between his three concepts are not that obvious and I find it difficult to get anything out of this classification.

The matching concept is commonly used in the literature on the functioning of labor markets (see, e.g., Granovetter 1981; Sørensen and Kalleberg 1981). Mark Granovetter, in particular, has emphatically pointed out that matching involves both parties in the labor market and both searching and signaling. He is very critical of theories that do not recognize this: 'Employers as well as employees search, and employees as well as employers try to read signals from the other side of the market ... Furthermore, an adequate theory would have to incorporate both searching and signaling, whereas present theories consider these as sequential activities' (Granovetter 1981: 26). In the author's own empirical research, matching is shown to be a complex process in which employers and jobseekers are involved in a mix of information search, signaling, and negotiations over pay and working conditions (Granovetter 1995). Another conclusion is that networks play a very important role in the process and the perhaps most interesting observation concerns the role of contacts with whom one has 'strong' and 'weak' ties respectively (Granovetter (1995: 51–62, 148–53). Acquaintances are by definition weakly tied to an individual and can usually bring in more new information about job openings than close (strongly tied) friends can do. The reason is that acquaintances move in different circles and often know things that are not already known by the individual.

Selection also takes place in relation to separations that can be a choice on the part of the employer or the worker, or both, to terminate an employment contract. It is generally hard to draw a sharp line between voluntary and involuntary quits. No doubt an employer and a worker may want the same, but sometimes they claim they want the same, although one of them is forced to accept the other's decision. When initiated by the individual worker, separation means dropping a job for another job or something else. The employee may find it difficult to make the decision to quit, but it is often not a big deal for the employing organization, at least not if it has a large workforce. To be laid off is, however, likely to be a much tougher experience for the individual. When an organization is about to reduce its personnel, decisions must be arrived at regarding those to be given the opportunity to stay and those who are to go. There may be conflicts between seniority principles and the need for people who can have a long career in the organization. Those involved in the selection process will also have to consider legislation and agreements on employment protection, seniority rules, etc.

To sum up, selection in the labor market involves choices to be made by employers and workers/jobseekers respectively, between individuals and between jobs, as long as the one individual must be preferred ahead of others and the one job must be preferred ahead of others. This holds for both recruitment and separations and the important question is of course, as Fevre tells us, what criteria (values) people use as the basis for their decisions. The discussion on discrimination is about these issues and it is next on my present agenda.

Discrimination and selection

It is common among sociologists to understand discrimination as a 'negative' concept. One encyclopedia even suggests that it 'can be simply defined as prejudice transformed into action' (Magill 1995: 373). However, discrimination in the selection of people to jobs may also have to do with the fact that when there are more applicants than vacancies some individuals must be rejected. Although frequently hard to take for those turned down, this can be done in a 'fair' way, that is, on the basis of criteria that all involved consider impartial. Discrimination is then a matter of sorting out the individuals who best fit these criteria.

The criteria applied in labor market selection processes differ from one case to another and they are not always made explicit or even recognized by the actors making the choice. Nevertheless, in modern societies, selection is generally regarded as fair and legitimate, if universal, 'objective' principles of merit are applied. We know that deviations – due to friendship, kinship, nepotism, favoritism, prejudice, etc. – from these principles exist, although it is often difficult to obtain reliable information on how widespread they are. In everyday speech, many of these deviations are described as discrimination and this is probably the most common meaning of the word; it refers to unequal or 'unfair' treatment. Another possibility is, however, to distinguish between 'fair' and 'unfair' discrimination and it is perhaps the best compromise (Noon and Blyton 2002: 262).

Just as in the public debate, all of my examples in this section refer to employers' conceivable discriminatory practices, but the same kind of reasoning can in principle be applied to jobseekers. When employers are accused of being unfair, it may not be very difficult for them to explain why an individual has been rejected. The reason is that there are many different criteria used in selection processes and that they appear in a variety of combinations. One thing needs to be emphasized in this connection; if employers – because they are negative or prejudiced toward women, immigrants, colored people, homosexuals, or some other category – do not select the most qualified individuals to jobs they come out with a less than optimal solution. In the end they have to pay the costs for it, given that their competitors in the market choose other strategies. The universal principles of merit have an ally in market competition, insofar as it puts pressure on employers to select the best possible individuals to jobs; this is an important mechanism operating against unfair treatment. However, if all rival employers adhere to, for example, racist practices, no competitive advantages or disadvantages will appear.

Statistical discrimination in recruitment processes refers to a situation in which inequality or unfairness is a by-product, because employers are not able or consider it too costly to get all the relevant information about the candidates for a job. Instead they take a shortcut by using information about category membership; to illustrate how this works we can take a simple example. Let us assume that there is a small employer who needs a person for a project that must be finished, at the very latest, within three years and who has two candidates for the job: a young man and a young woman. Although the man is somewhat less qualified, he is chosen on the grounds, perhaps not explicitly told, that a young woman may have a baby and then stay at home with her newborn child for some considerable time. The fact that both candidates may become parents during the three years does not alter this conclusion; it is the expected likelihood that they will stay at home with the child that matters and there is no question about the gender bias in that respect. Obviously, this choice can be considered unequal or unfair treatment, but the employer in the example may have no intention to downgrade women; it is just a rational choice in a situation in which nobody knows, or even can know, what is going to happen, but in which some forecasting is needed. The employer may even regret that women are more likely than men to stay at home when a child is born in the family, but this is something that a small firm can do little about and for which it is probably not willing or does not even have the capacity to pay the costs.

Discrimination, in one sense or another, also takes place with respect to separations. In the event of downsizing, when some individuals are to be picked out to leave their jobs, there is – as in other selection processes – a risk of unequal and unfair treatment. Employers no doubt need to keep workers with experience and specialized skills and knowledge, but it is not always very clear what criteria should be applied to evaluate their qualifications and irrelevant factors may intervene in the process. Moreover, experience and specialized skills and knowledge may be used as 'cover' terms to secure that other, not so respectable, kinds of preferences are permitted to determine the outcome. At the same time, we should be aware that, for example, legislation providing extra employment protection for older workers can be considered discriminatory, although its intention may be to protect these workers from being treated unfairly.

A related concept is that of 'affirmative action' referring to measures intended to counteract unequal or unfair treatment. This type of intervention can involve anything from simple forms of encouragement of underprivileged categories to quotas (see, e.g., Bacchi 1996; Bergmann 1996; Cahn 1995; Skrentny 1996). Its ultimate implication is that people who are not the most qualified could still get a job, because they belong to an underprivileged category. In other words, universal principles of merit and competence are, to some degree, set aside for other selection criteria, under the assumption that the latter will make up for existing inequality or unfairness in society, that is, it might be relevant to talk about inverted discrimination or counter-discrimination.

Whatever conceptual solution we choose with respect to discrimination, the crucial aspects regarding selection in labor markets are what criteria are being used and how they are applied. These criteria are not always made public, but even in the event they are we may not be sure what has actually decided the outcome. It is common that many different factors are weighed together and sometimes actors want to hide the real motives behind their decision or they might not even be aware of them themselves. Such circumstances do not make selection criteria easily accessible to the observer.

Employers and workers

Once employed, workers are expected to carry out work in return for a wage or salary. The employment contract implies that the employer – in exchange for more or less specified remuneration – can be in command of workers' time and effort, within some reasonable limits, in order to get certain work tasks done. As the one party has resources to hire workers and the other is more or less forced to earn a living, the relationship is often asymmetric from the outset. The asymmetry is particularly accentuated when the employer is a large and powerful organization rather than, for example, just an individual. Nevertheless, workers have at least some autonomy; to develop this somewhat further we can benefit from considering the notion of principal–agent relationship.

The principal–agent perspective

Dating back to Roman law, the term 'agency' refers to relationships between two kinds of actors: principals and agents (see, e.g., Ross 1974: 215–16; Jensen and Meckling 1976; Donaldson 1990). In a labor market context, the two parties can be depicted in the following way. One actor, the principal, has some work to be carried out and therefore employs another actor, the agent, to do it. The underlying stipulation is that the former decides what is to be done; in other words, it is a power relation-ship. If the assignment is to be accomplished, however, some authority must be delegated to the agent; hardly any work can be done without at least some autonomy on the part of the individual performing it. Delegation is in turn accompanied by 'a degree of underfulfillment of the wishes of the principal by the agent, which is termed *agency loss*', as 'the interests of the principal and agent are inclined to diverge' (Donaldson 1990: 369; emphasis in original). Another presupposition is that perfect monitoring is impossible. The literature on agency relationships is rather occupied with the normative task 'how to structure the contractual relation (including compensation incentives) between the principal and the agent' so as to 'to maximize the principal's welfare given that uncertainty and imperfect monitoring exist' (Jensen and Meckling 1976: 309–10).

It is not my intention to contribute to the solution of this task, but I think that the principal–agent perspective keeps us aware of two important things. First, it emphasizes that the two actors are involved in a power rela-tionship. Second, it makes us aware of certain limits for the exercise of power by the principal. In order to carry out work on behalf of the princi-pal the agent must have some room for autonomous decision making. Although the size of that room varies substantially from one job to another, there is always a potential for diverging intentions and, accord-ingly, for conflict. As explained in more detail below, it is often not very clear what an assignment involves or whether, in a given situation, the principal knows better than the agent what to do or how to do it.

Principal–agent or, to return to our 'normal' terminology, employer–worker relationships are thus power relations. The two parties affect one another in many different ways, but they do not have equal capacity to do so. Power is a matter of being able to get things done and to have power over someone else means to get one's will through despite the other party's will. This is a standard Weberian concept, defined by Max Weber (1978: 53) himself as 'the probability that one actor within a social relationship will be in a position to carry out his own will despite resistance, regardless of the basis on which this probability rests'. We should, however, avoid treat-ing the exercise of power as a one-way process; also actors in subordinate positions can exercise counter-power that affects those in dominant positions.

When analyzing the interaction between the two main parties at the workplace, we must keep in mind that the relationship may be more or less asymmetric. Sometimes there are just two individuals, as when a person hires a cleaning help. It may seem to be a rather equal basis for interaction when only two individuals are involved, but the two may actually take part on very unequal terms. The employer is likely to have more resources – especially if the cleaning is no one-time event but contracted on a more regular basis – and those who carry out such jobs are frequently not the most privileged. Yet, we should not *a priori* rule out the possibility that the worker has a dominant position in relation to the employer or at least some considerable counter-power. For example, the employer may be an old woman who has some small savings and who cannot do the work herself due to fading physical strength, while the cleaning help is a university student who just wants to earn a little extra money. However, the relationships between employers and employees are often very asymmetric with employees under a disadvantage. On the one side, we may have huge transnational companies or large public sector institutions and on the other side just individuals. If a large employer wants to set up conditions that are unacceptable to the employee, there is little that he/she, as a single individual, can do to resist this, although the union or some other agency may be called in.

Work organization and work orientation

Employers organize work activities and how to do this and what the outcome will be are therefore vital questions for them. Workers, for their part, generally have a different point of departure for participating in the organization's activities. Asking them what they want to get out of their job, a first answer may be 'income', as money is commonly a significant factor. In the classic study *The Affluent Worker*, done by John Goldthorpe, David Lockwood, Frank Bechhofer and Jennifer Platt (1968: 37–9), this is called instrumental work orientation. It means that work is principally seen as a means to achieve other goals. The main function of a job is to give people an income that can be used to satisfy their various needs. Accordingly, this orientation implies a clear division between work and leisure and that workers have a calculative attitude to the employing organization; they mainly look at the economic return in relation to their effort. Goldthorpe and his associates (1968: 41; emphasis in original) stress that '*all* work activity, in industrial society at least, tends to have a basically instrumental component' and this is indeed an important observation. Although it can be expected that a 'pure' instrumental work orientation is more widespread among people engaged in routine manual work, we do not have to question that higher-level employees also worry a great deal about their income; at least, there is no evidence indicating anything else.

Moreover, the researchers' classification includes two other types of work orientation, referred to as 'bureaucratic' and 'solidaristic' (Goldthorpe *et al.* 1968: 39–41). The first of these types, bureaucratic work orientation, is obviously elaborated with Weber's view of bureaucracy in mind. It means, among other things, that the relationship between the employee and the employer is supposed to have a long-term character. Salaries are not directly tied to a particular amount of work done but are an expression of the position an individual has and, in addition, of seniority. Employees can look forward to advancement both in terms of career and income and it is then required that they are positively committed to the organization's activities. Work and non-work cannot be clearly separated from one another.

Solidaristic work orientation is the third type and it is based on the prerequisite that work is a group activity. A group can be anything from the immediate work team to the employing organization as a whole. The crucial aspect is that individuals have some fairly strong degree of identification and loyalty with the collective in question. When identification relates only to a smaller group inside the workplace, these workers may very well have a negative relationship to the employing organization as a whole and to the employer. It is nevertheless assumed that the solidaristic orientation usually means strong ego involvement in work activities and that work cannot be separated from life outside it.

The last two types of work orientation direct our attention to the fact that people may be committed to their work and loyal with the employing organization (or work team). In other words, this perspective has an obvious resemblance to the analysis of the service class (see, e.g., Erikson and Goldthorpe 1993: 41–2; Goldthorpe 2000: Ch. 10; see also Chapter 3 in this book). Loyalty and commitment are to a large extent associated with the degree of trust that different categories of workers enjoy. This whole idea reflects the fact that the employer–worker exchange can take on various forms and that motivation is a significant element in people's work orientation. Instrumentality means that the individual is motivated mainly by the money and, as suggested above, this is a decisive or at least a very important reason for almost everybody who takes a job. With regard to the bureaucratic and the solidaristic types of work orientation, described by Goldthorpe and his colleagues, we find other phenomena with implications for work motivation such as ego involvement, career ambitions, organizational commitment, social relations, and group loyalties.

Organizations make up a distinctive field for sociological research and numerous studies have been carried out over the years. The main topics are – to put it in very broad terms – how organizations get work done, to what extent and how they rely on workers' different types of motivation, and what control mechanisms they use. Within the field, different theoretical traditions have developed, such as classical organizational theory, Taylorism, Human Relations, and Human Resource Management (see, e.g., Etzioni 1964; Perrow 1986; Blyton and Turnbull 1992; Legge 1995; Casey 2002). Sometimes the traditions of organizational study are classified into larger categories, for example as to whether they depart from an X or a Y theory of human beings (McGregor 1985). The basic idea is to distinguish between different employer orientations. Employers and managers who set out from X-type theories suppose that people are unwilling to work, that they do as little as possible for what they get, and that they have to be controlled throughout the work process. This way of reasoning is often associated with Taylorism. Taking instead Y-type theories for granted implies the opposite position; it is then assumed that people want to work and that they need not be forced and controlled but should be given wide possibilities to organize their activities themselves. Such views are typically found within the Human Relations School of organizational thought.

Many authors have tried to show that strict control – based on a negative interpretation of how human beings think about their jobs – has negative effects on the work process. They suggest that loose control may lead employees to do as little as possible and to obey formal rules without taking the consequences into account (see, e.g., March and Simon 1958: 36–47; Merton 1964: Ch. 5; Selznick 1949; Gouldner 1954). However, it has been difficult to show that 'participatory' or 'democratic leadership' and 'sympathetic supervision' increase worker morale and productivity (Thompson and McHugh 1995: 107). The huge amount of research done on these themes has not been able consistently to prove the validity of the main hypotheses (Perrow 1986: Ch. 3). Now, changes in the direction of less control are likely to be small, leaving the principal decision-making structures intact, and we can hardly expect that a little more relaxed control would automatically lead to better performance. It is difficult to see why workers, still in subordinate positions, would use their somewhat increased freedom just to work harder or more conscientiously for their employer.

An interesting question is to what extent humanistic perspectives are actually allowed to play a significant role in the everyday practice of work organizations. In his book *Labor and Monopoly Capital*, Harry Braverman (1974: 87) suggests that the outlook of the Human Relations tradition and of industrial psychology is to be found in personnel departments and schools of industrial psychology and sociology, whereas Taylorism rules in 'the world of production'; in his opinion, besides 'the bad odor of the name', the only reason why Taylorism is not considered a school of its own is that it has 'become the bedrock of all work design'. This was written more than thirty years ago and even if it did not exaggerate the situation for the time being it may do so today. Nevertheless, it puts the finger on an important aspect, namely that there may be a wide gap between theory and practice. Hence we should not immediately adopt the view that the latest version of humanistic organization theory – Human Resource Management (HRM), Total Quality Management (TQM), or whatever – has dramatically changed the practical world. However, we must be aware of the growth in the number of people with specialized knowledge and skills, which means that employers will have increasingly more employees who are particularly difficult to control.

There is an obvious temptation for researchers in the field of work organization to try to find the most suitable solutions for the one or the other party or both of them. An employer-oriented approach generally aims at making the organization more efficient and it is then rarely questioned, for example, who should decide and who should obey. The idea is just to provide solutions on leadership, motivation, and control issues that can contribute to increasing efficiency. It may, however, also be the other way around, that is, that the principal ambition is to reduce or eliminate the repressive, exploitative, and alienating features of wage-labor. This implies asking what subordination to machinery, monotonous work tasks, and tight work control mean for the workers and finding ways of removing various negative conditions like dangerous and unhealthy work environments as well as of increasing workers' influence. Of course, there is also the possibility of taking an in-between position; research is sometimes understood to be a bridge between conflicting parties, opening ways for improvements to the benefit of everybody.

My purpose in the following pages is to spell out some of the most important dimensions regarding how employers try to ensure that their workers do what they are expected to do. However, I also make some comments on workers' resistance. The work organization literature has its main focus on capitalist firms and their control of the work process, but there are also studies on public bureaucracies and other organizations. I keep the discussion on a general level and take examples from different sectors.

Work control and reactions to it

To begin, I briefly return to the issues of recruitment and selection, as they are very important also for work control. Amitai Etzioni (1964: 58–74; 1975: 255–64) has discussed the relationship between selection on the one hand and control and socialization on the other hand. His main point is that the latter two are dependent on the former, that is, if selection is done carefully there is less need for control and socialization and vice versa. Basing recruitment on strong selectivity, an employer may be able to recruit people who function well by themselves. Etzioni (1964: 69; 1975: 258–61) relates his discussion to his classification of three organizational types, called coercive (e.g., prisons), utilitarian (enterprises), and normative (churches, political parties). The point of departure for this classification is that organizations have members who are either employed or associated in some other way. For my purpose, of course, utilitarian organizations are most relevant; their members are employees and they are always selected. In contrast, the coercive type is not very selective and the normative type can be either way.

Among other things, Etzioni (1975: 260) points out that since utilitarian organizations heavily rely on the external educational system selectivity becomes particularly significant and this is further emphasized by the fact that they 'have relatively little control over the substance of socialization in these external units'. One possibility, though, is to practice 'reverse selectivity', that is, to dismiss people when they have proved not to fit in with the work task they have been assigned to. We can immediately see the problems with this method; it is costly and linked to quite a few obstacles – strong unions, seniority systems, etc. – not to mention the maltreatment of individuals that may occur. Anyway, employers have a lot to gain by being selective in recruitment, because it is a way of eliminating or reducing later costs for socialization and control of performance.

Once people are recruited to jobs, control of what they actually do becomes an issue. Richard Edwards (1979: 18) has suggested that systems of control contain three basic elements: (a) direction that refers to a mechanism by which employers specify work tasks; (b) evaluation that means procedures through which workers' performances are supervised and judged; and (c) discipline that stands for employers' ways of punishing and rewarding employees. All three of these dimensions are present in the discussion below, although it is structured somewhat differently. First, I make some comments with respect to directions; they are not control mechanisms in themselves but rather make up a prerequisite for all kinds of monitoring. The second dimension, evaluation, is here redefined and renamed as work control. It is the point at which the actual supervision is carried out and I add a number of aspects to it. Third, there is discipline or, as I prefer to say, sanctions; they are part of the control process and represent employers' efforts to affect workers' behavior.

Direction and the indeterminacy of jobs

As underlined by Edwards, direction is a prerequisite for all work control; if employers are not able to tell what should be done and how and when it should be done, there is nothing to control. Certainly, in some cases the obligations and expectations are clear from the outset, but in other cases they are not; jobs are in fact often associated with a considerable degree of indeterminacy. There are plenty of questions involved: how work tasks are defined, and when, how much, how fast, and under what other conditions employees are expected to work, as well as what remunerations should follow. More than a century ago, Sidney and Beatrice Webb (1897: 658) noted that 'the hiring of a workman, unlike a contract for the purchase of a commodity, necessarily leaves many conditions not precisely determined, still less expressed in any definite form'; this can be disadvantageous for both the employer and the worker but more so for the latter, not least because in 'any dispute as to the speed of work, or the quality of the output, the foremans' decision is absolute'. Even if foremen's and similar work organizers' decisions have become less absolute, the asymmetric character of employment relationships also today leaves its mark on situations as the one described.

There are at least two different ways of explaining the indeterminacy as to how job roles are to be performed. One is that things change across time and therefore cannot be accurately predicted (cf. Hyman and Brough 1975: 23–9). On the day a worker is employed, there may be some common understanding of mutual duties and expectations, but what will happen in a longer perspective is an open question. Continuous changes take place regarding demand for goods and services, technologies and technical equipment, organizational structures, etc., and they are in turn likely to affect employees' work situation. The degree of marketness has a significant role to play in these respects, since markets forces may compel employers to call for more work or other kinds of work than understood from the beginning. Particularly if contrasted with earlier agreements, changes that managers find necessary for the employing organization may meet with resistance among the personnel. As the parties will often have their own interpretations of what has previously been agreed upon, conflicts are rather likely to appear.

The second explanation behind the indeterminacy in the employer–worker exchange is that the employer does not know – or only vaguely knows – what is to be done or how it should be done. For example, social work agencies employ social workers to help people with financial difficulties, joblessness, drug addiction, and other problems, but it is often difficult for them to provide very clear instructions as to how this should be done. Although we may find a reasonable consensus about the desired outcome as well as relatively explicit rules of conduct, there may still be very different ways of achieving the goals.

Work control

Despite the fact that directions for jobs cannot always be clearly defined in advance, employers generally have an ambition to secure not only that the work they organize is actually done but also that it is done in an appropriate manner. I make a distinction between three different dimensions along which control can take place. The first has to do with employees' presence at the workplace, the second with how the work is carried out, and the third with the outcome, the goods or services produced. In addition, I suggest that we distinguish between direct and indirect forms of control. It will become clear in the discussion below what is more exactly meant by these various categories.

A first type of control focuses on workers' presence at the workplace when supposed to carry out their duties. This is sometimes not a very relevant question, since employees are not required to be very much at their workplace. University teachers can be taken as illustration; they are allowed to work at home, in the library, or elsewhere, except of course when they have a class, seminars, hours to meet with students, and administrative meetings. In many other jobs, however, there is basically just one place where the work can be done. An assembly line worker must be in the factory, a supermarket cashier must be at the check-out counter, a nurse must be in the ward where the patients are, and so on. In all these cases, it will create problems if employees – without any previous notice – stay away from the job and if they do not show up on time or leave the workplace early.

Visibility is an important factor for knowing whether workers are present at the workplace. As it is very clear in some jobs where a worker is expected to be and just about anybody can see it, control is easily exercised. The employer or representatives of the employer can do it, but there are also more indirect ways in which the same thing can occur. For example, a bus driver is supposed to drive a certain route day after day, following a certain schedule, and if the bus does not show up on time (with some tolerable delay taken into account) it is likely that someone will call the bus company. If a university teacher does not show up for class, the students will probably notify somebody responsible in the administrative staff. In other words, employers do not always have to exercise control themselves but can rely on being kept informed through other mechanisms. The methods of locating where people are have definitely been revolutionized by means of computers, cell phones, and other electronic devices, but the underlying issues of control remain very much the same.

Absenteeism is a problem for employers, most of all perhaps when it can be taken as a kind of reaction to working conditions. Besides taking a day or two entirely off, it happens that employees 'round off' the workday or take longer breaks than they are entitled to according to rules or agreements. Although there is a lot of variation across jobs and across workplaces in this respect, it is common that the working day has certain porosity due to employees taking it somewhat easy. The existing practices of limiting the actual hours worked can be looked upon as tacit agreements between workers and employers, perhaps involving some compensation for low wages or intensive working pace. When the costs for these practices grow, the employer has a choice between establishing stricter rules and finding some other way of improving the situation (cf. Gouldner 1954).

Second, supervision of the work process is a reality for large numbers of workers also in modern societies. Employers may consider it necessary to monitor the work process, because in their view employees do not carry out their job tasks fast enough or do not do them properly. Both of these aspects are related to the indeterminacy of the employment contract; it is not always clear what is required or expected. Work slow-down and working by the rule may also be mechanisms through which workers take something back when they feel disadvantaged and exploited. This attitude may in turn be due to the employer's exploitation of the indeterminacy of the employment agreement.

Monitoring does not necessarily require a supervisor to control every step of the worker. In fact, there are both direct and indirect ways of doing this and visibility is again crucial. For example, in a small restaurant the owner may, most of the time, directly observe waitresses' ways of performing their job, serving and treating guests. Still, if the owner is out of the restaurant for a few hours, it does not mean that the work is not observed; customers do it and if they experience problems they may let these be known. Of course, customers are able to see only a certain part of what waitresses do, so there are limits to this, but generally the visibility of workers' performances is an important factor, with considerable variation across jobs. To take a couple of other examples, whereas passengers can watch a bus driver in action, the interaction between a social worker and a client is largely hidden, for reasons of integrity, but the client can still report what has happened. There are numerous situations in which others than the employer (or representatives of the employer) monitor the work process; customers, clients, students, patients, and many others have such a role. It may be disputed whether the kind of feedback these categories provide is a good way of evaluating what employees are doing. Undoubtedly, in some respects, they have information that no one else can supply, but their own role in the process of caring, teaching, etc., is likely to affect their views in specific ways.

In the work by Edwards (1979: 18–22), we find a distinction between simple or personal control and more complex forms of control, mainly 'technical' and 'bureaucratic'. These latter forms are above all developed in large firms. Machinery can to some extent replace personal supervision, as it often has some built-in mechanism of control. A standard example is the conveyor belt where the worker cannot stop working – without causing substantial problems – as long as the belt continues to bring objects to be taken care of. Today computer systems furnish us with plenty of other examples of how employees can be supervised in their jobs.

Bureaucratic control is – to return to Edwards's typology – basically supervision by rule. In a situation where employers and management are not able to follow the work done more closely, certain rules are established for the employee to comply with. As was pointed out above, it may be somewhat indeterminate what a social work agency should do and how it should operate. In this kind of organization, where direct supervision cannot take place, the indeterminacy of the work process is to some extent compensated for by a set of bureaucratic rules. The organization thus has a mechanism at its disposal to control the interaction between the social worker and the client and afterwards it can be checked whether existing regulations have been followed or not. Yet, there are limits also to this; one aspect is that 'working by the rule' can create many problems for the employer, as hardly any work can be carried out successfully in that way. It has even been argued that 'there is no more effective means of organizational sabotage than a letter-perfect compliance with all the rules and a consistent refusal of employees to use their own judgment' (Bendix 1963: 445). It should be added, however, that there must not be formal rules;

informal norms, as part of the work culture, can be strong enough to function as control mechanisms. The whole atmosphere in a firm may convey more or less inviolable norms for employees, with respect to dress codes, the length of the working day, and many other aspects.

Some jobs are relatively easy to control, while others are not. Much of my discussion comes back to occupational and class divisions among employees. Generally, we can think of two principally different ways of handling the control issue. The employer has to make up his mind whether a tight control over work process is possible and desirable or whether workers should be trusted to do their best for the organization. As noted in Chapter 3, managers and professionals are normally admitted great or even complete discretion in decision making, simply because otherwise it will not be possible to get the work done. However, also lower-level workers can be entrusted a significant degree of autonomy.

Finally, the employer can control the product or the outcome of the work done. In the production of goods this is essentially rather simple, although it can be costly. It is basically a matter of checking whether a product – a screwdriver, a television set, a vacuum cleaner, etc. – does not have any construction defects and functions as it is supposed to do. In other cases control may be much more difficult, as with social workers' performances. The general goal of providing support for people with financial and other problems is not easily translated into useful criteria for assessing these performances. It may be found out how many clients have been put on social welfare and how many have been taken off it, but people may disagree as to whether an increase or a decrease in the number of welfare recipients means improvement. Such measures alone are often too simple to determine whether social workers have been successful or not in their jobs.

Sanctions

Control requires sanctions; otherwise it is only a halfway measure. In discussing sanctions, I return to some of the categories suggested by Etzioni and touched upon above. His classification of organizations correlates with three types of power or, in a later version, three types of compliance: coercive, utilitarian, and normative (Etzioni 1964: 59, 1975: 12–14). The three categories refer to physical, material, and symbolic means of control respectively and the following paragraphs are structured accordingly.

Although modern labor markets are supposed to be 'free', it should be remembered that over the decades physical repression has played a significant role in many countries. History is full of examples of harassment and persecution of militant workers and union activists. Violence has been used time and again when police and even military forces have been called in to put a stop to an industrial conflict. Repressive means can still be utilized, although they do not belong to the most typical features of the modern labor market. Besides, we should not forget that also workers have used violence, for example against people who continue to work or are sent for to work during a strike ('scab').

Utilitarian power refers to control over income and other economic resources. In this respect, employers have considerable power, as they pay workers' wages and salaries. Their ultimate sanction is to terminate the employment contract and such a measure may put workers in a difficult situation, if they have no other employment option, unemployment benefits to collect, or other kind of income on which to rely. Having some degree of job security written into the employment contract may mean nothing under normal conditions, but once there is redundancy it may be worth quite a lot, for example by implying severance pay during a certain period of time. In other words, for the purpose of reducing the conceivable harm of being laid off, legislated or agreed-upon clauses regarding employment protection are utterly important for workers.

Workers' corresponding method is to quit their jobs, exit from them (cf. Hirschman 1970), but this is an option of limited value, if no alternative job openings or other sources of income exist. Due to the asymmetry that often characterizes the relationship between employers and workers, an individual's voluntary exit may not be a very effective threat, but at least for a small employing organization its potential effects should not be underestimated. It can be rather devastating if an individual leaves, particularly if she belongs to some key category of employees and has vital job-specific skills, acquired through costly on-the-job training or long experience with the organization.

Threats of dismissal of workers can be compelling sanctions and individual workers' threats to quit can in turn occasionally be effective. Another common economic sanction, used by employers, is to tie remunerations to performance, but it requires that some reasonable way of measuring performance can be established. We must also mention control over promotions, as being promoted usually involves both financial and other significant consequences: a raise in pay, more interesting work tasks, better facilities, more fringe benefits, higher social status, etc. Not least in professional organizations or occupations, this must be considered one of the most effective sanctions that an employer can use, because it directly tells everybody how an individual is evaluated in comparison with others.

Work slow-down, working by the rule, absenteeism, and the like are often more or less individual protests to unsatisfactory working conditions but may nevertheless have a considerable economic impact, thus creating great problems for the employer. Yet, even if they feel dissatisfied with their working and employment conditions, workers as individual actors generally do not have much to come up with in terms of sanctions. It is above all by acting collectively that they can really put pressure upon their counterpart. This does not presuppose that they must go on strike; there are all kinds of other measures that can be turned into collective weapons.

Collective organizations and action

Collective action is probably first and foremost seen as the response of workers to a situation in which they are just too weak to act individually in relation to employers. The capitalist production process means the domination of capitalists over workers, but to some extent collective resistance from the latter can balance this. Claus Offe and Helmut Wiesenthal (Offe 1985: 178) argue that 'the capital ("dead" labour) of each firm is always united from the beginning, whereas living labour is atomized and divided by competition'. On the basis of this description, the authors continue: 'Workers cannot "*merge*"; at best, they can *associate* in order to partly compensate for the power advantage that capital derives from the liquidity of "dead" labour' (Offe 1985: 178; emphasis in original). The step to be taken is then to construct some kind of collective consciousness and organization and it requires that a number of obstacles can be overcome. It should be added that the situation within the public sector and other parts of the labor market is not all that different.

Besides trade unions there is also another type of employee organization that appears in the labor market, namely professional organizations. Normally, these do not participate directly in bargaining over wages, salaries, and work conditions, but they may nevertheless influence the exchange between employers and workers. There are actually many different ways in which professional organizations can exercise power; most importantly, perhaps, they are inclined to monopolize part of the labor market, by attempting to reserve certain jobs for people with specific qualifications and credentials only. Their role is therefore particularly interesting in relation to the recruitment criteria applied in these cases.

In response to the development of trade unions, employers have formed their own collective organizations. The literature on industrial relations generally pays less attention to these, because researchers have been more interested in the collective strivings of workers. Offe and Wiesenthal are right in emphasizing the relative unity of each capitalist firm in contrast to the atomized character of labor, but we should also keep in mind that firms compete with one another in the market and that their competition is often intense. For them to overcome their rivalry and act collectively toward workers often requires considerable organizational effort. Nonetheless, they may have plenty to gain from doing so, for example if they want to prevent accelerating wage bids or other possibly spiraling factors in a 'race to the top'.

The union is often thought of as *the* collective actor of workers in the labor market. Those who think that way may be justified in doing so, as this description is frequently the most adequate to be given. Workers' collective action does not, however, presuppose a formal organization. To get a better understanding of its development, we should start looking at the processes taking place before the rise of a union, possibly but not necessarily leading to its establishment.

The formation of a workers' collective

On the formation of a workers' collective, sociologist Sverre Lysgaard has given one of the best analyses in his book *Arbeiderkollektivet* (1961). Basing his study on interviews and direct observations, several decades ago, in a factory within the Norwegian pulp and paper industry, he was able to identify a number of conditions and processes that are important for such a development to occur. His study is a highly significant contribution to our understanding of how a workers' collective can develop and the emerging theory has clear connections with previous sociological work, above all the classical Western Electric (Hawthorne) studies and the interpretations of them (see, e.g., Roethlisberger and Dickson 1939; Homans 1951).

Lysgaard focuses on the social elements and processes behind the transformation of individual workers into a more or less integrated collective. Such a unit basically represents workers' entrenchment in relation to an insatiable technical-economic system, the firm; it is their defense mechanism. The emergence of a collective is promoted if three conditions are at hand. First, workers must have approximately the same position in the technical-economic system; they should have about the same type of work tasks, the same wage level, the same working conditions, etc. Second, physical proximity is important as a prerequisite for communication and without communication the collective has no chance to develop. Finally, there must be what is referred to as a common problem-situation. This means that workers face the same problems regarding, for example, wage systems, working hours, workplace safety, and threats of being laid off.

These three conditions make up the prerequisites for certain processes that are necessary for the workers' collective to evolve. Having fundamentally the same position in the hierarchy of the work organization is likely to create identification, as it is easy to identify with people with whom one shares the basic conditions of life or work. Identification in turn promotes interaction, but for interaction to take place some degree of physical proximity between individuals is required. People need to be able to exchange views about their situation to discover what they have in common. To some extent, communication can be prevented at the workplace; for example, workmates may not be allowed to talk with one another during work or it may be impossible due to a noisy environment or other obstacles. Still, because many individuals are gathered together most of the day and have common breaks, it is unlikely that they could be completely cut off from exchanging opinions. With the tremendous development of the electronic means of communication in recent decades, workplace conditions have of course changed very much since Lysgaard wrote his book, but this does not have to change the principles of the reasoning. Finally, with a common situation and more or less constantly interacting with one another, workers are likely to develop similar interpretations and feelings about what the problems are and what can be done to solve them. On the basis of a similar interpretation of the situation they may begin to act as a collective force; the workers' collective is in place.

Once established, the collective is held together by many different mechanisms. A whole ideology may emerge, providing a framework for how individual workers should define their situation and their role. With it also goes a set of norms with the function of keeping individuals in line. For example, it may be difficult for a worker to take the step to become a foreman, because this is likely to be looked upon as selling out to the employer. There are several social psychological processes – such as ridicule, isolation, and, ultimately, excommunication from the peer group – that operate to make workers comply with the collective's norms.

Lysgaard's book thus uncovers the social and social psychological processes through which a defense organization emerges to protect workers from the demands of an insatiable technical-economic system. It does not pay much attention to the formal organization of the union that is considered to be an analytically distinct category. Many sociologists in the field seem to have taken it for granted that collective action means union activity, but we must be cautious with such assumptions. However, in order for a workers' collective to become a stable social force that can stand up against a demanding employer, it needs a formal organization. Some kind of union is then the most realistic option, as it offers the structure and stability needed to counteract the power of the employer. There are hence different levels for the analysis of collective action and Lysgaard's analysis starts out from the basic level of interaction between workers and between workers and management at the workplace. A first question is whether a workers' collective can develop at all and, if so, we run into a second issue, namely whether the collective also materializes in a formal organization. Third, it may be reasonable to ask how the two interact.

Collective action and the role of unions

The trade union is no doubt often the major or even the only representative for workers, but we should keep the analytical difference between the two, above all because they may diverge in their outlook and standpoints. We can think of many reasons why discrepancies and conflicts between the representative and the represented emerge. Even besides the most obvious case with so-called yellow unions, organized, controlled, or strongly influenced by the employer, unions may pursue goals that differ from what their members want to see pursued. To put it simply, they may be either too radical or too conservative in relation to workers.

Time may be an important aspect; unions that were once 'true' representatives of workers and highly democratic sometimes turn into organizations that are mainly oriented toward self-preservation and in which officials carefully look after the privileges they have acquired. The perhaps most well-known account along these lines is that of Robert Michels (1962) who in the beginning of the twentieth century presented an analysis of the mechanisms that make also democratic organizations such as democratic political parties and unions turn into oligarchies. The author depicts this process interchangeably as a tendency and as an unavoidable development, no less than 'an iron law'. Although we must question the significance of many of the factors that Michels discusses as well as his 'iron law' perspective, he supplies a theory of how organizations may change across time and it contains several important observations.

The best arguments in this theory go something like this. Every organization of some size must have a division of labor; authority has to be delegated to a smaller number of individuals who, to begin with, appear as the servants of members. However, this will not be a long-lasting state of affairs; delegated authority inevitably leads to a monopoly of information and knowledge and sooner or later some people will become employed by the organization, as it will otherwise be difficult for them to have the time needed for the job. In protecting their own source of income, such officials tend to develop a conservative outlook. Monopolized information can be used for other purposes than those for which the organization was set up and we can thus observe a displacement of goals. Officials become interested in the mere survival of the organization and of their own privileges that go with it. Privileges are partly due to the interaction with other actors (elites) in the surrounding society. The conclusion is that the development of organizations is accompanied by a shift in the relationship between leaders and members: 'At the outset, leaders arise spontaneously; their functions are accessory and gratuitous. Soon, however, they become professional leaders, and in this second stage of development they are stable and irremovable ... Who says organization, says oligarchy' (Michels 1962: 364–5; capital letters changed to small).

A commonly used concept in the literature on workers' collective action and workers' organizations is that of interest. It is indeed a much debated notion, mainly because it can be conceived in two distinct ways, in subjective or objective terms. Both solutions have some obvious drawbacks. The subjective definition is problematic insofar as people may not be able to articulate their 'real' interests or they may articulate them falsely. An objective approach means that someone (the analyst) overrules (some of) the actors' own perceptions of their interests. This is not a tenable position and therefore it is largely preferable to treat the concept of interest as a subjective category, if we need to use it all. Yet, it may be reasonable to think in terms of objective necessities; for example, it can be argued that a diabetic must stay on diet in order to survive or, at least, to avoid deteriorating health and that a capitalist must make profits to avoid bankruptcy.

Actually, there is no need to use the concept of interest in these cases, but if we do, it can hardly be misunderstood. The problem above all appears when it is not all that clear what is necessary and when actors have different opinions about various options.

Some analysts of industrial relations argue that we should try to overcome the distinction between subjective and objective interests. In his book *Rethinking Industrial Relations*, John Kelly (1998: 24–6) deals with these issues within the framework of mobilization theory and I wish to make some comments on his contribution. Among other things, he suggests that we turn to Charles Tilly's attempt to combine the objective and the subjective perspectives. For Tilly, objective interests are rooted in people's social positions or, to be more specific, the relations of production. We should start out from these relations to predict 'the interests people will pursue on the average and in the long run', but at the same time rely, 'as much as possible', on how they define their interests themselves to interpret 'their behavior in the short run' (Tilly 1978: 61). It may be a good idea to infer hypotheses from the social positions that actors have and then study empirically whether they define their interests in the same way, but it seems that the crucial problem remains unsolved. We may find that people either define their interests in the same way as the researcher or that they do not, but in neither case is anything really accomplished. The long-run/short-run distinction does not help very much and phrases such as 'as much as possible' do not eliminate the confusion.

Kelly's own discussion of the concept of interests mainly stays within a subjective dimension. Although he maintains that the objective position of workers is the starting point for the analysis of workers' collective action, his two crucial categories are dissatisfaction and feelings of injustice. He emphasizes that in order for collective action to develop it is not enough that people experience dissatisfaction, but that such a feeling also has to turn into a sense of injustice. Kelly is quite right in this – and I shall return to it in a moment – but I cannot refrain from making the simple observation that at the bottom of the analysis there is not much of use in the concept of objective interest.

In order for collective action to occur, some reasonable consensus must be reached among participants on three issues: (a) 'what exists' and 'what does not exist'; (b) 'what is good' (or desirable) and what is not; and (c) 'what is possible and impossible' (Therborn 1980: 18; emphasis removed). This classification has some resemblance to Lysgaard's discussion on how the problem-situation is defined. With respect to what is desirable and possible, I go back to Kelly's discussion on the transformation of dissatisfaction into feelings of injustice. The author argues that people tend to attribute their difficulties to some kind of cause. When there is a problem at the workplace, employees look for possible explanations, and if the employer is found to be responsible for the existing conditions, they may feel treated unfairly. For collective action to take place the situation must not be conceived as unavoidable but as possible to change; workers have to believe that something can be done about the problem they experience. Furthermore, in the process through which collective action may develop, social identity and leadership also play important roles.

Besides the concept of collective action itself, Kelly makes use of a few other concepts outlined by Tilly: organization, mobilization, and opportunity. Organization covers those dimensions of a group's structure that are most important for its capacity to look after its interests, and mobilization refers to 'the process by which a group acquires collective control over the resources needed for action' (Tilly 1978: 7). Opportunity is not a very well defined concept in either of the two authors' discussions. According to Tilly (1978: 7, 55), it has to do with 'the relationship between a group and the world around it' – which is indeed easy to agree with but not very illuminating – and it is supposed to have three components: power, repression, and opportunity/threat. Despite this lack of clarity, opportunity must be considered a very decisive factor in collective action, given that such phenomena as repression and counter-mobilization are included in the concept. Kelly's own analysis of the circumstances under which collective action actually takes place tries to establish a connection between the cycles of union activity and the 'long waves' in economic development. This is an interesting approach that certainly concretizes the concept of opportunity and the author adds that we must also take the subjective dimension into consideration, that is, what people believe is possible. Finally, collective action is the outcome of the process in question and can take on different forms depending on the balance of the other factors mentioned.

Collective action is often assumed to require that workers calculate turnout and active participation among their colleagues as well as the possible or likely gains and losses of various actions and non-actions. Kelly rightly notices that mobilization does not have to be based on such self-oriented calculations; instead workers may very well join in because of loyalty to the cause or to the category of workers involved. If we were to adopt the perspective outlined by Mancur Olson (1965), it would be impossible to understand this. Moreover, as Kelly (1998: Ch. 5) elegantly shows, we would then have no theory that can help us explain why unions exist at all. This is not to deny that the issue of 'free riding', as analyzed by Olson, must be taken seriously. It is also essential how opportunity is judged; if the motive is just loyalty with the collective and workers think that the collective engagement has no chance to lead to any improvement for anybody, it will be difficult to make them participate in joint action.

One of the most important dimensions of opportunity is what Kelly refers to as counter-mobilization by the opposite side, which in his analysis includes both capitalist employers and the state. Employers also mobilize or organize to counter the actions taken or threatening to be taken by unions or groups of workers. Collective action is always interaction, both within the collective and in relation to outside actors who are supposed to be affected by it. With respect to the state, however, I think that Kelly's analysis is too presupposing; he treats it as simply supportive of capitalism. In the British case, during the Thatcher period, the empirical evidence may speak in favor of such an interpretation, but this is not enough for far-reaching generalizations. We should avoid the assumption that the state in its essence is functional for capitalism. This is, however, a topic for the section below on the state; before that I discuss another dimension of collective action: the efforts of some actors to monopolize part of the labor market.

Monopolization

Single employers as well as actors representing employers and employees may be able to monopolize the market to keep out competitors. Weber (1978: 43–6, 341–3) has developed some ideas along these lines by talking about open and closed social relations and above all about exclusion and exclusionary strategies. There are many different mechanisms that can be utilized for such purposes.

Ownership represents a type of exclusion. An actor who owns physical or financial capital can block the possibilities for others to achieve what they want. For example, a manufacturing company may own all the land available for industrial activity in a small community, in that way making it impossible for competing firms to establish themselves there. Due to this monopoly it will in addition have some substantial control over the local labor market; it can, for example, exert strong influence over wage levels and working conditions, although there may be unions and other actors (like the local authorities and the central government) that still have a say.

Also employees and their organizations use exclusionary strategies. It may be a matter of closing the door for people with another educational or ethnic background. The main aim is often to reduce the supply of workers within a given field in order to avoid that the market becomes flooded; if labor supply can be kept low, the chances are better that wages or salaries can be kept high. It is common that occupational associations or unions prevent outsiders from being recruited to jobs for which they do not have the 'right' qualifications. Weber (1978: 342) illustrates this with, among other things, 'an association of engineering graduates' and its attempts to maintain the legal and real monopoly for its members in relation to job applicants without diplomas. Exclusion is often associated with professional categories in possession of qualifications, theoretical knowledge, and skills that can be acquired only through higher education. Through credentials and certificates unqualified individuals can be kept out of certain positions, insofar as employers agree to this. An exclusionary professional strategy may also involve an effort to keep down the number of students taking the required education. The purpose is to prevent the market from becoming swamped with people with certificates, which in turn would make it easier for employers to hold back wages and other employee demands.

Frank Parkin has attempted to go further in examining the mechanisms of exclusion. According to him, the analysis must not be limited to the exclusionary strategies of the dominant group but include the reactions and counter-strategies by the excluded. In other words, we must consider also other forms of collective action, aimed at maximizing the remunerations and opportunities for a given category (Parkin 1979: 44–5). Strategies intended to open possibilities for the excluded are the other side of the coin and they are labeled usurpation (Parkin 1979: 74). The ambition is to provide the excluded with at least some of the resources and privileges that a dominant category has and these counter-strategies can involve all kinds of improvement, from smaller redistribution to total expropriation.

Social exclusion is thus according to Parkin not only exclusion in its original meaning but also usurpation. I do not deny the relevance of letting the analysis cover also the counter-strategies of the excluded, but it seems strange indeed to include these strategies under the concept of exclusion itself; the excluded try to open and not to close possibilities. It is a completely different thing that both strategies may appear simultaneously; Parkin (1979: 91) then talks about dual exclusion, for example when unionized employees take usurpatory action versus their employers, while, at the same time, they try to exclude other categories of employees. To my mind, only the second of these strategies can be considered exclusionary; the first is a matter of expanding opportunities.

The state

Following Parnes, we have one final actor in the labor market to deal with: the government or the state. Like unions and employers' associations, the state is also an actor that hires labor power. It is actually a very large employer, at least if we include local and regional governments in the concept, which is common to do. However, we are here interested in another role of the state, namely how it intervenes in the labor market by means of legislation and other measures. In the advanced capitalist countries, among other things, the state maintains a legal framework for labor market transactions, provides protection for those who cannot support themselves through gainful employment, contributes to the production of labor supply, and is more or less engaged in combating unemployment.

Theoretical considerations

Social scientists have come up with very different interpretations of the state in modern capitalist societies. Many, however, agree that the definition provided by Weber more than eighty years ago is a useful starting point. In a commonly quoted paragraph, Weber (1978: 65) suggests 'that it is possible to define the state itself only in terms of the means which it today monopolizes, namely, the use of force'. This definition touches upon something important, but it is often highly contested who actually has the legitimate right to the use of violence, for example in cases of civil war. In another text, Weber presents a more developed definition; again, there is a focus on the legitimate right to use violence, but some other aspects are also emphasized. The state is defined as an administrative apparatus, 'subject to change by legislation', and claiming 'binding authority', not only over its members, the citizens, 'but also to a very large extent over all action taking place in the area of its jurisdiction' (Weber 1978: 56). This is a more elaborated definition from which to start.

Yet, with the development of political democracy and the welfare state, other issues have come to the forefront. One crucial question is whether or to what extent state policies express the will of the majority of the population and there are different answers to it. Pluralist theorists, who after massive criticism have shown greater awareness regarding the significance of society's uneven distribution of resources, tend to emphasize that different elite groups must compete for power through the democratic process and that citizens therefore have a substantial influence over political decisions (see, e.g., Dahl 1961, 1982, 1985; Polsby 1980). It has been pointed out, however, that we should also look at the decisions that are not made, that is, the 'non-decisions', because dominant groups may bias the public agenda (Bachrach and Baratz 1970). Some have even gone one step further arguing that we need to overcome the behavioral focus of the previous approaches and take into account the '*latent conflict*, which consists in a contradiction between the interests of those exercising power and the *real interests* of those they exclude'; the latter 'may not express or even be conscious of their interests' (Lukes 1974: 24–5; emphasis in original). Once again we are back at the issue of 'real' interests and the same problems as indicated above thus apply.

Marxists tend to regard state institutions and state policies as geared into the reproduction of capitalist rule, no matter whether political democracy is at hand or not. While most contemporary analysts have abandoned the simple idea, once brought forward by Marx and Engels (1998: 37), that 'the executive of the modern state is but a committee for managing the common affairs of the whole bourgeoisie', they still have a tendency to see the state as basically functional for capitalism. The explanations suggested are, however, very different. One of them is that pro-capitalist opinions, values, and norms have a stronghold in the state apparatuses because their personnel are mainly recruited among the dominant groups in society (Miliband 1969, 1972, 1973). Others have been critical of this argument and emphasized the state's structural position in capitalist society and its relative autonomy in relation to social classes (Poulantzas 1972, 1973a, 1973b).

We find a range of other Marxist analyses too and they largely share the same problem. It does not really seem to matter what the state does and what policies are implemented; these policies are always assumed to be functional for the capitalist system (van den Berg 1988). From this point of departure follows a rather strange perspective on the welfare state. For example, welfare state expenditures for social insurance and income maintenance are typically interpreted as beneficial for the reproduction of capitalism, even if business leaders and pro-business organizations and political parties want to cut back on them. The view adopted on welfare state service production – healthcare, education, childcare, care for the elderly, etc. – is in the same vein. Some of these services are treated as fulfilling crucial functions for the capitalist system as 'ideological state apparatuses', for example by providing education for the reproduction of labor power (Althusser 2001: 85–126). Such a perspective cannot explain why neo-liberals and right-wingers have been so interested in shrinking these services or in privatizing them.

There is another Marxist-inspired approach, which has a somewhat different answer. It is the idea that the state in modern capitalist societies fulfills two functions; its main role is to promote the process of capital accumulation, but it also provides for people who cannot get by in the capitalist market (see, e.g., Habermas 1973; Offe 1984; O'Connor 1973; cf. van den Berg 1988: Ch. 5) The latter function is a consequence of political democracy through which also social categories without great resources can have a voice. By providing for people whose needs are not met by the market, the welfare state makes the system legitimate. It is, however, recognized that such measures can be costly and have detrimental effects on the capital accumulation process, for example by decommodifying labor power. This perspective emphasizes the contradictions that exist between the two tasks suggested, but – still in a functionalist way – it treats welfare state intervention as having mainly a legitimizing role. As I see it, welfare measures cannot be explained with reference to their possible function of legitimizing capitalism but must be understood in their own right. There has been a long political struggle regarding government provision of support to people in need and the social forces in favor of this kind of intervention have been rather successful in making it come true.

It is unsustainable to assume that permanent or essential relationships exist between capital, labor and the state. These relationships are at least partly open and they change across time. In making the case for such a perspective, I want to quote Paul Thompson and David McHugh (1995: 93; emphasis in original): 'The state does not function unambiguously in the interests of a single class; it is a state *in* capitalist society rather than *the* capitalist state, and it is an arena of struggle constituted and divided by opposing interests rather than a centralised and unified political actor'. Hence, we must acknowledge that state policies are to a high degree determined by the relative strength of social forces in society and this is also a major argument in the so-called power resources theory, suggesting that a strong labor movement can influence policies to improve the working conditions of ordinary workers, protect jobs, combat unemployment, provide a generous social security system, and decrease income differentials (see, e.g., Korpi 1978, 1983, 2002; Esping-Andersen 1985; O'Connor and Olsen 1998; Stephens 1979).

Notwithstanding, I add some points to remind us that every action is subject to certain structural constraints. Under normal circumstances, many state institutions are shaped not only to fit in with but also to support the functioning of the capitalist system. We can, among other things, mention legislation defining property rights and regulating contractual relationships in markets, including the labor market. The expression 'under normal circumstances' refers to a situation when capitalism has been in place long enough to obtain some reasonable stability. During transitional periods it may be quite different; for example, in the ongoing transformation of socialism to capitalism in Eastern Europe and Russia many state institutions are dysfunctional or contradictory to the new order and only slowly adjusting to it; others, however, may lead the march toward it.

When capitalism has become the unchallenged dominant mode of production, the state can be expected to have developed many relatively stable institutions that help the economic system to function. This does not mean, however, that all state policies must have this role. To a large extent, the policies developed depend on the balance of power between the principal social forces in society, but reforms that are assumed to go against the functioning of the economic system will have a non-negligible price. In the next section, I scrutinize these issues somewhat further.

State intervention in the labor market

The concept of state intervention in the labor market covers activities in both capitalist and non-capitalist sectors, including the role of the state as employer. For the present, I will exclude the latter aspect and focus on other kinds of state intervention. Many of these are directly supportive of the capitalist system, but this does not necessarily mean that they weaken the position of workers. Certain other policies may restrict the power of capitalist employers, in principle even to the point where the whole system run into difficulties. In addition, there are also policies with more or less indeterminate impact upon the relationship between employers and workers.

Thus, several options exist, but we should not assume that they are equally open; there are structural restrictions to consider. This insight is perhaps the only positive lesson to learn from the various attempts to develop Marxist state theory. Policies that reduce the power of capitalists or are detrimental to the functioning of the system have a price and the idea of 'structural limitations' can be illustrated as follows (cf. Wright 1978: 15–26). Let us assume that a labor government wants to make it more difficult for employers to get rid of workers, because there has been a dramatic increase of unemployment due to mass layoffs. It is possible for the government to do this, but at some critical point legislation may create larger problems than it solves. If employment protection becomes so strict that employers hesitate to hire people or even stop hiring, unemployment will rise even further, as employment is dependent on capitalists' willingness to recruit workers (which is in turn due to their power over jobs and over recruitment to jobs). A drastic reduction of that willingness may thus lead to the opposite from what was intended with the legislation. Such mechanisms make anti-capitalist measures, in particular system-threatening measures, less likely, but do not rule them out completely.

In concluding this chapter, I draw attention to some of the concrete ways in which the state intervenes in the labor market, besides being a large employer (cf. Furåker and Lindqvist 2003). First, with some cross-national variation, the state has a crucial role in establishing and maintaining rules for the interaction between employers and employees. Labor law provides rules with respect to the hiring and firing of personnel and regarding discriminatory practices in recruitment processes. It also regulates a whole range of other aspects of the exchange between employers and workers. Among other things, we find working time and work safety legislation and in some countries there is legislation concerning workers' participation in the employing organization's decision making. Yet another set of rules defines the terms for union activity.

Second, the state plays an essential role in providing economic subsidies to various actors in the labor market, both employers and workers/jobseekers. For example, firms sometimes receive subsidies for allocating their investments in remote areas. By far the most important part of this kind of state intervention is, however, income maintenance for people who do not have sufficient resources to support themselves. It involves social protection for individuals when they become sick, unemployed, elderly, etc. and hence touches upon one of the crucial aspects of the labor market, namely the economic necessity for people to earn a living from gainful employment. The underlying idea is that people should be supported only when they are unable to carry out paid work or have certain other reasons not to be employed or not to be at the workplace.

Countries differ concerning to what extent they provide income maintenance, which categories are eligible, the levels of income maintenance that are supplied, for how long benefits can last, etc. Some of them provide little in terms of these measures, whereas others are large spenders. The question is of course how people's willingness to hire out their labor power in the market is affected by welfare state benefits. I will come back to this discussion later and I will later also make some comments on the proposal of a citizenship or basic income, that is, an income that everybody would receive no matter whether they work or not.

Finally, there is government provision of various services, healthcare, education, etc. Although not always directly or only partly oriented toward the labor market, this type of state intervention is often very significant for the functioning of it, which can be illustrated by a few examples. Workers who need healthcare in order to remain in or come back to their jobs sometimes get it through the welfare state. The educational system imparts skills that are important or even necessary for individuals when they try to find employment. To take just one more example, public childcare makes it possible for both parents in a dual-earner family with small children to enter or to stay in the labor market.

One subtype of state intervention is active labor market policy, developed in a greater or lesser degree in various countries. It is a part of income maintenance policies, but I also want to emphasize the role of the state in solving two main problems in the operation of labor market: jobseekers' attempts to find jobs and employers' efforts to fill vacancies. By organizing public employment services and by providing labor market training and job creation programs, the state tries to find solutions to these issues. Normally, unemployment is considered the most serious problem, because it hits individuals who often have a very vulnerable position regarding income. Labor market policy measures are oriented toward income maintenance, as people are supported when they participate in training and job creation programs, but another aspect is what impact these programs have on the functioning of the labor market. We find a great deal of questioning in recent years as to whether active labor market policies really accomplish what they are set up for (cf. Chapter 5).

5
The Commodity Status of Labor Power

Individuals who offer their labor power for hire in the market commonly do so to support themselves; in the absence of other means of subsistence paid employment represents a crucial option to earn a living. In countries with a developed welfare state, citizens will be taken care of even if they refuse to work; at least in principle, no one will be allowed to starve. People are nevertheless under pressure to offer their labor power in the market, not primarily to avoid starvation but to survive at a 'normal' or even 'poor' standard of living. There is definitely a limit to the generosity provided; in contemporary affluent capitalism, with certain exceptions, working-age individuals cannot as a rule avoid gainful employment without suffering substantial income loss. Although many argue that it is not punitive enough, the welfare state does not entirely eliminate the economic pressure upon individuals who have nothing else on which to survive but their laboring capacities.

Furthermore, and more importantly perhaps, if a considerable proportion of those who are today gainfully employed would refuse to carry out paid work, the welfare state would become less able to support them. Large welfare state transfers require large government incomes and thus normally a significant proportion of taxpayers in the population. If the ratio between benefit recipients and taxpayers would be drastically increased, we can expect tougher rules and less generous benefits to be introduced. The system cannot be sustained unless most individuals behave according to the dominant norms; its functioning is based on the assumption that most of those who are able to engage in gainful employment should do so. Besides the welfare state, however, there are several other factors in operation to make people ready for paid work or for withdrawal from the labor market. This chapter takes a look at some of the most important mechanisms of commodification and decommodification of labor power. It is divided into three different parts that in turn deal with processes related to the economy, the family, and the welfare state.

The functioning of the economy

Processes within the economy affect the commodity status of labor power in several ways. I start by making a few comments on the general prerequisites for a labor market to exist: demand for labor power and people who are ready to hire out their capacities for work. The main part of this section, however, deals with other aspects. One refers to the processes through which the use value of labor power is being reduced or even eradicated. Another is about the possibility that employees can accumulate what might be called a 'surplus' income. Finally, I consider the role of self-employment, although the self-employed who do not hire others are not engaged in any employment relationship. They produce goods or services for sale and it is the outcome of this work that appears as commodities in the market and not their labor power. Still, since different employment statuses are communicating vessels, the development of self-employment affects the supply of labor power in the labor market.

Processes in the labor market

A first precondition for a labor market to exist is that some actors have a demand for labor power. It goes without saying that if capitalist and other employers did not have a need to employ workers labor power would not obtain commodity status. Capitalist employers are out to make profits and this requires people to be hired and put to work. Although they have no purpose to make profit, other employers – public sector institutions, voluntary organizations, and households – also have a demand for labor power, as they organize work to produce certain use values.

Moreover, the presumptive workers must have a reason to supply their capacities – be it a matter of economic necessity ('stick') or of the advantage or attraction ('carrot') of having a job and earning an income. The main underlying mechanism is the need for large population segments to support themselves and by offering their labor power for hire they are able to earn an income, even though some of them become unemployed, at least for a while. Actually, the socioeconomic structure rests on this economic necessity, but still we find categories of people – of working-age and fit for work – without a job and without having to look for a job. It is today no doubt possible to provide the mere means of subsistence for the whole population with relatively fewer people employed than ever before, but if the standard of living is to be kept at about the present level a large proportion of the population must take part in the production of goods and services. By emphasizing this economic necessity, I do not want us to disregard the attractions of having a job: good earnings, interesting work tasks, stimulating social contacts with workmates and others, etc.

Labor power's use value

It is sometimes argued that increasing segments of the population in the advanced capitalist world run a great risk of being left outside working life (see, e.g., Beck 2000; Gorz 1982, 1985, 1999; Offe 1996; Rifkin 1995). This can be interpreted in different ways: as a result of a general decline in demand for labor or in terms of increased difficulties for certain categories to meet employers' requirements or both. Some argue that we now witness the 'end of work' or the beginning of such a development. I return to this discussion in Chapter 9, but let me here just say that so far there is little empirical evidence in support of the 'end-of-work' argument. However, there are large numbers of unemployed, marginalized, and excluded individuals in the developed capitalist world. These individuals' capacities for work are not made use of in the labor market – in a way because their 'employability' is limited – and they will thus have to rely on their family, the welfare state, or charity in order to survive and avoid the risk of living in poverty. My discussion on labor power's use value is organized to fit in with the distinction between the three dimensions of labor power outlined previously: biological capacities, skills, and motivation.

First, labor power is always partly a matter of biological capacities. It is a renewable source of energy in two different ways: on a day-to-day basis and through the birth of new generations. Focusing on the day-to-day aspect, we can say that if employees' basic needs in terms of eating, drinking, sleep, mental balance, etc., are satisfied, they can continue to work week after week for many years. Eventually, however, aging will make itself felt, but it also happens that people, early in their lives, get diseases or are seriously injured in accidents. Illness and injuries may have nothing to do with jobs, but physically and mentally hard work takes its toll in terms of health and many employees get diseases or become injured at the workplace. There are thus two aspects to be taken into account: first, aging and other developments that occur independently of job activities and, second, the impact of work on people's health. The end result is well known; to paraphrase John Maynard Keynes, we can be sure that, in the long run, individuals' capacities for work will lose all use value; labor power's commodity status in the market will eventually go, due to processes and events at the workplace or outside it.

A worker whose physical and mental labor power has deteriorated, but who is nevertheless 'employable', might find another job that is less demanding. Employers are not, however, very inclined to recruit people with reduced capacities for work, because, among other things, their choices are based on what prognoses – age of course taken into consideration – can be made for the future. When labor power has no significant use value, its commodity status is in principle finished, although its bearer may stay in the labor market as unemployed for a period of time. To some extent, workers are decommodified by their jobs or by the interaction between work and other processes, including aging.

Second, there is the skill dimension and, to begin, we can note that the use value of a given set of qualifications is likely to change over time. On the one hand, employees get on-the-job training and/or are placed in formal training programs or other kinds of education leading to improvement of their skills and, in addition, long-lasting experience is likely to enhance their capacities. Accordingly, they become more valuable and more easily employable. On the other hand, jobs and the composition of jobs continuously change in the labor market. Skills that were once highly valued may suddenly – or, for that matter, slowly – become obsolete. It occurs that the use value of certain qualifications drops to nothing, but often the demand for certain skills declines without completely coming to an end.

When an individual's skills have become obsolete, something similar happens as when the physical and mental capacities of labor power lose their use value. The employee may try to find a job that is less demanding or requires a different set of qualifications. Another option is to enter the educational system to obtain new qualifications in demand. Sometimes it is not enough with just further education, because there may also be a need for de-learning of old ways of thinking and behaving. Lifelong learning has become a popular slogan for the continuous educational efforts that people have to expose themselves to (see, e.g., Edwards 1997; Field and Leicester 2000). It represents a way for the individual to retain or regain a use value in terms of qualifications and thus a degree of employability. One problem is nevertheless that people whose skills have become obsolete are often relatively old – aging is again an important factor – and therefore not always so eager to start all over again with education. However, we must dismiss the idea that older people cannot learn new things.

Third, workers' motivation or employment commitment can be expected to be affected by what happens at the workplace, in the labor market at large, or in life in general. Motivation should not be regarded as isolated from the two other dimensions above. On the contrary, it is most likely that people who are worn out or whose skills have become obsolete will feel less inspired to remain in their jobs or even in the labor market at all. This observation should not make us forget that many other factors also have an influence, positive or negative, on individuals' enthusiasm for a specific job or for paid work on the whole.

Although I doubt that the need for labor power is generally fading away, it is often too low (capitalism is an incessant story of unemployment) and it fluctuates with business cycles. Unemployment due to insufficient demand for workers is a major problem, but it has the advantage for the individual – compared to being unemployed because of bad health or obsolete skills – that if the labor market improves she may be asked for again.

The question is what the individual can do to improve her chances in the labor market in such a situation. One thing is to intensify the search for a job, as there are vacancies also in recessions. Another step that she can take is to lower her reservation wage, that is, the lowest price at which she is willing to hire out her working capacities. This would correspond to what happens in the regular consumer market, where merchants frequently organize sales to clear the stock and get rid of things that have not been sold in due time. To some extent, bearers of labor power can do the same but often only within narrow limits, because of restrictions defined in collective agreements or minimum wage legislation. It is also commonly difficult or impossible for the individual to accept just any wage or salary, insofar as it must provide some basis for a living.

If nobody wants to employ an individual, she may nevertheless remain in the market as unemployed, searching or waiting for a suitable job opportunity to appear, and this requires that the means of subsistence are provided through some other mechanism. To be unemployed implies that the commodity status of labor power is sustained. As pointed out in Chapter 2, to be in a job queue does not guarantee that one advances in a way that would be normal in other queues. Employers decide whom they want to recruit and they may prefer people who have just become unemployed instead of those who are long-term unemployed. In case nothing happens, the individual may cease looking for employment. The regular labor force surveys in developed countries refer to this as the discouraged worker concept. It refers to a situation where the individual is willing and able to take a job but has given up searching, because he/she believes nothing suitable will turn up. As the question in the labor force surveys is hypothetical – the individual is asked whether he/she would and could take a job if there were one – the empirical information on this category is somewhat shaky. However, it is not altogether fictitious; at least in some countries its size varies with business cycles (OECD 1995: 47–65). Thus, on the surface somewhat paradoxically, open unemployment in a local area may go up when the number of vacant jobs increases, for example through the establishment of new workplaces. The explanation is then that certain hidden dimensions of joblessness become visible when the demand for labor power rises.

We should also observe the ambiguity of the concept of discouraged worker. On the one hand, the word 'discouraged' seems to suggest that the individual is no longer motivated, although he/she used to be. On the other hand, if the individual is willing to take a job – which is part of the definition – he/she must have some motivation left. The non-employed who do not search for a job have no commodity status in the labor market, but the discouraged worker concept is based on the assumption that the potential is still there. At the same time, people might find it appallingly discouraging to continue being a jobseeker if nothing suitable ever seems to come up. Hence unsuccessful jobseekers' enthusiasm for work – and correspondingly also the use value of their labor power – can be expected to decline. However, empirical studies indicate that work motivation is high also among the long-term unemployed (see, e.g., Gallie and Alm 2000; Nordenmark 1999). Therefore, the fact that discouraged workers do not actively look for jobs appears to be related to the actual number of vacancies appearing in the market.

Avoiding employment

Decommodification of labor power means that individuals' capabilities for work are withdrawn from the market. As suggested above, due to developments at the workplace (in interaction with other processes such as aging), labor power may lose various aspects of its use value and its commodity status may thus not be sustained. In this section, I take one step further and ask whether the human capacity for work, even if its use value is maintained, can be decommodified through processes within the labor market. A few other decommodifying mechanisms will be identified and my aim is to spell out how they work.

If people can save money from their wage or salary, they will be able to stay away from work for a longer or shorter period of time. Since, in affluent countries, many employees' incomes are clearly above the mere subsistence level, it is possible for them to build up some economic buffer also from a relatively low income. Those who have small savings may keep them in reserve or spend them on certain more expensive things, such as a car or a condo, but they can also use them to buy themselves out of the labor market. A buffer can hence be utilized to avoid paid work, at least for some period of time, as in the cases when youths work hard for a while in order to save money for traveling to foreign countries, which is a rather common phenomenon. This kind of decommodified status does not last very long; after a few months or so the money is gone and the traveler usually has to return home and go back again to work or school. As another illustrative case, consider an individual who is close to the pension age and who has some savings after a long life with wage-work. He/she can thus quit the labor market before what is regarded as normal and this is more likely to occur when certain other circumstances are at hand, such as poor health or family members in need of care. Work motivation, or rather the lack of it, may also play an important role in making such a decision.

In both situations mentioned, the decommodified status is of limited duration. However, there are also employees who earn so much that they can leave their job at any time and still have all they need for the rest of their lives. Top-level managers often have a clause in their contracts allotting them large amounts of money, if they are fired from their jobs or even if they quit voluntarily. It may very well be a matter of being decommodified until retirement, which at least sometimes may mean quite a few 'years. Although such managers thus do not have to remain in the labor market, it is nevertheless common that they find other top jobs, which indicates that the motive for having paid work is not just the necessity to earn a living. Those who have no need to earn a living from gainful employment but remain in the labor market anyway can of course allow themselves to be selective and wait until something really attractive shows up.

For further examples we can turn to sports stars in tennis, soccer, football, ice hockey, basketball, racing, boxing, and several other sports. Many athletes are self-employed, but there are also employees among them. During their active period – which lasts for relatively few years – some can put enormous amounts of money aside. After a successful career they may have earned enough to refrain from gainful employment for the rest of their lives. Yet, when their sports career is over, athletes are commonly inclined to look for a job or to start their own business, as they are likely to be still rather young. They, too, can afford to be highly selective, since there is nothing that forces them to take just any job.

A concept that might be used in this context is self-decommodification. It would then refer to a situation in which an employee by saving money can quit work, permanently or temporarily. By refraining from immediate consumption he/she can set aside for future needs. However, the prefix 'self' gives certain connotations that might be misleading. For example, in dealing with the extremely high remunerations that selected managers receive, it seems deceptive to talk about self-decommodification, because these remunerations are after all taken from the surplus produced through the joint efforts by a larger collective. At least, we must not neglect the difference between a low-income earner who by making sacrifices is able to save some money to stay out of work for a while and a manager who can exploit a privileged situation to leave the labor market forever and still have everything needed and desired.

We here touch upon an aspect that can be expected to become increasingly more important in the future. Assuming that the average standard of living will continue to improve, it is likely that more and more people will be able to gather a fortune – small or large – over some decades of work. To this can also be added the property transferred between generations as gifts or through the rules of inheritance (see further below). If this kind of accumulation grows, we may have a situation in a not too distant future, in which, compared to today, a much larger proportion of the population – of course a well-to-do segment – has no economic pressure at all to be available to the labor market. How the labor market and society at large would be affected, economically and morally, is an important question and we should therefore already now start thinking in such terms.

The development of self-employment

Two different processes need to be considered with respect to self-employment in the history of modern capitalism. The first refers to the fact that large numbers of people working on their own have been made available to the labor market and this has happened through a process that might be labeled proletarianization. For a long period, the relative size of the farming population, mainly consisting of self-employed peasants, has decreased dramatically in all developed countries and today it often makes up but a few percent of total employment. A parallel development can be observed in several other industries, in which the petty bourgeoisie was large; thus, the proportion of artisans, small shopkeepers, and similar groups has decreased.

Although this transformation has been far-reaching, it has not come to an end in modern capitalism; also today we find that self-employed individuals in various sectors have to give up their position. When this change is rapid, the individuals themselves are forced to quit self-employment and instead offer their labor power for hire in the market. There is, however, also a slower variant; the members of an older generation keep their businesses until they reach the pension age, while their descendants do not or cannot take over but have to find something else from which to earn a living. As other sectors have expanded – for some time industrial production and later on the service sector – there have been plenty of opportunities for this second generation to become wage-earners. One significant aspect is that the young are generally more educated than their parents and they have often been recruited to white-collar jobs; to a large extent, they make up the new middle class. Using the terminology applied here, the historic development described can be characterized as a process of commodification. People – who used to support themselves through self-employment or whose parents did – have been transferred to the labor market and transformed into wage-workers. Instead of being or becoming entrepreneurs, they offer their capacities for work as a commodity for hire; wage-work is substituted for self-employment.

The second process to be considered goes in the opposite direction, that is, it can be referred to as decommodification. Individuals leave their status as wage-earners behind them and begin working on their own. In many economically developed countries self-employment has started to grow in certain sectors; it is not a matter of a revival of agriculture or small-scale manufacturing, but the 'partial renaissance' has occurred within the service sector, not least within certain new services related to communication and financing (OECD 2000: 160; cf. also Castells 1996: 220–1). Empirical data also suggest a great deal of interest among people to start working on their own (Huijgen 2000). To some extent, these data probably reflect unrealistic dreams, related to the fact that the contemporary ideological climate has for quite some time been very favorable toward self-employment.

The transition to self-employment sometimes goes by way of unemployment. A recent OECD study (2000: 163–7) cannot, however, confirm the 'unemployment push' hypothesis that expects such transitions to be particularly frequent in recessions, since the demand in the labor market is low in those times. The problem is, unsurprisingly, that there is also a counter-acting mechanism, because the opportunities for self-employment are also likely to be small during periods with low economic activity (cf. Meager 1992, 1994). Moreover, the unemployed are not always inclined to become self-employed, despite considerable efforts among governments to promote and support this (OECD 2000: 174–87; Meager 1992, 1994).

Family-related mechanisms

The family is another important social institution in modern societies. Individuals spend a great deal of their lives or even their whole lives in one or a couple of families and it is also crucial for the reproduction of labor power – both day-to-day and across generations – as well as for individuals' relationship with the labor market more generally. There are examples in history of how employers have had several family members or even whole families on their payroll, but even though such arrangements still exist, they basically belong to the past. In the modern type of labor market an employment relationship is normally a matter between the employer and an individual. Nevertheless, the family plays an important role for the individual's interaction with the labor market and for the commodity status of labor power.

Unless a family has other sources of income, one or several of its members must supply labor power to the market. In the one-breadwinner model the husband is expected to do this, while the wife's role is to stay at home to do the housework. Today the two-breadwinner model has gained considerable ground in developed capitalist countries (see, e.g., Crompton 1999). Nevertheless, female labor force participation rates are still clearly lower compared to male rates and women much more commonly work part-time. Another aspect should also be taken into account, namely the large numbers of families with only one parent who is then most often the mother (see, e.g., Duncan and Edwards 1997, 1999; Lewis 1997). Being alone with one or several small children creates great pressure upon the adult person to provide an income. On the whole, despite some very significant cross-national differences, the welfare state plays an important role for such families.

The size and the composition of a family are crucial factors for how much income it needs for consumption. With growing numbers of household members, the pressure increases upon the adults to supply their labor power in the market and the same may apply to teenage and older children. At the same time, however, there is a large amount of housework and childcare to perform. The ways of reconciling family obligations and needs for employment reflect the gender division of labor in society. A common solution is that the husband brings home the principal income through full-time employment, while the wife works part-time and uses more time on children and housework. If the family needs more money, either one of the two spouses or both may be able to put in more hours of paid work. Moreover, incomes can be increased when children, still living at home, reach working age and enter the labor market, insofar as they are prepared or urged to contribute. In any case, the economic pressure placed on the family is a crucial mechanism of commodification. For women who enter the labor market after a longer period of time at home, it implies some degree of defamilialization, that is, liberation from family obligations, although double burdens may be the overshadowing outcome.

However, we can turn the perspective around, thereby discovering that the family also can mean rather the reverse as to its members' relationship to the labor market. The advent of a newborn child, for example, has an obvious decommodifying impact, since the mother will have to stay at home for at least some period of time. More generally, all families with small children have plenty of responsibilities and this is a basis for decommodification, at least if no (sufficient) childcare is available. Someone has to carry out the tasks at home, which is in turn likely to put restrictions on the possibilities for labor market participation. There may also be other caring obligations in a family and they tend to have similar consequences. Actually, duties associated with small children and others in need of care bring about different kinds of pressure. On the one hand, they make higher incomes desirable or necessary, but, on the other hand, they require that someone is prepared to carry out unpaid work at home.

The family can have another decommodifying function too, by being a safety net for its members; individuals who are unsuccessful in hiring out their labor power in the market can get a haven there. Although economically developed countries have unemployment insurance systems for those who fail to find employment, these systems do not cover every situation or everybody and the family often plays the role of last resort (see, e.g., Gallie and Paugam 2000: 13–18). If one of the spouses is employed but the other cannot find a job and unemployment benefits are not available, the income at hand is perhaps enough for the household to live on. It may even be possible that the breadwinner can put in extra hours, at least for some period of time. Thus, a decommodifying element can be identified; through the safety net of the family the unemployed individual does not necessarily have to rush into any job available. In considering the consequences for a family when one of its members becomes unemployed, we must also take other aspects into account. For example, there are sometimes caring obligations (children, old parents) for which no direct solution is at hand; the unemployed individual may then be expected to engage in these unpaid duties and this is especially likely if it is a woman who is jobless.

A rather common situation is when a young individual reaches working age and is ready to enter the labor market but has to start with a period of unemployment. Youths without much or any previous work experience may not be entitled to unemployment benefits or only to very low benefits. The family can then continue to provide the means of subsistence. Unemployed youths do not have to live with their family in order to be supported by it, but this will lower the costs and solutions of this kind appear to be rather frequent, particularly in southern Europe (Gallie and Paugam 2000: 16–17). The more support the family is willing to provide, the longer the young unemployed individual can wait for a suitable job to appear; he/she does not have to take just anything available but can allow himself/herself to be somewhat demanding. Thus, again, a decommodifying aspect is involved, although it has a temporary character.

With respect to family relations we must also consider another element, the mechanism of inheritance, already touched upon above. Generally in our type of society, when people die, their property is transferred to relatives according to certain rules and these arrangements can affect the individual's relationship to the labor market. Inheriting sizeable assets will at least reduce but sometimes even eliminate the pressure on people to offer their work capacities for hire. Although being a family-related mechanism, inheritance is regulated by law and it is therefore also a government affair. In contemporary affluent countries, people on average own more assets, monetary and non-monetary, than ever before in history. These assets are enormously unevenly distributed, but an increasingly larger proportion of the population is accumulating resources – through inheritance and through the market – that can eventually liberate them from having to earn a living from wage-work. Presumably, taking a long-term view, this will have significant effects upon the labor market as well as upon class relationships in society and the family is a crucial institution in such a development.

The role of the state

As a next step in my discussion, I turn to the multifaceted role of the state or the welfare state in relation to the labor market. One aspect is legislation in connection with employment contracts. By providing statutory rules as regards such agreements, the state furthers the transactions between employers and workers. According to Émile Durkheim (1964: 114), for those who sign a contract it is important to know that violations to the conditions agreed upon can be acted against by means of legislative power; otherwise 'the obligations contracted for' would 'have no more than moral authority'. By upholding and enforcing rules concerning the employment contract itself, the state is crucial for the commodity status of labor power, but also other types of legislation are significant for the operation of the labor market, for example regarding work safety and working hours. The modern state provides some degree of protection from certain risks associated with having paid work and if the legislation functions as intended, at least some workers will avoid being worn out or injured. This means that labor power will preserve its use value longer and hence that its commodity status can be maintained longer.

Moreover, the state is often an important producer of services such as healthcare and education. There are many employees who would not be able to work, unless they were cured in public hospitals or similar institutions that of course also look after the non-working population. The educational system is to a large extent aimed at supplying workers with suitable skills for the labor market. This is not to deny the presence of contradictory goals within the schools; the goals advocated by big business and other elite interests may very well be in conflict with those of other citizens (see, e.g., Bowles and Gintis 1976). Healthcare and educational institutions do not have to be organized through the public sector, but this is to a considerable degree actually the case, although we find a great deal of variation across the advanced capitalist countries.

In the following, I focus on a few other aspects: social insurance, including labor market policy, and the role of the state as employer. Some of these polices are at the center of the discussion concerning how the welfare state is associated with incentives and disincentives for paid work. The main impact of the transfer systems is often assumed to be that they lessen the pressure upon people to offer their labor power in the market; in other words, it is the decommodifying function that is emphasized. As considered below, however, this is not the whole story; social insurance and labor market policy have a more complex role, as they also contribute to the commodification of labor power.

Social insurance

A main norm behind the modern welfare state is that working-age people – in passing a concept that is socially defined, that is, it changes when the dominant actors decide to redefine it – should be prepared to support themselves through gainful employment. Before going somewhat deeper into the particularities of this norm, let me make a few comments regarding the part of the population not supposed to be available for paid work. To begin, for those under working age, the basic principle is that their parents should support them, although there are many different benefit types for families or households, not least for lone mothers with small children (see, e.g., Duncan and Edwards 1997, 1999; Lewis 1997). These benefits have a part to play in people's decisions concerning employment and to some degree they may have a decommodifying effect by making paid work or long working hours less urgent.

Turning to people above working-age, we can start out from the fact that affluent countries provide some kind of old-age pension. The underlying idea is that when people reach the pension age they are considered to have done their part; thereafter they are allowed to enjoy some sufficient standard of living without having to worry about supporting themselves through paid work. Accordingly, the pension is potentially the ultimate decommodification mechanism; once the relevant age is reached, labor power can be withdrawn from the market forever. One qualification, however, needs to be appended; retirees may continue to work if they want to and can keep their job or find a new job.

For the remaining population, the predominant principle is that gainful employment should be the main way of earning a living. Nevertheless, there are exceptions to that norm and these exceptions can be classified into two major categories. The first is that if people have other sources of income – through property, family relationships, etc. – no public authority, at least not in the advanced capitalist countries, forces them to take a job. Compulsory measures of that kind are typically associated with state socialism under which working-age people without employment or enrolment in the educational system run the risk of being accused of 'parasitism'. The second exception refers to those who are unable to take on a job or to perform the job they have. What is counted as being 'unable' is, needless to say, also a matter of social definitions that continuously undergo change. The following situations exemplify what would today normally be considered legitimate reasons for people not to carry out paid work: having to take care of small children, having a severe handicap, being (seriously) sick or injured, and being in the educational system. In these situations people are not expected to have a job or to go to work for some period of time; there must thus be other mechanisms to provide for them and the welfare state is then often a highly significant institution.

One state of affairs needs to be given particular attention and that is unemployment. To be unemployed means to be inside the labor market – by offering labor power for hire people are by definition part of it – but it is a legitimate ground for collecting benefits. The unemployed have no work, but they are expected to be looking for employment and to be available in case vacancies occur. Actually, more or less suitable jobs become vacant all the time, even in recessions, and to be an active jobseeker is a standard prerequisite for entitlement to benefits. Another thing is whether or to what extent this principle is being observed in practice; people's availability for vacant positions may be checked more or less closely. I return to the policies related to unemployment in the section below on labor market policy.

The question is what the welfare state intervention does in terms of commodification and decommodification. To repeat, the welfare state is not supposed to touch the so vital mechanism underlying the hiring of labor power in the market – the necessity for people to support themselves from wage-work – but this is not to say that the intentions hold fully in practice. There is at least one clear exception to this principle, namely the old-age pension system. Pensions are paid to people no matter whether they have the ability to work or not and a universal system does not require previous gainful employment; benefits may be low but they are supplied anyway. Retirees are thus in principle decommodified, although they can continue to work if they want to and have a job.

Also with respect to other welfare programs, an element of decommodification – as I have defined it here – is always potentially present. I want to add one important specification, however, that can be illustrated in the following way. If, due to health problems, an individual is completely unable to work, income maintenance programs can just be seen as support to someone who is already forced to be outside of the workplace. An employee who has a heart attack will be taken to a hospital and is then, at least for a while, unlikely to be able to work at all. We may still talk about decommodification, although not caused by the welfare state but by the heart attack. Only if the sickness insurance makes it possible for the individual to stay away from work longer than he/she otherwise would have done can the welfare state be attributed an independent decommodifying role.

The main principle is thus, ideally, that the welfare state should step in when people cannot carry out work owing to reasons considered legitimate. Still, principles are one thing and their practical application is another and the focus should therefore be placed on the actual consequences for the functioning of the labor market. If everything worked out completely in line with rules there would be little to bother about, but as soon as we find a rule, we discover borderline cases and probably also some who abuse it. For example, the premise of the sickness insurance may sound like a simple principle – an employee should get some of his/her income loss covered in case of sickness. The question is, however, whether an individual's state of health prevents him/her from working or not. Most systems have some waiting period to make it costly to stay away from work just for one or a few days and this in particular hits people who are likely to have recurrent sickness periods.

When an employee becomes sick, some decision making will be involved. At the first crossroad the individual has to decide whether or not it is reasonable to stay at home away from work. In many cases this is a very simple choice, or not even a choice, as in the example above with the heart attack. Similarly, but still with borderline cases, if a nurse has got a cold, it would most often be considered irresponsible for her to go to work. In other cases, it may be much more difficult to tell – even for a doctor – how sick an individual is. The second decision comes if and when time for returning to work approaches; it must then be decided whether the individual is ready for work or whether he/she needs a longer recovery. Obviously, this decision entails an element of discretion left to the individual and the possibility of obtaining welfare benefits may have an impact on them. A major conclusion is nevertheless that if the individual cannot work under any circumstances, it is not the welfare state that is the mechanism of decommodification.

In an ideal world, people who are sick get sickness benefits and when they recover they go back to work; people who are unemployed receive unemployment benefits but continue to search for a job and when they find a job these benefits are cut off, and so on. Welfare state support has a decommodifying function if it allows individuals permanently or temporarily to withdraw from paid work in a way that they would not otherwise have done. Benefits cannot be attributed a decommodifying role if the individuals must stay away from work even without this kind of support. In other words, the crucial question is whether labor power is withdrawn from the labor market to a larger extent than it would have been had the benefits not been available.

There is a further aspect to consider, namely what is usually referred to as the 'entitlement effect' of welfare state programs (Hamermesh 1979, 1980). The argument is that the social insurance system encourages people to take paid work, because they will then be better off in terms of benefits if and when they need them. For example, pension systems are related to previous wages and salaries in such a way that people get higher pensions if they have had more income from employment. In other words, it pays to have been working before and, to some limit, the more the better. The system thus comprises a commodifying factor, increasing the incentives for taking paid work. Exactly the same thing can be said about other welfare state programs such as the unemployment and the parental insurance systems. There are certain work requirements for eligibility for the highest possible benefits or to be eligible at all.

Labor market policy

One kind of state intervention that has a special role as to the issues of commodification and decommodification is labor market policy. In addition to the cash benefits supplied to the unemployed, a key element in labor market policy consists of so-called active programs. The latter aim at helping people find jobs; they are, so to speak, on the commodification track. Unemployment benefits, in contrast classified as passive programs, are actually not, however, aimed at the opposite, that is, decommodification. The reason is that people receiving benefits are supposed to be available in the labor market, but in the public debate the decommodifying role of the unemployment insurance is nevertheless frequently taken for granted. In fact, both active and passive policies have a complex relationship to the questions of commodification and decommodification and this section spells out some of this complexity.

Although there is an emphasis on measures for the unemployed, we must be aware that labor market policy is to some extent also oriented toward the employers' main problem in the labor market, shortage of suitable workers, partly due to lacking employability of jobseekers. In fact, unemployment and shortage of labor might very well exist simultaneously, simply because of mismatch between jobseekers and vacancies. If this mismatch can be overcome, the two problems can be solved at once; there will be a decrease in both the number of unemployed and the number of unfilled jobs. By combining two dimensions, that is, whether measures are aimed at decreasing unemployment and labor shortage respectively, we can make a simple classification of labor market policies, including both active and passive programs. Table 5.1 shows a slightly modified version of a scheme that I have developed previously (Furåker 1986: 106–9).

In the upper left-hand panel of Table 5.1, we find programs intended to decrease both unemployment and labor shortage. For this purpose, the employment service is a key institution, since it can help employers and jobseekers meet. Other measures to be mentioned are labor market training and support for geographic mobility. Labor market training programs aim at making people employable in the market by providing them with skills that are in demand or will be so in the near future. Geographic mismatch is yet another problem that some governments have tried to eliminate through subsidies encouraging people to move. Subsidies may also help firms with difficulties of finding workers move to unemployment-struck areas.

The next panel, to the right, includes measures that are not aimed at decreasing labor shortage but at lowering the level of unemployment. For this purpose the government can either encourage employers to hire unemployed individuals by providing subsidies (these may be oriented to the recruitment of such categories as long-term unemployed, youths, women, and handicapped individuals) or directly create jobs, for example in sheltered workshops for people with disabilities. The underlying assumption is that certain categories of workers will have difficulties in the labor market, even if demand for labor is high. Subsidies are then a way of lowering the costs for employers, thus making the latter more interested in recruiting workers whom they consider less attractive. Regional policies can be another method of providing jobs to unemployed individuals; firms are encouraged to locate jobs to areas which they otherwise would have neglected when considering expansion. I also include early retirement pensions for labor market reasons in this category; early retirees are bought off from the labor market and this measure will lower unemployment without reducing labor shortage.

In the lower left-hand panel we find measures oriented at decreasing labor shortage but not unemployment. When there is insufficient supply of

Table 5.1   Labor market policy related to unemployment and labor shortage

Aims of measures	Reducing labor shortage	
Reducing unemployment	Yes	No
Yes	Matching unemployed to vacancies (employment service, labor market training, support for geographic mobility, etc.)	Direct and indirect hiring of labor power (sheltered workshops, subsidized employment) Measures for leaving the labor market (early retirement)
No	Increasing supply of labor power (activation of labor reserve; immigration)	Unemployment benefits Employment services to employed jobseekers

labor, the state can attempt to activate reserves, which may include campaigns to encourage housewives to enter the labor market and training programs to make them employable. Financial and other kinds of support for geographic mobility may be a further component among these activation measures. Reserves may also be taken from outside, through immigration, and policies regulating the flows of immigration are thus highly important.

This leaves us with one final set of measures on which to comment: those that do not aim at reducing either unemployment or labor shortage. Unemployment benefit schemes are here the crucial programs. When individuals receive unemployment benefits, they are expected to keep up the commodity status of their labor power, that is, they should be available to the labor market and take 'suitable' jobs at hand, but, of course, there is some room for them to avoid this; it should be emphasized that the classification in the table is focused on the intentions behind policies rather than their actual effects. In this last panel, placement services to already employed individuals are also included. The aim of these services is not to reduce either unemployment or labor shortage, although mobility among the already employed may have such consequences.

It should not be taken for granted that labor market policies function the way they are supposed to; intentions are one thing and actual consequences another. I therefore make some comments on how passive and active policies may affect the commodity status of labor power and let me begin with the unemployment insurance and other cash benefits. The crucial question is what mechanisms public authorities have at their disposal to ensure that people take jobs available. Much of the discussion about the unemployment insurance concerns this issue. A study by the Danish Ministry of Finance shows substantial differences across countries with respect to availability rules (Ministry of Finance 1998). The OECD (2000: 138–9) has in turn criticized the Danish study, mainly arguing that it does not help very much to know the formal regulation; it is necessary to look at its implementation and to do this is a much more difficult and demanding task. The criticism is undoubtedly justified, but we should be aware that there might be some positive correlation between formal rules and their actual application. To explore this relationship more carefully would require a burdensome and costly piece of empirical research.

There are plenty of studies on how unemployment insurance rules affect unemployment (see, e.g., Atkinson and Micklewright 1991; Atkinson and Mogensen 1993; Reissert and Schmid 1994; Nickell and Layard 1999; Sjöberg 2000). The results are somewhat divergent, but it seems possible to draw certain general conclusions. Thus we find that the duration of unemployment benefits may contribute to longer spells without a job, whereas there is no clear indication that benefit levels are very important. Anyhow, it appears that labor power is not offered in the market fully to the extent that might be expected had the unemployment insurance not existed; at least some element of decommodification is likely to be involved. However, the situation would not necessarily be problem-free if the unemployed had to accept just any vacancy straight away. An individual who does not fit in with the workplace or with the work tasks may soon become an employed jobseeker or even unemployed again and whenever someone quits a job for another there are always transaction costs involved. This is double, however, as when searching for employment an individual is largely better off if he/she already has a job; compared to being unemployed, it gives him/her more room to be selective and avoid rushing into just any opening that presents itself.

With respect to active policies it is not easy to determine precisely what role they actually play. It is a tricky task to decide whether they fulfill the commodifying intentions behind, that is, whether they lead to jobs for people. Due to deadweight, substitution, and displacement effects, active measures are not as effective as intended (Calmfors 1994). Based on empirical research there is now a growing body of knowledge as to how these measures work (see, e.g., Martin 2000; Martin and Grubb 2001; Robinson 2000). For one thing, labor market training does not seem to improve the chances of finding employment in the way expected. Moreover, it has been suggested that these programs have some 'lock-in' effect, which means that individuals participating in programs tend to be passive in searching for jobs. This suggests an element of decommodification, although the effect is limited in time, as training programs usually do not last very long.

Workfare

The ideas behind workfare date back to the 1960s when they came to the forefront of the public debate in the United States and later they have gained ground in other countries. Workfare is related to active labor market policy but is mainly oriented toward the poor, which can explain why it appears to have a more coercive character, reminiscent of workhouses in the nineteenth century. The argument is that the poor should not be allowed to stay on welfare but be forced to take jobs, which is supposed to be a way of breaking their dependency on benefits and of integrating them in society. Reforms along these lines were introduced and developed in the United States, both during the Reagan administration in the 1980s and the Clinton administration in the 1990s, as well as in the United Kingdom under the Thatcher government. Other countries have followed.

There is a growing literature on the issues associated with workfare policies (see, e.g., Lødemel and Trickey 2001a; Shragge 1997; Standing 2002). The possibly simplest definition points out that 'workfare is compulsory; is primarily about work; and relates to policies tied to the lowest tier of income support (social assistance)' (Lødemel and Trickey 2001b: xiv). It is in particular the repressive features of these policies that have been on the agenda in the public debate. There is no reason to go deeper into these discussions, but I want to bring up one of the arguments that, among others, Guy Standing (1999: 323–4) has formulated concerning the negative consequences of workfare programs. According to Standing, such programs are intended to strengthen the willingness among the unemployed and the poor to take a job – that is, to improve their work ethic – but it is argued that they fail to do so. It may be correct that workfare does not inject any much stronger work ethic among participants than there was to begin with, but if Standing had read Durkheim he might have reflected that the effect is perhaps most important for people in general or for those who with their tax money pay for the benefits. The support for the benefit system is likely to be dependent upon beliefs that clients deserve what they get. Thus, if clients are able to work, they are also expected to do it, and even make-work might then satisfy people's wishes to have some kind of reciprocity built into the system.

In other words, we might draw a similar conclusion as Durkheim (1964: 108) with respect to society's penal system: 'punishment is above all designed to act upon the upright people' and 'it serves to heal the wounds made upon collective sentiments'. His analysis requires, however, that the notions of punishment as expiation and as protection be reconciled. Punishment is certainly considered to be positive 'for the protection of society, but that is because it is expiatory' (Durkheim 1964: 109). It is assumed to be important for people to know that breaking the norms in society has consequences. Translated to the issues discussed here, we can formulate the following thesis; if the norm is that working-age people – unless they are incapacitated or have other legitimate reasons to be excepted – should earn a living through paid work, receiving benefits without deserving them is likely to be associated with popular disapproval. Consequently, it is above all the general work ethic in society that is reinforced rather than that of the unemployed and the poor.

To summarize, the state affects the commodity status of labor power in many different ways. It contributes to creating as well as preserving and restoring this status, but it also makes it easier for people, temporarily or permanently, to leave their jobs or the labor market as a whole. Yet, the discussion about the welfare state has primarily been preoccupied with the issues of decommodification or – to use another terminology – the disincentives of various programs and the risks that the systems are abused, with negative effects on public expenditures and the supply of labor. Although many worry about these matters, others do not think that the welfare state goes far enough with respect to decommodification. The latter want to see a completely different system allowing everybody a basic income. Given that this income is sufficient on which to live, people would no longer have to offer their labor power in the market; it would be the ultimate decommodification for everybody. This kind of proposal is dealt with in Chapter 9.

The state as employer

So far several kinds of state intervention in the labor market have been considered, but it remains to make a few comments regarding the state's role as employer. This role is very wide ranging in all the advanced capitalist countries; public sector employees make up a large proportion of total employment and they are found in central government apparatuses as well as in regional and local bodies. There is considerable variation between countries as to the proportion of personnel in the administrative and judicial systems, the military, and the police, but, to a large extent, the cross-national differences appear in the welfare service sector (see, e.g., Alestalo, Bislev and Furåker 1991). Especially in Scandinavian countries there are great numbers of employees in public welfare services, healthcare, childcare, care for the elderly, and so on, mainly organized at local and regional levels.

The state is thus an actor generating demand for labor power in the market. By creating jobs, it can be said to have a commodifying role and the public sector particularly recruits women to employment in the welfare service sector. It simply means that female (and male) labor power is pulled into the market, recruited to vacant jobs, put to work, and recompensed with a wage or a salary. Furthermore, we can observe that the state has even a double commodifying role by providing, for example, childcare services. On the one hand, these services make it possible for parents to combine parenthood with gainful employment; hence they provide assistance to people when they aim at hiring out their labor power in the market. On the other hand, childcare centers are also employers; they above all hire women to look after other people's children. A similar reasoning can be conducted with respect to other carrier services as well.

A complex set of mechanisms

This chapter has dealt with several factors that affect the conditions under which people offer or have to offer their labor power in the market. I have identified a complex set of forces in operation and in interaction with one another. Some mechanisms can be attributed a commodifying function and others a decommodifying function, but the one and the same factor may also have both kinds of consequences. Therefore we need to be careful in our attempts to assess their actual or potential impact on the commodity status of labor power.

It is a fundamental predicament of the human race that people have to work to create their means of subsistence. This does not mean that everyone has to work, but a large proportion of the population must do so, insofar as the present standard of living is to be upheld. In the absence of other resources, people in modern societies have to supply their capacities for work in the labor market. If employers are willing to hire them, they will be able to support themselves and possibly also other family members. There are several mechanisms that modify this fundamental predicament – the necessity to work – for at least part of the population. Those who are owners of sizeable monetary resources or other ample property can refrain from paid employment, entirely or partly and for longer or shorter periods. It is the non-propertied or the insufficiently propertied who have to offer their labor power in the market. To be self-employed represents a further possibility to avoid not work but wage-work; this requires some property, although an entrepreneur can get started and get on by means of loans.

Labor power must have a use value in the market in order to be hired. With education and on-the-job training this value can increase, but sooner or later a turning point will be reached. With advancing age, individuals' capacities for work will eventually come to an end. There may also be developments within the labor market that undermine the value of these capacities; owing to physically or mentally hard work, monotonous and repetitive tasks, etc., workers may become worn out faster than expected from normal aging. It also happens that they are seriously injured at the workplace and therefore become disabled to go on with the tasks they have. Another aspect is that skills may become obsolete because of technical and other kinds of change. We can thus identify a number of different mechanisms that make the use value of workers' productive capacities approach zero or the definite end point of the commodity status of labor power; to some degree the market itself contributes to the process of decommodifcation.

Employees who earn money in the labor market may be able to accumulate a surplus, which will allow them to refrain, if they want to, from paid work, at least for some limited period of time. Far from all individuals with savings make use of this opportunity, as there are many ways of spending or investing the money, but, now and then, some take a few months off to travel and others simply stop working before normal retirement age. Top-level managers and sports stars may be able to accumulate large sums of money that allow them to be independent of the labor market forever; it is then a matter of lifetime decommodification.

Another important mechanism in relation to the labor market is the family, not least for the reproduction of labor power across generations. The size and composition of the family lie behind the pressures upon its members to earn money from paid work. *Ceteris paribus*, the more individuals there are to support in the household, the larger the need for incomes. Increasing needs can lead to stronger pressure upon family members to work longer hours or to enter the labor market in the first place and thus possibly to commodification. However, caring obligations require that some non-paid work is carried out at home, which can be difficult to combine with gainful employment, that is, they may have a decommodifying effect. In addition, the family is a safety net, among other things when people become unemployed. It redistributes resources internally so that members without an income of their own get supported; in that way it has a decommodifying function, because the unemployed do not have to hurry to get a job. We must also be aware of the diverse transfers that take place between family members, among other things, between members of different generations (inheritances, gifts, etc.). In this way, people may receive more backing than through any of the benefits provided by the welfare state. Larger transfers are limited to the well-to-do segments of the population, but even smaller ones may have a crucial impact upon people's decisions about entering or staying in the labor market.

In this chapter, I have also considered the role of the state and, above all, that of the welfare state. Three things appear to be especially significant. First, the state maintains certain rules regarding the functioning of the labor market, such as legislation concerning employment contracts, and it is thus responsible for a type of intervention that has great significance for upholding the commodity status of labor power. There is also legislation on work safety and working hours that is similarly important, not least in the light of labor power's potential loss of use value, especially if it is harshly exploited at the workplace.

A second crucial aspect of the welfare state is that it provides support for people who are unable to work or who have reached the end of their working life. The definitions of inability and working age are social constructions and as such they are subject to change over time. To make some generalization, the major idea behind various social insurance systems – sickness insurance, parental insurance, unemployment insurance, etc. – is not that people should be supported for not working if they can but only if they cannot. Actually, the social insurance systems are decommodifying only to the degree that an individual would have carried out paid work if they had not existed. They must thus have an independent effect, making people withdraw from the labor market to a larger extent than they would have done without them. However, there are elements in the social insurance systems that must be regarded as having a commodifying function, usually referred to as the 'entitlement effect'. In order for people to get benefits or as high benefits as possible, they must have carried out a minimum of paid work previous to the period for which they claim support.

Labor market policy is a special part of the welfare state's arsenal of measures. The unemployment insurance is intended to support the unemployed, but not to withdraw them from the labor market and the main principle is that unemployed individuals who claim benefits should be available for paid work. In other words, the commodity status of people's labor power is supposed to remain intact. However, we cannot take for granted that, in practice, unemployment insurance works the way in which it is intended; in fact, we can even take it for granted that it does not so altogether. Other parts of labor market policy are directly oriented to commodification. The so-called active programs include a spectrum of measures such as employment services, labor market training, etc., for the purpose of getting people (back) into employment; whether they are successful in accomplishing this is an empirical issue. Even measures aimed at commodification may contribute to keep people outside the regular labor market; for example, training programs can be associated with a lock-in mechanism that makes people unavailable for jobs longer than necessary.

The state has a third role in the labor market as employer. In all advanced capitalist countries, public sector employment is a good-sized part of total employment, because the government has assumed responsibility, totally or partly, for several very different institutions: police, military, healthcare, education, etc. There has been an especially significant expansion of welfare state services during the second half of the preceding century, although in many countries some decline has occurred in the last two decades or so. In any case, today large numbers of people – and in particular women – are engaged in producing various kinds of public sector services. The state not only affects people's living conditions in general and thus their willingness to enter the labor market, but also it creates demand for labor in the market, which, again, is a crucial prerequisite for the commodity status of labor power.

6
Age of Services, Information, and Globalization

Most analysts agree that contemporary societies are undergoing rapid and significant changes, but there is a great deal of disagreement about how fast and comprehensive these changes are and what consequences they are likely to have. In this chapter I address a number of issues regarding the service sector, the role of information and knowledge, and the process of globalization. It should be emphasized that the three dimensions, although being analytically distinct, are interconnected. The most important question for this book is of course how various developments affect labor markets.

It is today common to claim that – with respect to the advanced capitalist part of the world – the industrial era belongs to history; the assumption is that industrialism is being replaced or has already been replaced by a new kind of socioeconomic system. This idea is associated with the theory of post-industrialism and it has by now been around for several decades. The range of labels that have been suggested to designate the emerging new social and economic order should make us somewhat suspicious of what this is all about. Post-industrial society is a frequently used label, but there are also several others such as the service, post-capitalist, knowledge, information, and informational society or economy (see, e.g., Bell 1976; Drucker 1994; Castells 1996; Singelmann 1978; Stehr 2002; Stonier 1983; Touraine 1971). More recently, globalization has come to the forefront in the analysis of social and economic developments, because it is assumed to represent a force with huge impact on these processes (see, e.g., Castells 1996; Held *et al.* 1999; Held and McGrew 2002, 2003a; Standing 1999).

Many observers are convinced that modern societies are moving toward a new destination or even that we have already arrived there, but it seems difficult for them to agree about a common characterization of the destination. Although the pictures presented by different authors are often very loosely put together, their impact on the contemporary debate has been great. It is therefore worthwhile exploring what various theorists claim has happened and to what extent they provide plausible forecasts. In some cases we are already in a position to know the answer to the latter question, as the predictions were made decades ago; in other cases it is too early to cast the final verdict, but we can scrutinize the theoretical framework to see whether it is likely to be useful and whether the available data point in the predicted direction.

The first transformation to be brought up is the expansion of service production. This is a phenomenon that has been discussed extensively in the social science literature for several decades. What we find is, needless to say, dependent upon how the notion of service is defined, and – as is soon demonstrated – there are different solutions in the literature leading to divergent empirical answers. As my reasoning is mainly theoretic, I do not introduce any new empirical information but rather stick to generally accepted and uncontroversial facts.

A second issue to be dealt with is the role of information and knowledge in present-day societies. Services in the field of information and communication have expanded and the microelectronic revolution has made communication and proliferation of information across the globe much easier. It is today possible to get into immediate contact with people in various parts of the world and we can have almost instant access to information about events that take place far away. The consequences for the production and exchange of goods and services as well as for many other aspects of human life are tremendous. Moreover, the expansion of the education system means that large proportions of the population now remain in school much longer than their parents did. There has also been a growth in the proportion of occupations that require well-educated workers and they are to a large extent service and information occupations.

Finally, I turn to the recent discussion on globalization and internationalization. This is a field filled with plenty of controversy and a rapidly growing literature dealing with all kinds of change, economic, political, and cultural; naturally, for my part, the economic and political dimensions are the most relevant. I also discuss some of the connections between globalization and internationalization on the one hand and the expansion of services and the role of information and knowledge on the other hand. Most significantly perhaps, the development of global interaction is forcefully facilitated by the new and continuously improving possibilities for dissemination and exchange of information.

The expansion of the service sector

In the immense literature that is written on the socioeconomic developments of modern societies, we find a great deal of attention directed to the expansion of service production. Concepts such as service, service sector, and tertiary sector are used interchangeably but often without being clearly defined. As a consequence of this, I start by considering some conceptual issues.

The service concept

As pointed out in Chapter 3, the most well-known theorist of post-industrialism, Daniel Bell, provides no systematic definition of the service concept. There is no such title word in the subject index of his major book *The Coming of Post-Industrial Society*, although 'service occupations' can be found. From the discussion in the book on these occupations, we may conclude that Bell (see, e.g., 1976: 127–8) has a wide definition, but his insistence that post-industrialism is a matter of 'a game between persons' suggests a narrower interpretation. On the whole, however, Bell's analysis seems to be in accordance with one (the broad one) of the two basic approaches to the service concept, described by, among others, Tom Elfring (1988: Ch. 2) and me (Furåker 1987: 124–9).

To follow Elfring, the literature contains two main ways of dealing with the service concept. The first is to consider it a wide-ranging category, and, as mentioned above, Bell's general perspective appears to be an example of this. It implies treating services or the service or tertiary sector as a rest category when agriculture and industrial production of goods have been taken away (see, e.g., Clark 1951: 401). The second approach results in a much more limited concept that takes several very specific characteristics as its point of departure. It is emphasized that services 'are immaterial, intangible, impermanent, made by people for people and consumable only at the instant of production' (Elfring 1988: 19). Many authors advocate a definition of services along these lines (see, e.g., Gershuny 1978: 55–9; Offe 1985: Ch. 4; Sayer and Walker 1992: Ch. 2).

The narrow definition of services might be regarded as theoretically more attractive than the broad alternative, since it does not refer to activities that are simply leftovers from other categories, but it is associated with several drawbacks. Elfring (1988: 19) points out that some examples of this definition given in the literature, such as haircuts and laundry services, are problematic, because the activities in question 'do change the physical appearance of a head (shorter hair) and a fabric (cleaner)' and their outcome will last for some time. We might look for better illustrations, but the major problem with this conceptual solution is its exclusion of a number of activities that most of us would count as services. For example, librarians who classify new books cannot qualify as service workers, obviously in opposition to common language. What these employees do in their jobs has a material dimension to it – books receive codes, they are put in a computerized catalog and in shelves according to their code number, etc. – and the outcome will probably remain until someone does a reclassification or the library is reorganized. Similar conclusions can be drawn with respect to other activities such as sending out pay checks for a company or revising its financial situation. In response to the difficulties in handling the notion of services, Castells (1996: 205) suggests that we begin by establishing distinctions between different types of services and this is also the approach adopted by analysts such as Joachim Singelmann (1978) and Elfring (1988).

Although Marx did not spend much energy on services, he made some remarks in line with the narrow definition. At one place in his texts, the activity of a singer is taken as an example and the author remarks that the performance cannot be separated from the performing individual (Marx 1963: 405). The singing can be enjoyed, but once it comes to an end, the pleasure is over; it is consumed simultaneously when it is produced. However, we should take into account that human memory has the capacity of preserving such experiences of pleasure; there are people who have strong memories of concerts that took place long ago. What is more, today the singer's performance can perhaps be bought in the form of a record or a video and people may be able to download his/her songs on the home computer. The once immaterial, non-permanent service has taken on a material and, if not eternal, a more permanent form. It is easy to agree with Manuel Castells (1996: 205) in his statement that the distinction between goods and services tends to become increasingly blurred.

As pointed out in Chapter 3, we should also be aware of the problems with statistical classifications. In international statistics, it is generally the basic activities of the employing organization that determine whether workers are counted as belonging to one or another sector and not what they actually do. Thus, cleaners in manufacturing firms add to industrial employment, whereas workers in cleaning firms are counted as part of service sector employment. In other words, outsourcing has direct effects on the size of the sectors, even if the number of people in each type of job remains exactly the same. Taking these problems into consideration as well as all the others mentioned above, I have not been able to find any workable solution; therefore, in this book, the question of how to define the service concept will be left unanswered and I consider services in the wide meaning of everyday language.

Post-industrial theory and services

The theory of post-industrialism is an attempt to describe and explain the overriding societal developments that economically advanced societies go through, including the expansion of services. Before turning to the issue of service sector growth, we need to look somewhat further at some of the theory's underlying assumptions. Daniel Bell (1976: xii) emphasizes that 'no unilineal sequences of societal change' and no 'laws of social development' exist. It follows that we should avoid interpreting his analysis as an attempt to opt for a process of convergence between nations. The author is also careful to point out that he does not deal with any specific nation but regards the concept of post-industrial society as 'an analytical construct' – apparently an ideal type in the Weberian sense of the word – to make sense of the changes taking place in 'advanced Western' nations (Bell 1976: 483). This approach implies generalizing certain features from reality to make us see the characteristics of a phenomenon in a more pure form. Any given unit can be compared with the analytical construct and we can then judge how well they correspond to one another. However, we must question whether in fact Bell does not base himself on just one specific nation; it seems rather obvious that the United States is the model behind his post-industrial scheme.

Some of the main themes of post-industrialism were covered in Chapter 3. A major idea is that production of services, or, rather, of certain kinds of services, is expected to become central in the advanced economies. Although at least partly agreeing with the post-industrialist scenario, Castells stresses that there is not only one model of occupational change in the developed world. He maintains that the United States fits well with the predominant image of post-industrialism, whereas Japan represents a rather different pole. During 1970–90, the United States had an expansion in the proportion of managerial, professional, and technical occupations and of clerical and sales workers, while the proportion of craft workers and operators decreased. Japan, however, 'appears to combine an increase of the professional occupations with the persistence of a strong craft labor force, linked to the industrial era, and with the durability of the agricultural labor force and of sales workers that witness the continuity, under new forms, of the occupations characteristic of the pre-industrial era' (Castells 1996: 217).

Singelmann (1978: 10) has noted that social scientists have commonly assumed 'a sequential shift of employment', proceeding from agriculture and other extractive industries to manufacturing and thereafter to services. This is the conventional model and it has its origin in a few older studies (Fisher 1935; Clark 1951). A basic supposition is that the sequential employment shift reflects economic progress and increasing national incomes. Departing from that idea, Singelmann (1978: 85–107) has tested the impact of national income, international trade, and urbanization on the development of the service sector. His conclusion is that these factors do not unambiguously explain how far the expansion of services has gone. Moreover, we cannot find just one single model of development in these respects, as Europe is different from North America and both differ substantially from Japan.

Also Bell (1976: 127–8) has discussed the transition from goods to services and has then pointed out that services to some extent expand, because they are needed in connection with the production and distribution of industrial goods; transportation, finance, and insurance represent typical examples. Additionally, with increasing national incomes, people spend a lesser proportion of their money on food at home but begin to visit restaurants more often and they start to look for durables, luxury items, travel, entertainment, sports, and the like. There will thus be an expansion in many different kinds of services. A further aspect is that 'a new consciousness begins to intervene', as people realize that in order to live a good life they need healthcare and education as well as 'a decent environment' (Bell 1976: 128). The growth of services in these areas is a significant element in the development of post-industrial society.

No matter how the process is to be explained, using services in a broad sense, we must admit that there has been a considerable shift toward service production in the economically developed countries. In a long-term perspective, and relatively speaking, jobs in extractive and manufacturing industries have declined, while employment in the tertiary sector has expanded dramatically. One aspect is of course that industrial production is continuously being relocated; the new division of labor appears to involve more services in the advanced capitalist countries but more manufacturing in certain other parts of the world (cf. Castells 1996: Ch. 2).

The age of information and knowledge

There is a huge literature on the development of knowledge and information society. It is a very common claim that these phenomena are becoming increasingly important in modern societies. Authors such as Toffler (1980), Stonier (1983), and Naisbitt and Aburdene (1990) have expressed tremendous expectations as to what the age of information will render possible. It will, according to Toffler (1980: 19), lead us to a civilization that can be 'made more sane, sensible, and sustainable, more decent and more democratic than any we have ever known'. In contrast, there are authors who take a critical view to much of the discourse flourishing on the knowledge and information society (see, e.g., Schiller 1996; Webster 2002). The increasing role of knowledge is also a crucial theme in the early versions of post-industrial theory and this theory will again be at the center of my discussion. To begin, I consider the conceptual issues.

The concepts of information and knowledge

Regarding the concept of knowledge, Bell (1976: 175; emphasis removed) comes up with an explicit definition; it is seen 'as a set of organized statements of facts or ideas, presenting a reasoned judgment or an experimental result, which is transmitted to others through some communication medium in some systematic form'. He does not, however, provide a definition of information but simply emphasizes that knowledge must be distinguished from news and entertainment. Furthermore, there is a comparison with the views of some other analysts. Among other things, Bell points out that his concept is narrower than the one proposed by Fritz Machlup (1962: 21) who has a subjective point of departure and defines knowledge in terms of 'the meaning which the knower attaches to the known'. The latter author also suggests that 'to *inform* is an activity by which knowledge is conveyed; to *know* may be the result of having been informed' (Machlup 1962: 15; emphasis in original).

Others have formulated other solutions; for example, Tom Stonier (1983: 19) has outlined a conceptual chain, hierarchical in character and including not only knowledge and information but also 'data', defined as 'a series of disconnected facts and observations'. In order to be transformed into information, data must be selected, sorted, summarized, analyzed or organized in some other way. By being processed in such manners they are made useful for varying specific purposes. The next step is that information is structured to become 'knowledge', which is necessary for insight and judgment. Nevertheless, it remains difficult to keep the three concepts apart and the author tells us that they are used rather loosely throughout the book, 'because what is information at one level may only be data at the next' (Stonier 1983: 19).

Although they differ in emphasis and lack in precision, the definitions of knowledge and information proposed by authors such as those above will suffice, insofar as we need them only for the purpose of general reasoning. It appears to me that the most important point is to establish and maintain some dividing line between knowledge and information, between, roughly speaking, on the one hand, structured and theorized data and, on the other hand, scattered facts. The lasting vagueness of the concepts involved will be a problem only if we want to go beyond the general discussion level for a deeper theoretical penetration or engage in empirical research. We can, however, leave that out for now. I next turn to the question of how post-industrial theory conceives the growing role of knowledge in social and economic developments.

Post-industrial theory and knowledge

For Bell (1976: 212) post-industrial society is a knowledge society both because 'the sources of innovation are increasingly derivative from research and development' and because the knowledge field accounts for increasing proportions of the gross domestic product (GDP) and employment. These conclusions do not seem to be controversial, but at least two points warrant some further discussion.

First, it may be true that knowledge is becoming increasingly more important, but it is not obvious why this should be considered a characteristic difference between industrial and post-industrial society. The gigantic technological progress that has taken place during the industrial era and that has made industry so highly productive is based upon knowledge and the diffusion and exchange of knowledge. Various results from both basic and applied research have continuously been transmitted to manufacturing firms, despite the fact that such results cannot always immediately be put into practice. Research is also a great part of the activities within certain industrial firms themselves such as pharmaceutical manufacturers. A related observation is that the information technology is closely attached to industrialism (Kumar 1988: 29–31). It cannot reasonably be argued that the transition to information technology appeared only with the decline of industrial employment in the advanced capitalist world; actually it has very much contributed to that decline.

The second issue has to do with what has actually happened with job requirements in terms of skills and education. As was previously shown with reference to the work by Castells, there has been a substantial increase in the proportion of professional and other occupations that demand long education and expert knowledge. The service sector evidently supplies large numbers of jobs for highly qualified workers, but, at the same time, we must keep in mind that it is very heterogeneous. A significant proportion of service jobs do not demand much theoretical knowledge but are above all a matter of manual labor (Harrison and Bluestone 1988; Esping-Andersen 1993, 1990: 206–17). Actually, the sociological literature provides a great deal of discussion and disagreement on these issues but little empirical research. As mentioned in Chapter 2, some believe that upgrading is the typical pattern, others that degradation is the overriding trend, and yet others that polarization is the most significant feature in recent developments. It is impossible to find systematic empirical support for the degradation thesis, but which of the remaining two gives the most adequate picture of contemporary reality is open to interpretation.

There are many difficulties in determining whether certain jobs require more skills than others or whether they require more skills today than previously. We have no standard way of measuring what it actually takes to carry out different work tasks. The education demanded might be an option, but it is only a rough estimate that cannot really capture the full complexity of job contents and, as will be shown below, it also has some other drawbacks. A further reason behind the problems to come up with robust conclusions is that we have very little research covering whole labor markets. This is related to the measurement difficulties and to the fact that such studies are costly to carry out. As a result, we are left with a scattered picture, based on anecdotal evidence, case studies and non-standardized data from different industries in different countries. Despite the lack of solid empirical evidence, some authors have apparently been tempted to make far-reaching generalizations.

One important distinction to make is that between what jobs actually require and what education and skills incumbents have. If we register that people on average are more educated today than before, it does not immediately allow us to conclude that today's labor market demands greater skills. There is also the possibility that people have more education than needed (cf., e.g., Åberg 2002). If they are overeducated, how do we explain this? Part of an answer might be that the education system has expanded, because people tend to increase their human or cultural capital just to be competitive in the labor market. It is then understood that employers have a preference for recruiting highly educated people, even if vacant positions do not really necessitate that prospective incumbents have very great skills and knowledge. Employers are thus assumed to take educational achievement as an indicator of an individual's ability and to use it as a criterion for selection.

As to the specificity of post-industrialism, Bell goes even further by arguing that is not just a matter of the knowledge field taking larger proportions of GDP and of employment:

> 'What is distinctive about the post-industrial society is the change in the character of knowledge itself. What has become decisive for the organization of decisions and the direction of change is the centrality of *theoretical* knowledge – the primacy of theory over empiricism and the codification of knowledge into abstract systems of symbols that, as in any axiomatic system, can be used to illuminate many different and varied areas of experience' (Bell 1976: 20; emphasis in original).

This is indeed a far-reaching claim associated with a number of corollaries. In Bell's eyes, whereas for a long time the entrepreneur, the businessman, and the industrial executive have been the dominant figures, in post-industrial society the time has come for scientists and the engineers of technology. These latter categories do not have to make up a majority in terms of employment – neither did the industrial top figures – but they will take a leading role in the central decision making in society: 'In the post-industrial society, production and business decisions will be subordinated to, or will derive from, other forces' than the 'business civilization'; 'the crucial decisions regarding the growth of the economy and its balance will come from government, but they will be based on the government's sponsorship of research and development' (Bell 1976: 344).

The last part of the quotations contains yet another element in Bell's treatment of knowledge society: the assumption that governments and overriding societal planning will come to play an increasingly more important part. It represents a very typical way of thinking in a period when Keynesian solutions were backed up by large numbers of politicians and economists and cost-benefit analysis was discussed as a way of going beyond the limits of single firms' cost-revenue calculations. Bell does not argue that post-industrialism is a kind of socialism, but he envisions more of societal planning and political steering. In this respect, his predictions have not been substantiated by history; the text clearly belongs to an epoch before the ideological turn to neo-liberalism, the shrinking support for government intervention in the economy, and the breakdown of state socialism in the Soviet Union and eastern Europe.

With the arrival of knowledge society, the class structure is presumed to undergo significant changes. According to Bell (1976: 359), there are two main conclusions to be drawn in relation to this, namely, first, that the social stratum of scientists or, to use a wider term, 'the technical intelligentsia' must 'be taken into account in the political process' and, second, that science itself has a specific ethos, making scientists act differently from other categories, such as businessmen. Therefore the changes in the class structure must be conceived of in somewhat different terms than before. Bell (1976: 361; italics removed) argues that class no longer denotes 'a specific group of persons but a system that has institutionalized the ground rules for acquiring, holding, and transferring differential power and its attendant privileges'. He continues by saying that in the United States there are three main sources of power: property, skills, and political office. Although property tends to lose its role as the decisive basis for class dominance, the three sources still coexist, making the whole situation relatively open.

Alain Touraine, another pioneer theorist of post-industrialism, has suggested a straight answer to the question of what has happened, or will happen, with the socioeconomic structure in the new society. He does not hesitate to draw rather strong conclusions about changes in this respect: 'If property was the criterion of membership in the former dominant classes, the new dominant class is defined by knowledge and a certain level of education' (Touraine 1971: 51). In other words, occupational categories whose position is based on knowledge, skills, and long education have come to replace or will replace the old propertied power-holders. Whether this had happened or would happen is not clarified, but since Touraine's text was written more than three decades ago, the change should have taken place by now. Actually, there is very little evidence in support of this argument. The whole idea of a new class of professionals and intelligentsia (or of a professional-managerial class) has been highly debated and contested over the years and other authors have provided much more interesting analyses (see, e.g., Gouldner 1979; Konrád and Szelényi 1979; Walker 1979).

The discussion on the knowledge society involves the question of whether the fundamental structure has been changed. If ownership of capital is no longer a decisive factor in determining class dominance – or as a decisive factor as it used to be – does that mean that capitalism is done away with? Is post-industrialism a non-capitalist or a capitalist society? Apparently in order to avoid misunderstandings, Bell has felt obliged to provide some clarification on this question. In dealing with the developments of the United States, Japan, Western Europe, and the Soviet Union, he declares that 'post-industrial society does not "succeed" capitalism or socialism but, like bureaucratization, cuts across both' and that it refers to 'a specification of new dimensions in the social structure which the polity has to manage' (Bell 1976: 483).

The idea of post-capitalism

One author to provide a clear-cut answer on the question of capitalism is Peter Drucker and he knows to tell us that the new order is post-capitalist. We should note that he does not use the word post-industrialism, although his analysis is kindred. According to Drucker (1994: 6–7), we already live in post-capitalist society, but it is not 'non-' or 'anti-capitalist' as several capitalist institutions continue to exist. Above all, the free market will not be replaced, as it has turned out to be the best mechanism for economic integration. It may thus seem that the author has chosen a strange terminology, but, in other respects, the new order is supposed to have a very different structure compared to capitalism. The main economic assets used to be capital, natural resources, and labor, but this is not the case anymore; today it is knowledge. Therefore, the dominant group in society will be 'knowledge workers'. Unlike employees in the old society, knowledge workers own both the means of production and the tools of production – 'the former through their pension funds which are rapidly emerging in all developed countries as the only real owners, the latter because knowledge workers own their own knowledge and can take it with them wherever they go' (Drucker 1994: 7).

In post-capitalist society there is also a second principal class of service workers who do not have very much education but make up the majority of the working population. Drucker is worried about the risk for open class conflict between the two major classes. In order to avoid such a conflict there must be a rapid increase of productivity among service workers, similar to what has happened within industry. It is acknowledged that they need to 'attain both income and dignity', which requires both 'productivity' and 'opportunities for advancement and recognition' (Drucker 1994: 86). If such a development does not occur, it will be difficult to escape from a severe class conflict between knowledge and service workers.

A fundamental problem with the picture painted by Drucker is that it has scanty reference to empirical facts. For example, his conclusion that pension funds 'are rapidly emerging in all developed countries as the only real owners' is not based on any much deeper empirical investigation than some simple figures on the growth of pension funds. It is, however, one thing to grow and a very different thing to be 'the only real owners'. In order to be able to draw the latter conclusion we would require at least some analysis of what is happening with the ownership structure. Moreover, it is not clear why Drucker brings in pension funds, as he has already declared that it is knowledge and nothing else that is important. In my view, the expansion of pension funds should be taken most seriously, because it is likely to have great impact on present and above all future economic developments; in that sense Drucker is on the right track, but his analysis leaves a lot to be desired.

Knowledge workers are, according to Drucker, the dominant social category, but how does he account for certain other, previously so important categories? What, in his opinion, has actually happened to the old ownership class, the bourgeoisie, and to the industrial working class? There is in fact no analysis behind the swift conclusion that the two main categories are now the knowledge workers and the majority of less-educated service workers. Additionally, the idea that class conflict in post-capitalist society can be avoided only with a growth of productivity in services is too easily copied from the development of the industrial sector, in which increased productivity has been a significant mechanism to reduce the conflict between capitalists and proletarians. As we all know, services are not always possible to rationalize, at least not to the same extent as the production of goods.

There is no reason to pay more attention to Drucker's shallow analysis; it can just be taken as an example of how thinking that is based on neither thought-out theory nor robust empirical study can sail away and end up in amazing and ill-founded conclusions. Instead we turn to a very different way of treating the role of knowledge and information in contemporary societies. A major contribution in this respect is Castells's three-volume analysis of the information age, in which the idea of informational society is formulated.

Informational society

The three volumes written by Castells are to a large extent empirical, presenting all kinds of data, not least on labor markets. Even so, there is a theory behind it, and it is connected with post-industrial thinking. Castells (1996: 25–6) admits being indebted to that approach, but he is also critical of it. This might explain why he has developed his own conceptual scheme, although the reason is never clarified. However, the new scheme presented is not very different from that of its predecessors. To begin, Castells (1996: 14) mentions that Bell (and Touraine) locates the distinction between pre-industrialism, industrialism and post-industrialism on a different axis than that covering capitalism and collectivism or statism. Since the two axes can be combined, we get industrial capitalism, industrial statism, etc. As far as I can see, these combinations are very much in accordance with Castells's own conceptual elaboration, but there are some differences that need to be observed.

Castells's approach involves a distinction between mode of production (capitalism, statism) and mode of development (industrialism, informationalism). With the new technologies of information and communication appearing toward the end of the twentieth century, capitalism has taken a great leap forward and what we have today is capitalist informationalism.

Mode of production refers to 'the structural principle' for the appropriation and control of the surplus that may be generated in production (Castells 1996: 16). During the century that we have just laid behind us, two major such systems existed: capitalism and statism. There is no further explanation of what is meant by 'structural principle' and it might seem that this mode of production concept is close to a standard Marxist concept, but, as will be shown, this is not entirely the case.

By using the concept of mode of development, Castells (1996: 16) wants to capture 'the technological arrangements through which labor works on matter to generate the product, ultimately determining the level and the quality of surplus'. The relevance of this concept is best illustrated by the examples he furnishes. First, in the agrarian mode of development, expansion of the surplus equals quantitative increases of labor, land, and other natural resources. Second, the industrial mode of development has a corresponding mechanism in the use and spread of new energy sources. Third, the distinctive features of informationalism lie in the role of 'technology of knowledge generation, information processing, and symbolic communication' for productivity, and, although knowledge and information have always been important, the new thing is 'the action of knowledge upon knowledge itself as the main source of productivity' (Castells 1996: 17).

It should be observed that Castells makes a distinction between 'information' society and 'informational' society. While the first concept has to do with the 'role of information in society' – and this role is considered to be important in all societies – the latter refers to 'a specific form of social organization in which information generation, processing, and transmission become the fundamental sources of productivity and power, because of new technological conditions emerging in this historical period' (Castells 1996: 21 n.55). This conclusion is drawn without any genuine empirical substantiation.

Moreover, the author tells us that his own theoretical approach is developed around three other main concepts: production, experience, and power. Production is defined as 'the action of humankind on matter (nature) to appropriate it and transform it for its benefit of obtaining a product, consuming (unevenly) a part of it, and accumulating surplus for investment, according to a variety of socially determined goals' (Castells 1996: 15). It is also maintained that production involves class relationships and that they are crucial for how the product is being used for consumption and investment. An essential question is how the concept of *matter* is defined. In the words of Castells (1996: 15), this concept 'includes nature, human-modified nature, human-produced nature, and human nature itself, the labors of history forcing us to move away from the classic distinction between humankind and nature, since millennia of human action have incorporated the natural environment into society, making us, materially and symbolically, an inseparable part of this environment'. Accordingly, production also includes services, taken in the broad meaning of everyday speech.

The next concept, experience, means 'the action of human subjects on themselves, determined by the interaction between their biological and cultural identities, and in relationship to their social and natural environment' (Castells 1996: 15). It seems to be aimed at covering identity formation or something similar but must be considered overly indistinct. Some clarification is provided, though, when we are told that experience is built around gender and sexual relationships, with a basis in the family and so far characterized by men's domination over women. An obvious question is why the concept should be limited to gender/sexual relationships; no rationale is provided as to why such a narrow definition is brought forward. As this aspect shall not be dealt with any further in this book, I willingly just leave it with that.

Power, finally, 'is that relationship between human beings which, on the basis of production and experience, imposes some will upon others by the potential or actual use of violence, physical or symbolic' (Castells 1996: 15). This echoes some kind of Weberian definition and a few lines further on in the text the author emphasizes the role of the state as the monopolist of legitimate use of violence. However, it is also suggested that 'what Foucault labels the microphysics of power, embodied in institutions and organizations, diffuses throughout the entire society, from work places to hospitals, enclosing subjects in a tight framework of formal duties and informal aggressions' (Castells 1996: 15).

Another important aspect of informational society is its connection with what is referred to as 'network society', which is founded on 'the convergence and interaction between a new technological paradigm and a new organizational logic' (Castells 1996: 152). The latter is related to the ongoing technological change, but it is not dependent upon it and would apparently exist also on its own. If I understand it correctly, this is the 'specific form of social organization' that we met above in the distinction between information and informational societies. In very formal terms, the network society is defined as a set of interconnected nodes. A node is in turn – to use a strong understatement – confusingly defined as 'a point at which a curve intersects itself' (Castells 1996: 470). Concretely speaking, it can refer to very different phenomena such as national councils of ministers in political networks; coca fields, secret laboratories and landing strips, local dealers, and money-launderers in drug-traffic networks; and television systems and news teams in media networks.

What is particularly characteristic of networks is that they 'are open structures, able to expand without limits, integrating new nodes as long as they are able to communicate within the network, namely as long as they share the same communication codes (for example, values or performance goals)' and they are therefore 'appropriate instruments' for globalized capitalist firms, in which, among other things, innovation and flexibility play a crucial role (Castells 1996: 470–1). Nevertheless, networks are 'a source of dramatic reorganization of power relationships' as 'switches connecting the networks (for example, financial flows taking control of media empires that influence political processes) are the privileged instruments of power', which means that 'the switchers are the power holders' (Castells 1996: 470–1).

Furthermore, Castells (1996: 471) maintains that network society is still capitalist; it has not implied a change in the dominant mode of production, at least not thus far. Network capitalism has two distinctive features; it has a global character and it is largely structured around financial flows. The author even talks about the 'electronically operated global casino', arguing that the 'real economy' could be called the 'unreal economy', because 'in the age of networked capitalism the fundamental reality, where money is made and lost, invested or saved, is in the financial sphere' (Castells 1996: 472). In other words, it is claimed that the financial networks are more important than the actual production of goods and services, which, to my mind, is a serious misrepresentation turning socioeconomic structures and processes upside down.

Now, what is all this about? To begin, Castells is an old Marxist, a fact that is reflected in his terminology, but at the same time he makes some obvious deviations from conventional Marxism. We may ask whether the author's own conceptual framework represents improvement and, if so, in what respects. A decisive distinction in his analysis is that between mode of production and mode of development. Castells is certainly right that it should be possible to combine two sets of concepts in different ways: industrial capitalism, industrial statism, etc. In traditional Marxism, the general concept is mode of production that in turn includes two dimensions: relations of production and forces of production (see Chapter 2). Accordingly, in combinations such as industrial capitalism and industrial statism, 'capitalism' and 'statism' refer to the social relations and 'industrial' to the technical side of production. Such a solution is by the way precisely in line with the terminology of axial principles suggested by Bell (1976: 11) who bases himself upon Marx on this point. The distinctions mentioned allow us to do what Castells considers important: to make the combinations exemplified above. No other motive is suggested as to why he introduced his conceptual innovation of mode of development and it is difficult to see that anything has been gained by it.

The Marxist scheme already has a concept for basically the same phenomena that Castells wants to capture with the notion of mode of development. Therefore his concept seems to be merely redundant, but we need to take one more aspect into consideration. It emphasizes a dynamic dimension (development) and suggests progress, which means that the possibility of stagnating or degenerating productive forces is excluded. This is not a satisfactory solution for a general theoretical tool intended to be applicable across nations and centuries. Instead, it is preferable to have an open concept that does not imply any specific direction of change. Although progress is an obvious historic trend, it should not be taken for granted and it should not be written into our conceptual apparatus.

A few words must also be said about another of the basic concepts in Castells's analysis: power. I have no strong objections to how that concept is defined, but it does not play a very significant role in the book. For example, the discussion of networks leaves the impression that power has become less important, although it is claimed that people who control the nodes in a network are the real power-holders. Castells raises the question of whether we can identify a global capitalist class, but his answer is negative. He points out that 'sociologically and economically' there is no such class but only 'a faceless collective capitalist, made up of financial flows operated by electronic networks' (Castells 1996: 474). This seems to imply that the social categories localized at the center of economic and financial networks are just string puppets. At the same time, however, the author suggests that the capitalist classes have not vanished, but that they can be found only in certain areas of the world.

The definition of networks is bizarrely formal: it refers to a set of interconnected nodes and a node represents the point where a curve intersects itself. It is impossible to see any point at all with such a concept; it appears to be a simple blunder. More importantly, Castells depicts networks as open structures, despite the fact that we discover, among his examples, rather closed structures such as clandestine drug-dealing networks. In addition, the idea of open structures is reminiscent of lack of control and absence of power relationships. The empirically relevant task must be, as I see it, to study the degree of closure or openness in networks and to examine who are the actors with the power to control participation.

Nevertheless, compared with many other post-industrial accounts, the analysis developed by Castells has some advantages. He gives a valuable description of the socioeconomic order and its continuous transformation and his perhaps most important observation is that this order is still capitalist, which positively distinguishes him from certain other authors concerned with the 'information society' and the 'information age'. There are too many analysts who have taken ownership of capital to be *passé* without really providing any valid and effective arguments for it. By contrast with this, Castells emphasizes the growing role of information, while at the same time not losing sight of the overriding socioeconomic structures that are not easily transformed. However, he supplies a rather vague and pointless treatment of several concepts. Castells also seems to believe that the notion of power has a more important role than it actually has for what he is doing. Mode of development is a conceptual innovation, but it must be considered redundant, because we already have the concept of forces of production. I certainly prefer the latter, because it does not presuppose 'development' but is neutral with respect to the direction of change and therefore more useful. Unquestionably, forces of production tend to 'develop' – or at least they have done so in the course of history – but that does not have to be written into the concept itself. With a neutral concept, we leave the possibility open that there may be very little change, stagnation, or even regression.

Globalization and internationalization

In a short period of time, globalization has become one of the catchwords through which much of the contemporary debate on economic, political and cultural developments is channeled. It has even been suggested that globalization is 'the new grand narrative of the social sciences' (Hirst and Thompson 1999: xiii). Numerous books and articles have been published on this topic and if we did not know better – that trends do not last forever – we might be inclined to think that there is an insatiable demand for such texts. David Held and Anthony McGrew (2003b: 19) have argued that the discussion on economic globalization hovers around four topics: whether economic activities have been globalized, 'whether a new form of global capitalism, driven by "the third industrial revolution", is taking hold across the globe', how far economic processes remain 'subject to proper and effective national and international governance', and 'whether global competition spells the end of national economic strategy and the welfare state'. With this outline of the issues involved, it should be clear that the way is paved for controversy.

Globalization is frequently discussed in relation to the concept of internationalization and the two notions are often used interchangeably. It is obviously difficult to distinguish them from one another, but internationalization is sometimes primarily assigned the function to clarify what globalization is, which implies that the latter concept holds the front position. Although this whole debate is largely independent of the original post-industrial theory, I begin by making some observations on the relationship between the two.

Post-industrial theory and globalization/internationalization

The early literature on post-industrialism does not generally have very much to contribute to the analysis of globalization and internationalization. At least we do not find much in the publications by Bell and Touraine, despite the fact they both bring up some international questions for discussion. There is a very simple reason for that; at the time when these authors published their major works on post-industrialism, the international issues debated were related to the Cold War and to the development or underdevelopment of the Third World. After the fall of the Berlin

Wall and with the speedy economic growth in certain newly industrialized countries, the whole situation has become very different.

One topic discussed by Bell (1976: 112–19) is the possible post-industrial convergence between the United States and the Soviet Union or between capitalism and socialism. Bell does not endorse the idea of such a convergence, because it 'is based on the premise that there is *one* overriding institution that can define society', that is, on something that he does not believe in (Bell 1976: 112; emphasis in original). Although accusing Marx for having such a single-minded view, Bell uses the Marxist concept of mode of production to illustrate his point. On the basis of the distinction between social relations and 'techniques' (or, we might say, relations and forces of production), two types (capitalist and socialist) of industrial as well as post-industrial societies can be identified (Bell 1976: 114). In this context, Bell also suggests that we make a distinction between convergence and internationalization. Convergence is taken to refer to a process through which societies, with their different institutional combinations, tend to resemble one another on the same dimension or confront the same kind of problems. It does not follow, though, that they give the same response to upcoming problems and the reason is that their organizations differ. In contrast, internationalization is taken to refer to the adoption of similar styles, for example in painting, music, or architecture, and the spread of scientific knowledge and technology.

Without going deeper into the convergence discussion, we can conclude that Bell's treatment of international topics is rather unconnected to the issues brought up in later debates on globalization. There are, however, some later post-industrial writings that have contributed to this discussion and among them Fred Block's book *Postindustrial Possibilities* (1990) can be mentioned. Block utilizes the terms 'internationalization' and 'international economy' that for some other analysts must be kept distinct from 'globalization' and 'global economy' (see further below). At the same time, his distinction between two different ways of analyzing the world economy appears to coincide with the standard division between globalization and internationalization.

According to Block, there are two major ways of looking at the international economy and these two approaches run through much of the discussion on economic globalization. First, the world economy can be taken as the point of departure; we then look at how nation states try to 'interfere with' its dynamics 'by erecting tariff barriers or by subsidizing their foreign trade' and such measures are 'conceptualized as political interventions in the economic realm' (Block 1990: 16–17). This is precisely what those who use the concept of globalization do, although many of them would go further in their conclusions about the effects on nation-states. The second approach reverses the order between the global and the national, arguing that the system of rules for international economic transactions is created politically, through a process of negotiations among nation-states; it is the power relations among and within nations that shape the laws and norms for exchange and cooperation within the international economy. Authors who claim that globalization is a myth or at least strongly exaggerated subscribe to this latter perspective and also have a preference for using the term internationalization.

Block (1990: 17) continues by maintaining that, after World War II, the United States – the country which is the author's major concern – has been dominant in the international arena and 'the particular direction of US influence has in turn been shaped by the relative power of different domestic social and political actors'. There is an essential insight in this; it is not anonymous market forces that have created the rules of the game. Instead this has to a large extent been done by the United States – in cooperation with other powerful nations, we must add – that consequently also has the ability to change the rules. Moreover, the policies that have been developed express the relative strength of various social forces within the dominant countries.

The most direct connection between post-industrialism and internationalization in this analysis refers to the role of services. To those who assert that the United States is under pressure from low-wage countries, Block emphasizes that its imports mainly come from other developed countries. Another, and for our discussion more important aspect, is the following. Services that are, or rather must be, produced domestically make up 'the dominant and growing share of what consumers in the United States purchase' (Block 1990: 19). What the author has in mind is, for example, healthcare, restaurant meals, and local transportation. Therefore, even if there is intensified international competition in the markets for manufactured goods, it is a competition 'over a diminishing share of the consumer dollar': 'The shift to services means that [the] developed economies actually become in some ways less international over time, since internationally traded goods represent a diminishing share of total consumption' (Block 1990: 19).

Yet, in contemporary societies, there are other types of services that have a weak domestic basis, for example those related to modern communication technologies. Some of these services can easily – and often even more easily than goods production – be moved from one place to another; as one example we can mention call centers that are now rather often established in certain low-wage countries far from the customers serviced. In other words, when empirically analyzing the consequences of a growing tertiary sector, we must look carefully at what industries are actually growing. Block has an important point that many services have a robust domestic basis and quite a few of them, such as childcare and care for the elderly, must stay that way. Furthermore, caring and many other activities cannot easily, if at all, be rationalized, which implies that they will continue to require a great deal of personnel; I return to this aspect in Chapter 9.

Conceptual considerations

A first issue that needs to be considered is what globalization means. Assuming that there is a process of internationalization, what reason do we have to replace that concept with that of globalization? What is so specific with the present development that it cannot be covered by the concept already at hand? It is worth being repeated that the two notions are often used interchangeably, although for some authors it is indeed important to maintain a distinction between them. The differences suggested in the literature can be depicted, for example, as follows: 'Internationalization refers to exchanges between nation states – across borders – and has occurred over the centuries. It is not new. Globalization, however, refers to exchanges that transcend borders and which often occur instantaneously and electronically, and is new' (King and Kendall 2004: 140). Similarly, international relations have been said to be '*inter*territorial', '*cross*-border exchanges *over* distance', in contrast to global relations that count as '*supra*territorial', '*trans*border exchanges *without* distance' (Scholte 2003: 88; emphasis in original).

It is not easy to make sense of these distinctions; not least, it seems strange to describe globalization as different from internationalization on the basis that the first is new and the second is not. The core of the argument, however, lies in the distinction between two types of exchange, although it remains to clarify their respective features. What is then actually the difference between crossing and transcending borders and between interterritorial and supraterritorial exchange? Also, strictly speaking, how important is it that exchange takes place 'instantaneously and electronically'? In fact, Castells takes this as his starting point in claiming that a global economy is something distinct from a world economy. While the latter has to do with the spread of capital accumulation across the world, a global economy instead refers to a system that can 'work as a unit in real time on a planetary scale' and although capitalism – for a long period of time – has been expanding, 'it is only in the late twentieth century that the world economy was able to become truly global on the basis of the new infrastructure provided by information and communication technologies' (Castells 1996: 92–3; emphasis removed). Unquestionably, we should make our definitions as simple as possible, but this is perhaps too unsophisticated in being solely based on the new information technologies without any reference to other aspects.

Peter Dicken (2003: 305; emphasis in original) has claimed that internationalization is a matter of '*quantitative*' processes and 'the simple extension of economic activities across national boundaries', while globalization means '*qualitatively* different' processes, in which these activities are not merely extended geographically but are in addition – and this is the crucial aspect – subject to '*functional integration*'. Internationalization and globalization are assumed to coexist, but only very few industries are supposed to be truly global. A key concept is that of production chains, which are coordinated and regulated by both business firms and the state. There is a good point in emphasizing functional integration in the way Dicken does, as well as in keeping the analysis industry-specific. The focus is then placed on the shallowness or depth of integration processes in various industries, which implies that some weighting is required to decide whether the economy as a whole can be characterized as globalized.

Held and McGrew (2003b: 4) have formulated one of the most influential definitions of globalization; they take it to signify 'the expanding scale, growing magnitude, speeding up and deepening impact of interregional flows and patterns of interaction', linking 'distant communities' and widening 'the reach of power relations across the world's major regions and continents'. This is an all-purpose definition that can be used to study economic as well as political, cultural or whatever processes we are interested in. However, it leaves out the question of how to draw the line between globalization and internationalization; the two authors apparently do not bother much about finding an answer to that.

For Paul Hirst and Grahame Thompson (1999: 10) a global system entails that 'distinct national economies are subsumed and rearticulated into the system by international processes and transactions', whereas an 'international economy, on the contrary, is one in which processes that are determined at the level of national economies still dominate'. Although recognizing the 'trends to increased internationalization' and the concomitant 'constraints on certain types of national economic strategy', the two analysts claim that, for the time being, we are far from a global economy (Hirst and Thompson 1999: 4). The paramount argument is that the process of internationalization has not hitherto dissolved the nation-state's capacity for governance; it is assumed to be a fallacy that the nation-state is completely overrun by the economic development in the world (see also, e.g., Weiss 1998). Globalization is thus regarded as essentially a myth.

Five major critical points are presented in support of the conclusion that the globalization thesis exaggerates current developments (Hirst and Thompson 1999: 2–3). The first is that the highly internationalized contemporary economy is not unparalleled; internationalization has been a long process with distinct conjunctures since the 1860s, when an economy based on industrial technology began to spread across the world. The authors even argue that in some respects the present international economy is more closed than the system was during 1870–1914. They also strongly request a historical perspective in order to make it possible to see what is new and what is not new with the current changes.

The third, fourth and the fifth arguments all concern companies. According to Hirst and Thompson, genuinely transnational companies are not that many (most companies are multinational or national) and there is no clear trend toward an increase in numbers. Moreover, capital investments in developing countries are not very impressive and have not led to any great expansion of employment. With the exception of a few newly industrialized countries, the Third World is very much marginalized in these respects. Therefore the world economy cannot be considered truly global; there is no smooth flow of resources across the globe but a concentration of trade and investments in Europe, Japan, and North America.

Finally, Hirst and Thompson (1999: 2–3) point out that the main economic powers, the G3, have strong influence over financial markets and other economic conditions: 'Global markets are thus by no means beyond regulation and control, even though the current scope and objectives of economic governance are limited by the divergent interests of the great powers and the economic doctrines prevalent among their elites'. Thus, they share the view with Block that the development of the world economy does not prevent the domination of specific nation-states. However, they suggest that in a fully globalized economy, which is actually considered to be very far from the reality in which we live, there would be little room for the nation-state to formulate its own policies: eventually, 'the hitherto hegemonic national power would no longer be able to impose its own distinct regulatory objectives in either its own territories or elsewhere' (Hirst and Thompson 1999: 13). Instead a whole range of international bodies – from transnational companies to international voluntary organizations – are likely to become more powerful, leaving national governments behind.

Held and his colleagues (1999: 11) have pointed out that a main problem with Hirst and Thompson's approach is that they tend – as do 'hyperglobalizers' who are convinced that globalization will bring about a borderless economy with little influence for the nation-state –'to conceptualize globalization as prefiguring a singular condition or end-state, that is, a fully integrated global market with price and interest equalization'. This is an important argument; it appears to be preferable to look at globalization as a process rather than to define an ideal type of global economy. Still, the criticism brought forward by Hirst and Thompson should be taken seriously, not least their emphasis on the indispensability of historical comparison. When new trends come to the forefront in the public debate, there is great demand for skeptical voices to ensure that the discussion is not completely carried away. All theories simplify reality, but intellectual fashion often makes people go too far in simplifying things and shunning complicating facts. In this case, it is facilitated by the fact that we have no easy method of distinguishing globalization from internationalization.

The discussion on globalization is by no means politically innocent; various actors have something to gain or lose from the way in which a given situation is described. Nation-states may encounter increasing difficulties in pursuing national policies, for example when they attempt to set standards for working conditions and to combat unemployment. If people believe that globalization is such an overwhelming process, as do some authors, they will see no way of avoiding its negative consequences and therefore give up fighting against them. Hirst and Thompson (1999: 6) have given their own version of this point, which is worth quoting at length:

'The notion of an ungovernable world economy is a response to the collapse of expectations schooled by Keynesianism and sobered by the failure of monetarism to provide an alternative route to broad-based prosperity and stable growth. "Globalization" is a myth suitable for a world without illusions, but it is also one that robs us of hope. Global markets are dominant, and they face no threat from any viable political project, for it is held that Western social democracy and socialism of the Soviet bloc are both finished'.

Moreover, to repeat from what I have pointed out before, the assumption that globalization has weakened role for the nation-state perhaps hides the fact that some nation-states are more powerful than others. A fundamentally divergent interpretation is that strong nation-states are 'midwives' rather than victims of internationalization (Weiss 1998: 195–6). The new order of global governance through institutions such as the International Monetary Fund and the World Bank may even represent another kind of imperialism, in which leading capitalist countries have acquired new mechanisms for domination and control (see, e.g., Petras and Veltmeyer 2001; Gowan 1999; see also some of the contributions to Held and McGrew 2003a). From this perspective, globalization is imperialism in disguise; such an interpretation is not the full story, but it should not be left out of consideration.

Globalization, information technology, and competition

For my purpose, the most interesting aspect is not globalization or internationalization *per se* but the possible impact of these processes on labor markets and labor market institutions. We can think of many of possible consequences: reorganization of the division of labor, restructuring of industries, changes in levels and composition of employment in single countries, homogenization of labor laws, new forms of immigration control, etc. This section is, however, concentrated on a more overriding issue: the role of competition in the economy. In the event of intensified competition we can expect significant changes in labor markets, directly or indirectly through the markets for capital, goods and services.

It is a general characteristic of capitalist market economies that actors compete with one another. As emphasized in Chapter 4, there is rivalry between employers as well as between workers, which is not to deny that cooperation also exists. Competition varies from time to time as well as geographically and industry-wise, but, overall, it has probably increased over more recent decades. It is related to several other factors and two of these appear to be particularly important: the new information technology and globalization. In saying this, I go along with the argument put forward by Castells (1996: 239) that 'lean production, downsizing, restructuring, consolidation, and flexible management practices are induced and made possible by the intertwined impact of economic globalization and diffusion of information technologies'.

As other types of technological innovation, the new information technology is itself very much an outcome of competition (cf. Castells 1996: 81). Capitalist firms participate in a contest with one another, based on demands to obtain and, if possible, enhance profitability. To be successful in that respect they must develop their means of production, among which information and communication technologies have become highly significant. The rapid development of these technologies over the past decades is to a large extent the result of competitive pressures. As a consequence, we find that productivity has risen, but it is not productivity gains *per se* that motivate capitalist firms; it is the prospects of high or increasing profitability.

In passing, the absence or presence of competitive pressures has had tremendous impact on historical developments. Actually, this can help us see why really existing socialism was never able to catch up with the technological advantage of Western capitalism but remained technologically inferior, which ultimately contributed to its collapse. Soviet-type state socialism no doubt competed with capitalism, but internally its mechanisms of competition were too weak. One of the most well-known statements by Marx (1971: 21) is that when the relations of production become fetters for the development of the productive forces they are likely to be transformed. His thesis seems to be applicable in this case, although he of course did not have socialism in mind but referred to capitalism and pre-capitalist modes of production. There is a deep irony in this, as Marx's view was that socialism would liberate and unfold the productive capacities of human societies. Although many different and interacting factors must be considered in explaining why things did not develop that way, the main conclusion is unambiguous – really existing socialist countries have completely failed to live up to Marxist expectations or hopes.

Returning to contemporary capitalism, we must also recognize that the new information technology in turn affects competition; they mutually affect one another. One effect of the new information technology on competition is that it makes everything much faster. There are many different aspects of this and one is the role of information and communication for the transactions in financial markets. The speed of such transactions has increased enormously over the last decades and, in fact, today they can be done without any significant lag at all, as noted by Castells (1996: 93):

'Capital is managed around the clock in globally integrated financial markets working in real time for the first time in history: billion dollars-worth of transactions take place in seconds in the electronic circuits throughout the globe'. Thus, if some investors fear that a firm will not make the profits expected, they can sell their stocks at once and transfer their capital to other objects. Other actors will immediately be informed about such moves and take their steps accordingly. As a result, firms are subject to rapid changes in the financial markets and this increases the pressure upon them to be competitive and successful. It also creates a narrow focus on short-term reports; firms must promptly show positive results or developments or at least create the impression that great profits are likely to be reaped within a near future.

The new technology of information and communication has also affected the relationship between consumers and producers. Customers can be informed more quickly – and they can be better informed – about the existing supply of goods and services and producers learn faster how people's taste and consumption patterns change. Paul Baran and Paul Sweezy (1968: Ch. 5) noted many years ago that 'monopoly capitalism', with its inherent tendency of generating economic surplus, has a strong need to increase sales. Fashion then comes to play a significant role; producers and dealers have a lot to gain from creating consumer trends and making people fashion-oriented. They thus devote large resources to advertising and sales promotion and their efforts are facilitated and governed by the new ways of disseminating commercial messages. A related development is the expansion of 'niche' markets for certain categories of buyers. Overall, with the new information technology, the communication between producers and consumers is speeded up.

For firms, the new technology increases both pressures and possibilities and it has great impact on the production process itself. It is in this connection that the notions of 'flexible specialization', 'just-in-time', and 'lean' production have become widely spread (see, e.g., Piore and Sabel 1984; Womack, Jones and Roos 1990). By means of advanced information and communication technology, various elements in this process – for example, semi-manufactures, raw materials, machinery, and labor – can be coordinated in a much more efficient way than has ever been possible before. A major method of reducing costs is to minimize stores and storage capacities and by instead intensifying the flow of production factors and improving the timing of them, large productivity gains can be made and profits can thus be increased.

Competition occurs at the level of nation-states and regions, insofar as politically and territorially defined units strive to accomplish the best possible economic development. Nation-states have not become insignificant, but their role may have been modified. With intensified rivalry over investments and jobs they must create an attractive business climate either by furnishing good conditions in terms of education, transportation, and other services or by offering low costs in terms of wages, taxes, etc. Castells (1996: 256–64) brings up the question of national competitiveness in discussing whether the diffusion of information technologies affects employment levels. He finds no systematic correlation in that respect, but his conclusion is nevertheless that competitiveness determined by economic strategies and sociopolitical contexts are important for the creation and destruction of jobs.

It is not unusual, however, to deny the idea of intensified international competition. For example, John Kelly (1998: 60–5) is not willing to accept the explanatory role ascribed to competitiveness and his reasons for this seem to be ideological; the author apparently does not want to supply arguments in favor of a trade union strategy that means concessions to employers. It is supposed to be a 'fashionable idea that one of the major tasks of industrial relations research is to trace out the logic of competitiveness by exploring employer responses to market pressures, such as human resource management, and then seeking to investigate union and worker responses to those initiatives' (Kelly 1998: 64). Employee strategies are not on my agenda here, but we may still ask how to explain the attitudes and behaviors of the counterpart. In my view, it is unlikely that employer demands are nothing but fabrications to keep workers and their organizations in line.

We find other examples of how the notion of intensified competition is met with reservation and disbelief. Hirst and Thompson (1999: 133) maintain that the discourse on international competitiveness has great impact on almost every relevant actor – companies, public institutions, and individuals – but should be treated with the same caution as the globalization thesis itself. Consequently, and recalling what has been noticed before, they consider it a myth and not an innocent myth; these ways of reasoning are taken to be ideological justifications for certain proposals and actions: 'Company strategy and public policy are alike concerned to match supposed international challenges' and individuals are expected to be 'competitive', which translates into being 'flexible', 'innovative', 'imaginative', 'entrepreneurial', etc. (Hirst and Thompson 1999: 97). Moreover, despite the arguments presented above, we find that also Castells (1996: 86–7) is somewhat skeptical to the concept of competitiveness, regarding it as 'an elusive, indeed controversial, notion' more suited for countries and regions than for firms; in the latter case he prefers the notion of 'competitive position'. Yet, he attaches strategic importance to competitiveness due to, among other things, the increasing interdependence of economies.

One point to be added is that when new challengers are admitted to a market it may only temporarily lead to more competition, because sometimes one or a few large newcomers become completely dominant and drive others out of business. We should thus watch out for the temptation to exaggerate the significance of competitiveness, but certain facts cannot be ignored; competition exists and firms that do not reach some minimum of performance actually go bankrupt. This puts pressure upon management, which in turn partly passes it on to workers. The issue is not always the risk for financial losses but the fact that profitability prospects look better somewhere else; for employers, the threat of capital flight is one way of putting power behind words. Moving to another country with lower wages, less labor market regulation, and less generous social security systems can be a way of lowering costs and therefore of securing better long-term profitability. We should not, however, just think in terms of 'a race to the bottom'; it is not costs alone that count in market competition. There are significant advantages to be attributed to countries with well-functioning, reliable institutions and infrastructure; in other words, there is also a 'race to the top'.

With respect to the possible effects of globalization on labor supply, we can recall from Chapter 3 that Castells (1996: 232–40) has raised the question of whether it makes sense to talk about a global labor force. His answer is that – with the exception for certain professionals and scientists – so far it does not. Nevertheless, the main conclusion from his discussion is that the interdependence of the labor force across the world has increased. Three mechanisms are brought up as explanations behind this augmented interdependence:

> 'global employment in the multinational corporations and their associated cross-border networks; impacts of international trade on employment and labor conditions, both in the North and in the South, and effects of global competition and of the new mode of flexible management on each country's labor force' (Castells 1996: 234–5; emphasis removed).

On the whole, international migration has been extensive during more recent decades, but we should remember that it has also been substantial during certain earlier periods. There are evidently large numbers of people who want to move from poorer to richer countries and who actually also do it; some of them are refugees from political, religious, or other kinds of repression, whereas others mainly have economic motives. At the same time, there are rather strong legal, social, cultural, and economic obstacles for people to overcome in order to be successful in entering new countries and new labor markets (see, e.g., Brochmann and Hammar 1999; Castles and Miller 2003).

It seems likely that there will be more migration as borders are opened up, the international division of labor is reshaped, and great fluctuations appear in the demand for labor across countries and across regions. If the supply of labor increases in the most developed part of the world, it may lead to intensified competition in the labor market, but this does not necessarily mean that wages must be lowered or that unemployment must rise. In the short run, some effects of that kind may appear, but immigration will also generate new jobs, as it adds to the number of consumers. The development in the United States since the beginning of the 1990s is an instructive example of this. Despite very large flows of immigration, unemployment continued to decrease all through 1992–2000, and the small upturn after that cannot be blamed on these flows.

New times, new labor market relations?

Contemporary developed societies and their labor markets have undeniably undergone many significant changes over the last decades. Although we should be cautious with the use of labels, we are not entirely misguided in talking about a new age of services, information, and globalization. Having browsed through a huge literature on the service, information, and globalized society, however, I must conclude that it often tends to exaggerations. The problem is located both in the descriptions of what has happened up to now and in the predictions about the future. Authors are apparently tempted to go a little too far in their conclusions about past, ongoing as well as expected future changes. These developments are frequently quite impressive in themselves without having to be magnified.

What are then the main conclusions to be drawn from the observations and the analysis made in this chapter? We find several developments with great implications for the labor market, but instead of enumerating details – significant as they may be – I want to emphasize two main aspects. The first is the changes in the composition of jobs and of jobholders in the labor market and their concomitant effects in society. Second, the balance of power between the main actors in the labor market is continuously undergoing change and this is partly due to what happens with the composition of jobs and of jobholders. The development of competition, related to the expansion of information technology and the globalization of markets, is another factor, which I believe has a significant impact on power relationships.

Changes in the composition of jobs and jobholders

To begin, the changes in the composition of jobs in the labor market – a major theme in post-industrial theory and this also holds for the information society thesis – is that industrial employment tends to decline and service employment to increase. Many observers have pointed out that, to a large extent, services are related to industrial production and cannot be treated as separate from it. One problem is also to distinguish the production of services from the production of goods, as the borderline between the two is increasingly becoming blurred. I have been unable to settle that issue and I even doubt that it is possible. Moreover, as a consequence of the process of internationalization and globalization, manufacturing jobs have to some extent been allocated or reallocated to poorer countries where wages are lower and social security legislation and benefits are weaker. Thus the post-industrial scenarios outlined for our part of the world need to be modified in several ways or at least interpreted cautiously; yet, what can be loosely referred to as service sector employment has apparently expanded, while at the same time there has been a decline in manufacturing employment.

In relation to this development I want to take up two important aspects and the first one refers to changes in the occupational structure and the class structure. A crucial feature of the present picture is that the relative size of the traditional working class has declined. Since the industrial prole-tariat is a major social force behind collective solutions at workplaces and in society at large, we can expect significant social and political conse-quences to follow. The labor movement, including both political parties and trade unions, has been weakened with great impact on various condi-tions in society. A weakening of the labor movement does not mean, however, that it has become completely powerless; it still has some sub-stantial power and cannot be counted out.

What is more, it does not follow that social class has lost its role. With the growth of the service sector, the professional-managerial occupational groups have expanded. These categories are mostly employees – although there is a considerable proportion of self-employment in the sector – and their rela-tionship to employers is at least partly similar to that of other workers. The main difference is that they, within the social division of labor, have execu-tive power or the authority of being experts, in turn associated with various premiums. However, many service sector jobs are similar to – and sometimes worse than – traditional working-class jobs in terms of payment and working conditions. Although no expansion in the proportion of disadvantaged service employment can be confirmed (cf. Esping-Andersen 1993, 1990: 206–17), there are large categories with a socioeconomic position close to or even inferior to that of the industrial working-class.

Another consequence of the expansion of the tertiary sector is the huge inflow of women into the labor market; the labor force has been feminized. In, for example, healthcare, education, childcare, and care for the elderly we find many occupations with affinity to long-established 'female' tasks and, not surprisingly, female employees make up the vast majority of the workforce in these occupations. Still, women work part-time to a larger extent than men and on average receive lower pay; they are also under-rep-resented on the higher levels of workplace hierarchies, often even in indus-tries where they make up the majority. The division of labor generally remains gendered in society, both horizontally and vertically, although in some fields the traditional patterns have started to break up. Certain work-places and occupations have obtained a much more balanced gender com-position, which is a crucial factor if work cultures are to be changed.

There are many other significant effects of the feminization of labor markets; among other things, it means that the one-breadwinner family is substituted for a two-breadwinner model. This has important consequences for family life, although the gender division of housework has not at all been altered to the same degree. At least as long as women work part-time, they remain secondary providers, but in some places we discover increasing proportions of women on full-time contracts, which can be taken as a small sign of a possible future challenge to male dominance. The greater role of women in the labor market has many other consequences too; for example, with only one breadwinner it is relatively easy for a family to move from one place of residence to another, but with two spouses who need employment – and in particular if we assume two full-time jobs – it becomes much more difficult.

Changes in the balance of power

Due to technological development, industrial production, as well as many other activities, has been dramatically rationalized over the past decades. This has led to a decline in the proportion of traditional industrial workers, usually considered to be the most important counterforce to capitalist power. As a consequence, the resistance to employer demands has been weakened, perhaps not as much on the factory level (because there are still large factories) as in society at large. The unionization rate has declined in many of the advanced capitalist countries, although not in all; in some it has even increased (for some further discussion on this, see Chapter 7). However, the decline in terms of membership is not the only negative development; collective bargaining has become more decentralized and fragmented and unions have lost some of its influence in societal decision making. Moreover, unemployment has generally been much higher in recent decades than before the first oil crisis in the 1970s (Korpi 2002). In total, there are some indications of a shift in the power balance in the labor market and this shift has been to the advantage of employers.

The development of competition is another important factor, associated with both the new information and communication technologies and the processes of internationalization and globalization. No matter whether the claim of intensified competition is sometimes exaggerated, we should not avoid paying attention to it or disregard it as false, because when borders are opened up for trade and investments, it is necessary for employers to step up their efforts to rationalize production, reduce costs in other respects, or increase sales. This may imply demands for downsizing, for work organization changes, for wage adjustments, etc., and for deregulation of the institutional framework related to these dimensions. Nation-states, too, must try harder to secure investments and jobs within their territories. However, competition also contains the seed for its opposite:

monopolization. Some firms go bankrupt, others are bought up by the winners, and in the end there may be fewer actors in the arena.

In any case, a period of stepped-up competition is likely to contribute to a shift in the power balance between employers and employees, as it paves the way for stronger demands on workers. Also the relative decline of the industrial working-class and the long-term rise in unemployment are important factors behind this power shift. The working-class and its organizations are more likely than others to have a collective orientation and to fight for collective solutions of various problems and this counter-force has been weakened. Competition is primarily an element in the capitalist sector, although it makes itself felt in the public sector too, not least due to pressures on public finances. In many countries, the public sector has been subject to retrenchment and restructuring; sometimes under the banner of neo-liberalism but sometimes without any pronounced ideological basis, quite a few governments have conceded to employer demands and implemented reforms. They have been willing to make certain changes in the direction of deregulation of statutory law, privatization of public property, and retrenchment of social welfare expenditures. Still, with a few more spectacular exceptions such as the neo-liberal experiments in the United Kingdom and New Zeeland, we should be aware that the policy changes in the advanced capitalist world have often been rather modest.

In sum, competition in markets for goods and services can be expected to affect labor markets by making employers put pressures upon workers for adjustments. Firms under strong competitive pressures must make all kinds of improvement with respect to products, technical equipment, organization, and personnel. Many of these changes translate into demands for worker flexibility as regards employment, skills, working hours, wages, and various other dimensions (for some further discussion, see Chapter 8). This whole development has provided arguments for employers to be tough also in their demands on governments. The latter are given a choice: make adjustments in labor market regulation and social security systems or face the consequences of doing nothing, which implies downsizing, closures, transfers of jobs to other countries, and higher unemployment. Employers might have inflated their demands, but everything is not taken out of the blue; there is real pressure upon firms to adapt to change and it calls for more labor market flexibility.

A general question is whether the developments described have had or will have any substantial impact on the fundamental structures of capitalism. The positions that different authors take on this issue are indeed divergent. For example, as described previously in this chapter, some believe that we are now living in post-capitalist societies, whereas others are eager to point out that the advanced Western societies continue to be capitalist in nature despite great changes. In my view, the former position cannot be defended; all available evidence speaks in favor of the latter. Fundamental socioeconomic structures are resilient; they have some built-in solidity and are not very easily transformed. They are no doubt affected by various kinds of change, but yet they seem to survive, sometimes perhaps in an adapted form. Social scientists should take it upon themselves to study these processes more closely and I repeatedly return to the issues of change and continuity in the remaining chapters.

The fact that employers have been far from totally successful in their demands is related to two sets of factors. First, it must be kept in mind that there is some significant resistance both on the part of workers, including their organizations, and on the part of governments. These actors have made many concessions and adjustments but far from everything demanded. The relative stability in welfare state arrangements is an indicator of how important these institutions are for large segments of the population and, concomitantly, it gives us some idea why we discover quite a lot of popular resistance to neo-liberal solutions. A second reason why changes have been relatively moderate is that employers neither always easily find the best solution nor agree on what it is. This is in turn a consequence of two of my foremost points in Chapter 8, namely that employers also look for stability and that different flexibility mixes can be used to obtain basically the same outcome.

Many employers have been very eager to pursue certain reforms, but others have not felt that union or government regulation is such a big deal. The need for stability in firms should not be underestimated; employers are often utterly keen on retaining their workforce, or at least the core of it, because high turnover of personnel can be very costly. Even when increased flexibility is vital for the survival of a firm, pragmatists usually find some mix of solutions that can satisfy various actors and still work approximately as desired. Despite this, employers keep on trying to push back government regulation, union influence and other forms of collective action. This would allow them to have more flexibility on their own terms such as more tightly performance-related pay systems, wider use of fixed-term contracts, and better adjustment of working hours and work schedules to business operations. They have to some extent been successful, but not totally, in pursuing such goals; I return to these issues several times in the remaining chapters.

7
The Individual–Collective Aspect of Employment Relationships

Ideal-typically we can characterize employment relationships as collective or individual. To qualify as collective these relationships must be regulated through arrangements that go beyond the individual worker. One way of implementing that kind of regulation is through bargaining between employers and workers or their representatives. Such bargaining may involve several workplaces, locally, industry-wise, nationwide, etc. Government intervention is another collective mechanism that partly settles the working conditions for all or for specified categories of employees. As illustrations we can think of statutory rules on working hours and work safety regulation. Also the social insurance system entails collective security by providing benefits when people are hit, for example, by sickness or injury.

There are thus different ways of regulating employment relationships collectively. In contrast, an individual solution ideally means that the employer and the worker make their deal without any interference by unions, governments, or other organizations and institutions. All interaction between an employer and a worker is of course social, as it involves two actors, but this is not sufficient to make it qualify as collective in this context. Leaving ideal types behind, we must recognize that employment relationships in real life comprise both individual and collective elements; there are all kinds of combinations in that respect. Even if general wage levels are decided through bargaining between employers and unions, some room is still often left for individual solutions and, at the same time, there can be legislation defining minimum wages. Similarly, working hours may be determined in a mixed way and within the limits set by the law.

Collective organization is largely indispensable for workers when they want to put power behind their demands; it is a crucial counter-power for those who have little else in terms of resources at their disposal. As mentioned in Chapter 4, Claus Offe and Helmut Wiesenthal (Offe 1985: 178) argue that under capitalism each firm has a kind of unity to begin with, whereas workers need to associate to make up for this, which requires the formation of collective consciousness and organization. In the absence of a collective organization, the individuals who hire out their labor power remain atomized and divided. A different way of expressing basically the same perspective is to phrase it as Jelle Visser (1996: 15) does in claiming that individual bargaining may sometimes 'be a euphemism for unilateral decision-making by the employer, given his superior power over individual or unorganized workers'. In other words, without having the collective behind him/her, the individual usually has little say in relation to the employer.

This chapter deals with the collective–individual dimension of employment relationships and several sociological arguments related to it. Among other things, I take a look at some recent developments and at how they are interpreted by different authors. One rather often used concept is that of de-collectivization, more or less synonymous with notions such as disaggregation and fragmentation (Hyman 1992: 151). It refers to a decline in collective arrangements and it can be due to a variety of social processes and mechanisms. Another and similar concept is individualization that is assumed to end up in individualistic orientations and attitudes: it can be a significant element in a process of de-collectivization, but the latter notion is more comprehensive.

The discussion below is organized in the following way. To begin, I focus on de-collectivization processes and a key question to be addressed is what has happened with unions and how to explain it. The next item on my agenda is the thesis of individualization, by many sociologists assigned a front position in their descriptions of contemporary society. Some interpretations of this thesis – that are particularly relevant for the analysis of labor markets – are presented and scrutinized. Subsequently, I turn to certain social characteristics and processes and contrast them with the tendencies toward individualization. My focus is on the collective character of work, the occurrence of social comparisons, and the trend toward professionalization.

De-collectivization

There are numerous phenomena that can be regarded as signs of de-collectivization, that is, a process through which collective solutions and identities lose, totally or partly, their significance. Deregulation, privatization, and welfare state retrenchment are often dealt with in such terms, but the conclusions to be drawn are not always that unambiguous. We can take employment protection legislation as an example; in this respect there has been a great deal of discussion about the need for deregulation and we know that quite a few countries have relaxed their statutory rules. For a large number of OECD member states, a systematic comparison has been done on the strictness of such legislation in the late 1980s and the late 1990s (OECD 1999: Ch. 2). On the indicators presented in the study, most countries score lower at the later point in time. Nevertheless, a main conclusion is that 'there has been quite high persistence in national systems of employment protection regulation over the past ten years' (OECD 1999: 86). In other words, some deregulation has taken place, but it is not that overwhelming.

De-collectivization has also manifested itself in the privatization of public activities in many Western nations (see, e.g., Martin 1993; Parker 1998; Saunders and Harris 1994; Whitfield 1992). It has been a matter of activities such as communications and transportation, supply of water or electricity, healthcare, childcare, care for the elderly, and education. Non-governmental owners have been allowed to take over existing activities or to set up new activities. We find considerable differences across countries regarding the degree of privatization, among other things because the initial proportion of public ownership shows great variation among them. Privatization no doubt means de-collectivization, but it is unclear how it affects the collective–individual character of employment relationships. In itself, a change of ownership does not alter these relationships; in order for this to occur, it must be accompanied with other changes.

Furthermore, during the last decades, public welfare provisions have been cut in many advanced capitalist societies (see, e.g., Korpi and Palme 2003). If the social protection supplied by the welfare state is being limited, the individual may be left more to the willpower of the employer. For example, if government schemes for part-time pensions are restricted, it will have an impact on older workers' employment situation; worn-out workers may have to work longer hours than for which they are capable or accept a substantial loss of income. Nevertheless, it is difficult to make strong generalizations with regard to the effects of welfare state retrenchment on employment relations.

For the topics treated in this book, the most important de-collectivization process has to do with union membership and influence; there are plenty of statistics and research suggesting that, on the whole, trade unions in the economically advanced Western world have been weakened during recent decades. However, this development is not even and some evidence points in the opposite direction. The degree of unionization is probably the best indicator to look at, but also other aspects need to be taken into consideration, such as coverage of collective bargaining, degree of centralization and decentralization in bargaining, and participation in general societal decision making (see, e.g., Ackers, Smith and Smith 1996; Goldfield 1987; Kjellberg 2001, 2002; van Ruysseveldt and Visser 1996).

Regarding the development of industrial relations in Europe during 1980–95, Visser (1996: 31) notes that the trade unions have been particularly hit, as 'their power in the external labour market is being eroded, their contribution to macroeconomic management marginalized, and their role in regulating employment relations in firms disputed'. The conclusion is that 'unions were rarely in the driving seat' and these words do not appear to be an overstatement (Visser 1996: 32). Adding non-European countries such as the United States and Australia to the analysis rather strengthens this conclusion (see, e.g., Galenson 1994: Ch. 1; Kjellberg 2001: 25–8; 2002: 68; OECD 1994: 184–5; 1997: 70–4). Moreover, data point in the same direction for the years after 1995; thus, since the beginning of the 1980s, the main international trend is that the strength and influence of trade unionism have been damaged, above all reflected in declining unionization rates. The development of union density is not, however, the same every-where; change has been far-reaching in some countries but very small in others and figures are to some extent headed in opposite directions. For example, in a couple of decades, we find a substantial decrease in France and the United States but an increase in Finland. The general pattern is, however, that unions have been weakened and the decline in unionization rates appears to be the most indisputable trend. Let us see how the lower-ing union density has been explained in the literature.

Explaining the decline in union density

There are plenty of books and articles that deal with the reasons why unions have met with increasing problems in recruiting and retaining members (see, e.g., Brown 1990; Goldfield 1987; Hyman 1992; Kelly 1998; Kelly and Waddington 1995; Standing 1999: 199–203). Surveying the most important explanations suggested in the literature, I find it convenient to classify them into five categories. A first type of explanation focuses on changes in the composition of the workforce. Certain categories of workers are less inclined to join unions and if their proportion of total employment increases, unionization rates will fall off. The typical example is women, who have heavier family obligations than men and consequently devote relatively less time to paid work; their labor force participation is lower and they more often work shorter hours. All of this is likely to make it less important for them to join a union. Another gender factor to consider is that unions are male-dominated and therefore represent men better than women (see, e.g., Colgan and Ledwith 1996, 2002). However, to some extent, the picture needs to be modified; for example in Sweden – where the female employment rate is not so far from the male rate – women have passed men in terms of unionization (Kjellberg 2001: 267, 2002: 50).

Second, a related argument can be made with regard to kind of jobs and workplaces. It is, for example, well known that unionization rates are linked to the size of the workplace (see, e.g., Goldfield 1987: 131–4; Gallie *et al.* 1998: 104–6). If the proportion of jobs in small units grows, union density can be expected to decline. There is also a discussion about the dif-ferences between, on the one hand, services, in particular certain new types such as information technology (IT) or IT-related services, and, on the other hand, manufacturing industries, the traditional stronghold for trade unionism. We should observe that unionization rates are frequently rather high in the public service sector (see, e.g., Kelly 1998: 41–2; Kjellberg 2001: 375, 2002: 47–8). Another example of the role of job characteristics is provided by, among others, Guy Standing (1999: 199), who points out that people in non-standard jobs are less unionizable. In fact, his argument seems to represent a combination of the first and the second type of explanation given here. Standing emphasizes that temporary workers, part-timers, and other non-regular workers have increased in numbers and that they are less likely to join unions. Empirical evidence verifies that both part-time and temporary workers score relatively low on union density (see, e.g., Gallie *et al.* 1998: 104–5; Kjellberg 2001: 273–5, 395).

A third kind of explanation has to do with competitive pressures in the economy and the connected labor market insecurity. Richard Hyman (1999: 104–5) has given three reasons why unions have a harder task to justify their role and actions in a time of intensified competition. First, they may have to make concessions, for example trading off pay increases – or even accept pay reductions – to help employers not only survive but also enhance their ability to be successful in the market. Second, competitive pressures may foster 'enterprise egoism', which in turn may lead to an acceptance of deregulation of national or sectoral statutory rules. Finally, with intensified competition tensions are likely to increase between winners and losers in the workforce: 'The logic of market relations is that competition reinforces disparities of power within as well as between classes' (Hyman 1999: 105).

We find a very different stand on these issues in the work by John Kelly (1998: 60–5). He takes a negative attitude to the alleged explanatory power of competitiveness, and, as noted in Chapter 6, his position appears to be motivated by ideological and strategic considerations. Kelly is unwilling to provide ammunition to a union strategy that simply means yielding to employer pressures. The assumption is that the discourse of intensified competition is used to pave the way for various kinds of worker concessions. Evidently, Kelly wants to avoid a situation in which workers or unions envisage nothing but a choice between two negative outcomes: accepting employer demands or pricing the firm out of business or out of the country. The demands for competitiveness may be exaggerated, but it is an enormous overstatement to contend that they are entirely invented; they cannot be discarded on such grounds as explanatory factors behind employers' strategies and concomitant union adjustments.

Competitive pressures tend to enhance insecurity among employees. According to Standing (1999: 199), increasing labor market insecurity has made it more difficult for unions to recruit members, not only because fewer workers have employment, but also because it becomes easier for employers to resist unions. The first part of the argument seems to go beside the point. With respect to union density, the number of employees does not matter; it is the *proportion* of them who are unionized that counts or should count. Members who become unemployed should not be included, but there may of course be a great problem with how the statistics are organized. However, if members who become unemployed stay with their organization and are included in the calculation, *ceteris paribus* the unionization rate will *increase*.

The second part of Standing's argument is that insecurity helps employers resist unions, but exactly what mechanisms are involved, and how they operate, is not explained. At any rate, it seems to be in line with Hyman's perspective as outlined above. More insecurity is an expression of stronger employer advantage, but – as Standing himself points out – with the Ghent system, that is, a benefit system controlled by unions, there is an incentive for workers to join unions and this becomes particularly important in a recession with increasing threats to jobs. Besides, financial support in case of unemployment is not the only thing for which workers look in response to labor market insecurity; they often need other types of collective protection as well, for example when employers want to change working hours or other working conditions. Actually, the fact that workers have a vulnerable position in the labor market, and therefore experience insecurity, is a fundamental cause behind the emergence and development of trade unions.

Fourth, many authors emphasize the role of employers and the state in pushing back support for unions and this seems to be especially common among those who deal with the United States and Britain (see, e.g., Goldfield 1987: Chs. 9–11; Kelly 1998 : 60–5; Standing 1999: 200–1). For example, Standing underscores that capitalist employers have become tougher and that many governments have introduced anti-union regulations. Kelly (1998: 61) argues that we have seen 'a rise in employer militancy that expresses itself in four ways: hostility to union recognition, derecognition, antipathy to collective bargaining, and attempts to bypass and marginalize workplace trade unionism'. He also calls attention to the role of state in various endeavors to break up union resistance and power. The counter-strategies put forward by employers and governments are no doubt highly important, but we must still ask why these actors have been successful. For Kelly (1998: 61), it appears as an end in itself for ruling groups to preserve their power and he claims that they always attempt to find new ways of doing this. Economic and competitive pressures of the kind discussed above are thus played down, but it is hard to see why such pressures would not be part of the changing balance of power. By defining the situation of firms as subject to uncompromising competition – requiring cost reductions, productivity increases or expanding market shares – employers have a strong argument to use against workers. This may not be the only explanation, but it would be a mistake to exclude it from the discussion on how to account for employer power.

Finally, some authors have emphasized the role of individualism for the decline in unionization. One example is a well-known article by Henry

Phelps Brown (1990) who contrasts the collectivism of previous industrial epochs with the situation in the second half of the twentieth century. It is pointed out that workers have become more affluent and that ownership of cars and homes has spread. Moreover, Brown mentions the growing proportion of employees in small workplaces and the increased attention paid to education and training for self-improvement. There are hence many factors that contribute to the emergence and expansion of individualistic values and attitudes. A relevant question is, though, why there is such a great variation in union density between countries that hardly differ that much in these respects. Without a persuasive answer to that question, it seems difficult to believe that the diffusion of individualistic values would be such a decisive factor behind the weakening of unions, although it may very well have some part to play. As noted above, there are several other explanations available as to why this impairment has happened. All the same, besides Brown we find several other authors who also regard individualization as a crucial development in contemporary societies and they have actually taken the idea a considerable step further.

The individualization thesis

The concept of individualization has various meanings in the literature, but it is generally part of the view that both working life and society at large undergo changes that undermine traditional orientations related to collectivities such as the family, the working class, and the local communities. These processes are commonly explained by the development of modernity; it is the emergence of the modern outlook and world view that has facilitated individuals' liberation from social binds as well as from traditional or religious beliefs, values, and norms. Some argue that 'late' or 'reflexive' modernity means yet another step through which people are increasingly forced to choose their own life trajectories (Lash and Wynne 1992: 2–3).

According to Ulrich Beck and Elisabeth Beck-Gernsheim (2002: 8), the historically new development during the second half of the twentieth century implies that what 'was earlier expected of a few – to lead a life of their own – is now being demanded of more and more people and, in the limiting case, of all'. The authors point out two new elements: 'first, the democratization of individualization processes and, second (and closely connected), the fact that basic conditions in society favour or enforce individualization (the job market, the need for mobility and training, labour and social legislation, pension provisions etc.)' (Beck and Beck-Gernsheim 2002: 8). This development thus involves both structural and subjective or cultural elements: expectations or pressures put upon people to regard themselves as responsible for their own fate and changes in the socioeconomic structure, including the labor market. One reason why Beck and

Beck-Gernsheim's analysis must be considered particularly interesting for the discussion in this book is their view that the labor market is the 'motor' of individualization; I will return to that shortly.

It is easy to see the implications of the perspective suggested, above all – to use the words by Rosemary Crompton (1998: 128; emphasis in original) – 'that increasing individualization, if indeed it is under way, would be contrary to the development of social classes, particularly the development of *collective* class *identities*'. Among other things, as a result we must expect workers to become less interested in the type of solutions that unions represent. Although many maintain that collectivism belongs to the past, few argue that the process is already completed; the assumption is rather that it is in progress. From the quotation above, we understand that Crompton has some reservation as to whether the individualization thesis is at all correct and, as a minimum, I think that we need to scrutinize it further to see whether or in what respects it makes sense. If it is found to be plausible, significant consequences will follow for the labor market in modern societies; we can then predict a weakening of class identification among workers and of support for collective organizations. The willingness to join trade unions and take part in their activities is likely to fade away and workers can instead be expected increasingly to develop individual strategies to pursue their interests.

The idea of an individualization process is not new. *Inter alia* – and for some perhaps surprisingly – such ideas appear in the work by Karl Marx and Friedrich Engels. They looked upon capitalism as a mighty force capable of sweeping away traditions and social ties founded in an older form of society. Marx's whole analysis of the labor market, as dealt with in Chapter 2, implies that individual workers, 'free' wage-workers, relate to their labor power as their commodity in order to get the most out of the exchange with the capitalist. This kind of individualized relationship is a basic element in the capitalist labor market and, as a result, there is 'no other nexus between man and man than naked self-interest, than callous "cash payment"' (Marx and Engels 1998: 37). Moreover, the two authors put forward an ideal of the full development of individuals' capacities and energies that was assumed to be possible only with communism.

However, Marx and Engels (e.g., 1998: 42–50) took the view that workers pulled together in the factory under capitalist authority and close to the subsistence level must and will, sooner or later, overcome their individual relationship with the employer. Workers' situation would make them develop common values and demands that eventually would lead to collective action. In other words, life in the capitalist factory was endowed with the prerequisites for the formation of a more or less united proletariat. After having pointed out that the mass of people had been transformed into workers, Marx (1976: 211) gives the following account: 'The domination of capital has created for this mass a common situation, common interests.

This mass is already a class against capital, but not yet for itself. In the struggle ... this mass becomes united, and constitutes itself as a class for itself. The interests it defends become class interests. But the struggle of class against class is a political struggle.' There are different opinions about whether working class identity and proletarian collective action ever at all developed the way Marx and Engels expected, but their whole idea in this respect stands for the opposite of individualization.

Let us also recall Émile Durkheim's (1964) classical analysis of the development of the division of labor and its consequences for the forms of solidarity in society. The crucial distinction is then that between mechanical and organic solidarity. In a society where the division of labor is low, Durkheim argues, people are fundamentally in the same situation, which is reflected in the relations between them. Mechanical solidarity prevails, based on the homogeneity of individuals and involving a strong *conscience collective*, unambiguous norms and tight social control with little room for individualism. However, the division of labor advances with the development of technology and commerce; people become more specialized, they do different things and thus in a sense have less in common. As a result, another kind of solidarity, organic solidarity, tends to evolve; it implies a much weaker *conscience collective* and leaves essentially more to the individual. This might mean that society becomes atomistic and even breaks down, but such tendencies are generally counteracted by the necessity that people cooperate in order to survive. Nevertheless, the emergence of organic solidarity may not be enough; there is a continuing risk that disaggregation and anomie will spread.

Durkheim (1964: 5) suggests that in order to avoid anomie there must be 'a group which can constitute the system of rules actually needed' and this is the 'corporation or occupational group'. The state is supposed to be too far apart from the economic activities to fulfill such a role. Instead it must be a group with enough knowledge of the functioning of the specialized fields of economic life; the intermediate occupational group then appears to be the only organization that can induce individual actors to comply with common norms and rules. We may indeed have strong misgivings regarding Durkheim's proposal for how the problem of social integration and social order is to be solved, but the way he formulates the issue remains relevant.

In the contemporary discussion on individualization, Beck and Beck-Gernsheim (2002: xxi) are eager to distinguish their perspective from that used in neo-liberal economics of 'the autarkic human self', arguing for a social-scientific concept labeled 'institutionalized individualism'. This latter perspective can be found among a large number of sociological theorists. A main theme is that individualization is a structural feature of highly differentiated societies, the integration of which is not endangered but rather made possible by it. What is important, then, is that the 'central institutions of modern society – basic civil, political and social rights, but also paid employment and the training and mobility necessary for it – are geared to the individual and not to the group' (Beck and Beck-Gernsheim 2002: xxi–xxii).

However, Beck and Beck-Gernsheim (2002: xxii) take one further step by claiming that individualization means 'disembedding' of the individual from his/her social existence 'without reembedding'. We should note that in his earlier book *Risk Society*, Beck (1992: 128; emphasis removed) presents another view: Disembedding is then supposed to be followed not only by 'loss of traditional security' but also by re-embedding and the latter stands for – whatever that means – 'a new type of social commitment'. Such a turnaround of perspective ought to have significant consequences for the conceptualization of the individualization thesis, but to my knowledge neither Beck nor his co-author has commented upon it; this is so surprising that we may even ask if some kind of trivial mistake is involved. In a foreword to their book, Zygmunt Bauman (2002: xvi, xvii) has called attention to the idea that 'no "beds" are left to "re-embed"' and expresses some worry that individualization will lead to the 'corrosion and slow disintegration of citizenship'. It remains to be answered what happens with social integration, if no re-embedding takes place.

The analyses worked out by Beck and Beck-Gernsheim cover a whole range of issues – among them issues related to the family – and given the focus of the present book there is no reason to go into all of them here. Interestingly enough, the two authors explicitly identify the labor market as the 'motor' behind the process of individualization, which makes their perspective particularly relevant for my part; I therefore take a closer look at what they are saying in this respect.

The labor market as motor of individualization

In Beck's book *Risk Society* and in his and Beck-Gernsheim's later book, *Individualization*, the labor market is treated as the motor behind the individualization process. As a matter of fact, the section on this in the latter book is essentially a copy of the analysis in *Risk Society*. My summary and quotations refer to both of the two publications or to one or the other interchangeably. The authors mention three dimensions as particularly important: education, mobility, and competition (Beck 1992: 92–5; Beck and Beck-Gernsheim 2002: 31–3). Let us see how the argument goes.

To begin with education, it might appear strange to think of it as a dimension of the labor market, but Beck and Beck-Gernsheim look at it in the light of people's future job situation. Schooling implies that individuals have to make choices and plans for the future, as it will affect their coming labor market position and, consequently, their whole life biographies. Besides, education provides the basis for reflexivity that, among other things, may create problems for the survival of hierarchical job structures.

It is also related to the selection of individuals and thus to their expectations of upward mobility. Since the latter presupposes the presence of a hierarchy, there seems to be some tension involved, given what was just said about hierarchical job structures. The labor market or, to be more precise, the demand for labor in the market is a decisive factor behind mobility that is not only a question of climbing career ladders but also refers to other types of change, for example a switch of occupation or of place of residence. Among the possible effects of mobility we find that existing social ties and support arrangements may be broken off. The individuals are thus more or less left all by themselves and they are made responsible for their personal destiny. Finally, we have to consider the competition in the labor market between individuals who offer their labor power for hire. It makes it necessary for people to advertise and market their individuality, that is, their unique qualifications and experiences, and it tends to isolate them within the groups to which they belong.

The three dimensions identified – education, mobility, and competition – are evidently interdependent and they are likely to reinforce one another. It can, in addition, be expected that their interaction reinforces the process of individualization. Apart from education, mobility, and competition, Beck suggests that also other factors promote individualization. Two examples are provided: first, the collective upward mobility and the increased standards of living (leading to a diffusion of exclusive consumption patterns) and, second, the juridification of labor relations (Beck 1992: 95). It is not obvious on what grounds the latter aspect is supposed to advance individualization.

We must observe that Beck and Beck-Gernsheim do not have very much to say about the decline in union density. They argue that increasing layers of people have become dependent upon the labor market and that trade unions may not be capable of handling this. The reason is that 'wage labour risks ... do not necessarily set up *any* commonality', but instead require 'social, political and legal measures which in turn bring about the individualization of demands' (Beck and Beck-Gernsheim 2002: 37; emphasis in original). No evidence is furnished in support of this assumption and there is no explanation as to why risks connected with wage labor would not generate at least some 'commonality' but only individualized demands. Nor is it clear why political and legal measures should lead to individualization; in my view, they actually represent the opposite, collective solutions to various problems.

A crucial element in the individualization thesis is that class distinctions are supposed to be obliterated; they 'will pale into insignificance beside an *individualized society of employees*' (Beck 1992: 100; Beck and Beck-Gernsheim 2002: 39; emphasis in original). Social groups tend to lose their identity both in terms of their self-understanding and in relation to others. Their potential to become a politically significant social force is thus also hampered. Instead, in order to deal with social problems people are obliged to form new political and social alliances (Beck 1992: 100–1; Beck and Beck-Gernsheim 2002: 40). There will be temporary coalitions between different groups in different situations, whereas permanent conflicts will develop along ascribed characteristics such as race, gender, and ethnicity.

For Beck and Beck-Gernsheim (2002: 39), 'class society' is essentially 'defined in terms of tradition and culture', whereas a society of individualized employees is based on labor law and 'socio-political categories'. How the latter claim should be interpreted remains unclear, as no further clarification is provided. Anyhow, the allegation that class distinctions will disappear does not presuppose the end of inequality; the idea is instead that inequalities are redefined into individualized risks. It is also maintained that various social problems are increasingly understood in terms of individual characteristics and shortcomings, although no empirical evidence is supplied in support of this generalization. To my mind, welfare state provisions in case of sickness, maternity, handicaps, old age, etc., stand for precisely the opposite, namely that individual risks have become socialized. Given how they define class society – see the quotation above – we should not be surprised at Beck and Beck-Gernsheim's conclusion regarding its development. The fading away of this kind of society appears to be a simple corollary to the assumption that people's ties to tradition and culture are undermined or cut off. Thus class does not mean much, if anything, any more.

Being 'entrepreneur of the self'

Another version of the individualization thesis is related to entrepreneurship or the ideal of entrepreneurship. Robert Reich (2002: Ch. 5), who has brought forward the idea that self-employment will become more common, illustrates this clearly. Without using the word itself, he describes a process of individualization, that is, a development in which individuals increasingly appear as atomistic market actors, hunting for perpetually better products, services, and jobs, or for 'terrific deals' as his term is. In this context, we must concentrate on the ideal of being an entrepreneur rather than on real entrepreneurs, as the latter do not offer their labor power in the market but produce goods and services to be sold to customers. Additionally, as long as they do not hire other people to work for them, they are not involved in any employment relationship and thus simply remain outside of the labor market (see Chapter 2). Nevertheless, the ideal of entrepreneurship with its emphasis on individualism is important also in employment relationships.

The relevant aspect for my discussion is that entrepreneurship represents an ideal with conceivable impact on employment relationships. Such an ideal may be one way of thinking about individualization without necessarily using the term, as in the notion of the 'entrepreneur of the self'

(Gordon 1987: 300, 1991: 42–4; du Gay 1996: 180–4, 1999: 85–7). This notion means that life becomes a project and that people define their own life projects; it implies that social systems and actors adopt the enterprise form as their 'generalized principle of functioning' (Gordon 1991: 42). Autonomous and choosing individuals are supposed to make the best for themselves, not least in relation to their employers. Even unemployed individuals can be regarded, and regard themselves, as engaged in an enterprise to maintain or to rebuild their own human capital.

In order to be 'entrepreneur of the self' in an employment relationship, the individual worker must have opportunities for self-development, self-responsibility, and empowerment. Thus, substantial organizational change may be required, for example as regards performance-related remunerations and participation and responsibilities in management activities. Workers are simply supposed to develop a relationship with their employers of the sort that entrepreneurs generally have with business partners. Along similar lines, Rosabeth Moss Kanter (1990: 9–10) has coined the expression 'post-entrepreneurial revolution' to designate strategies that take 'entrepreneurship a step further', to the internal organization of traditional corporations, thereby building 'a marriage between entrepreneurial creativity and corporate discipline, cooperation and teamwork'. According to the author, such a model is attractive, because it presumably brings more satisfaction and rewards to the individual employee, who is consequently likely to become more motivated.

The question is whether this is anything more than a new management ideology. However, if the discourse of enterprise would become the generalized principle in the functioning of social and economic systems, it would no doubt have strong impact on individuals' relationship with their employers. As employee commitment is supposed to increase at the workplace, we might anticipate not only collectivism but also instrumentalist work attitudes to vanish. At the same time, commitment implies loyalty and in that sense entrepreneurship within an organization is not merely a matter of individualism but involves another kind of collective identity and responsibility. In other words, we should keep away from one-sided perspectives; individual and collective elements appear in many different combinations and they are often intertwined in a complicated way.

The individualization thesis under scrutiny

In this section I take up a number of problems – related to the individualization thesis – for discussion. First, I make some remarks on the problem of historical comparisons. As can be gathered from the form of the word, the concept of individualization refers to a process and this implies a comparison with something past. All conclusions about the process as well as about the present are subsequently dependent on how the past is conceived. Second, I return to the issue of class, as it is also part of the debate on individualism and collectivism in the labor market; this time the focus is on the possible implications of individualization regarding the relevance of the class concept. Third, I provide some general comments on the relationship between individualistic and collectivistic values and strategies; this is a more complex relationship than it at first seems. Finally, I discuss the issue of social integration in an individualized society.

Historical comparisons

As regards the disaggregation thesis, which apparently includes the individualization thesis, Hyman (1992: 159) remarks that it relies 'heavily on a mythologized vision of the past: a golden age when workers were spontaneously collectivist, and labour organizations joined ranks behind a unifying class project' and he continues by saying that, 'of course', history 'was never like this'. It is an elementary fact that there has been competition, division and atomization among workers as long as there has been a capitalist labor market. Hyman recalls the historical conflicts between craft and general unions in Britain to underline the lack of novelty in the disaggregation thesis. The remarkable thing was rather that collective identities could be developed at all, as cooperation was spontaneously no more likely to arise than conflict. Activists had to put in a lot of effort to achieve mobilization for the common goals.

The 'mythologized' picture of the past – linked to some versions of the disaggregation and individualization theories – exaggerates workers' previous ability to set aside their internal divisions and create powerful collective organizations. However, the problem is not only that the description of earlier epochs is distorted (which may mislead at least those who are not historians themselves), but also that this prepares the way for a biased interpretation of the present. If we believe that workers used to be unanimously collectivistic, we must conclude that the present is different; the romanticized depiction of the past has the function of making it easier for those who believe that collectivism is evaporating to state their case.

Even if the past is not romanticized, it can be skewed in a way that has serious implications for the analysis of the present, as shown by the following illustration. A main theme in individualization theory is that individuals increasingly become responsible for their own fate. When people remain unemployed – to use the example given by Bauman (2002: xvi) in his foreword to Beck and Beck-Gernsheim's book – it is perhaps suggested that they have not learned 'the skills of winning an interview', that they have not tried 'hard enough to find a job' or that 'they are, purely and simply, work-shy'. Bauman points out how individuals may be blamed for their predicament, but it remains to be examined whether this has become more common in contemporary societies. Beck and Beck-Gernsheim (2002: 24) claim that unemployment and other social problems used to be treated as 'blows of fate', but today, they continue, things are different and individuals now blame themselves. This conclusion is not based on any empirical evidence and I seriously doubt that such data can be provided. It seems very unlikely that – some decades ago or whatever time frame the authors have in mind – less responsibility was put on the unemployed themselves for their situation. Interestingly, in this connection, Bauman (2002: xvi) stresses that individualization itself 'is a fate' and 'not a choice'.

Besides, even without comparisons with the past, the notion of an individualized society – as Beck and others have formulated it – meets with difficulties in terms of empirical evidence. Reporting results from the British Job Insecurity and Work Intensification Survey (JIWIS) – a study aimed at scrutinizing the effects of flexibility, intensification of everyday life and insecurity on people's social relationships – Jane Nolan (2002: 117–19) concludes that she was unable to find support for the picture presented by Beck and others about individualized attitudes. Most of the respondents did not show the attitude that Beck (1992: 131–7) has called 'self-reflexive' and that implies an 'obsession' with one's own biography and individual career and performance.

The class issue

It has become rather common among certain sociologists to believe that class is no longer a significant concept. They sometimes want to abandon the concept altogether, quite often with reference to the process of individualization. As mentioned in Chapter 4, authors such as Beck and Beck-Gernsheim (2002: xxiv, 203ff.) insist that class should be counted among what they call 'zombie' or 'living-dead' categories. Jan Pakulski and Malcolm Waters take an even stronger position in their book, tellingly called *The Death of Class* (1996). The impact of the process of individualization appears in their discussion about ethics. It is pointed out that a crucial difference between the working-class and the middle class can be found on the issues of collectivism and individualism (Pakulski and Waters 1996: 123–4). Whereas the working-class favors collective and mutual solutions in production as well as in distribution, the members of the middle class are suspicious of collectivism and instead emphasize individualism, individual ambition and success. The authors then claim that, in the second half of the twentieth century, the process of individualization has gone so far that 'the values of manual workers have become indistinguishable from those of the middle class' (Pakulski and Waters 1996: 124). In other words, we should not expect to find any class differences whatsoever in terms of individualistic and collectivistic orientation.

These assumptions are indeed easy to falsify, as there is a huge literature indicating that class is more or less strongly correlated not only with various aspects of people's life chances but also with their political attitudes and other opinions (see, e.g., Wright 1985, 1997; Marshall 1997: Ch. 2;

Svallfors 2004). Even though there may be a process of individualization, collective identities have not disappeared. To mention one further example, analyzing Swedish survey data from 1997, Tomas Berglund and I found that – compared to white-collar workers and in particular higher-level white collars – manual workers were much more inclined to agree that unions are needed and much less inclined to say that the best would be to negotiate with the employer individually (Furåker and Berglund 2003).

In contrast to Pakulski and Waters, other advocates of an individualization thesis – such as Manuel Castells – take a more cautious stand in relation to the class issue. Castells (1996: 475–6) argues that informationalism and globalization make labor 'disaggregated in its performance, fragmented in its organization, diversified in its existence, divided in its collective action', as it 'loses its collective identity, becomes increasingly individualized in its capacities, in its working conditions, and in its interests and projects' and dissolves 'into an infinite variation of individual existences'. Yet, he does not presuppose that the working class is vanishing or that the concept of class is becoming insignificant. There is an assumption of an ongoing individualization process, but it remains indeterminate how far it has gone and will go.

In Chapter 3, my view with respect to class was formulated and all of my arguments do not have to be repeated here. Still, it seems that the logic of this chapter requires at least some further comments, so let me add a few points related to the issue of individualization. Returning to the description given by Beck and Beck-Gernsheim, we can recall that education, mobility, and competition are treated as the crucial underlying factors, supposed to foster individualism. I think that this assumption is beyond doubt, but that the reasoning is more applicable to some social classes or strata than to others. The whole scheme – to get an education, be willing to move to the available jobs and to compete with others over them – means more to higher-level white-collar workers (or the professional-managerial class) than to manual workers. In other words, individualization is not an equally relevant development for everybody, but with a continued expansion of jobs requiring professional knowledge and skills individualism will spread. This implies that the individualization thesis must not be ignored, but the key factor is then changes in the class structure and not the death of class.

Another aspect is that having a more downright instrumentalist attitude toward work – an attitude that is likely to be more widespread among manual workers – may allow more room for individualism, or certain kinds of individualism, than other work orientations such as the bureaucratic and solidaristic forms defined by John Goldthorpe and his colleagues (see Chapter 4). The mechanisms involved are actually rather double-edged. Employees with a bureaucratic or a solidaristic work orientation must at least partly sell out or commit their souls by adopting some of their employer's perspectives and philosophy, which makes a difference compared to those who do their job only for the money. In a way, the latter workers have a relatively independent position, because they are less obliged to internalize employer norms and standards (cf. Savage 2000: 126–7, 2001: 98–100). Those at higher levels of workplace hierarchies may have more freedom and room for individuality in their jobs, but at the same time they are more closely tied to the goals and norms of the organization.

A crucial issue as regards class is whether people under certain conditions define themselves in terms of class identities and interests. They no doubt have some inclination to do so and this goes not only for blue-collar and white-collar workers but definitely also, and sometimes even more so, for capitalists. In case a labor government threatens to increase corporate taxes or to make employment protection legislation stricter, it would hardly come as a surprise if capitalists react collectively against such proposals and perhaps take direct action against them. Correspondingly, when an employer makes plans for layoffs, workers are likely to express some common worry and possibly also develop some joint counter-strategy. Today, labor governments do not very often implement reforms that go against business interests, but layoffs continue to take place and now and then downsizing provokes considerable collective reaction and resistance from workers.

Collectivistic and individualistic values

People may support unions and other collective organizations for different reasons. Compared to ordinary members, trade union activists and ideologically committed individuals can be expected to regard the collectivistic moral values associated with unions as especially important, while ordinary members are relatively more likely to pay attention to instrumental motives (Hyman 1992: 160). Ideological commitment is no doubt essential, but it does not have to be present for workers to join in; also instrumentalism can be a basis for collective efforts to evolve. Unions may simply represent the best solution in instrumental terms and supporting them does not necessarily involve any weighty moral or ideological values. There is unquestionably sometimes a choice between a collectivistic and individualistic strategy, but various combinations of strategies are possible.

One issue is whether unions are able to handle the consequences of an individualization process. If not, they are likely to run into problems keeping and recruiting members and workers will then turn their backs on them and seek their own ways of dealing with employers. Trade unionists are sometimes assumed to 'react with alarm and despondency', because they find nothing but egoism, isolation and atomization, particularly among younger workers (Zoll 1996: 82). In practice, unions are more or less able to cope with the tendency toward individualism, that is, to adjust their activities to it and consequently to maintain their role and influence in the workplace and in society as a whole (see, e.g., Bacon and Storey 1996; Deery and Walsh 1999).

It can be repeated that instrumental motives do not have to translate into individualism, since they may also pave the way for collective action. Likewise, workers must not give up their individuality because they consider it a good idea to pursue some of their interests through organized struggle. Choosing a collective strategy on certain workplace issues does not have to imply very strong commitment and it must not interfere with strategies chosen on other issues. A main conclusion is that people may very well express individualism in some respects and, at the same time, collectivism in others. With increasing diversity among broad categories of workers, we must expect the former to continue to spread. The critical aspect is nevertheless whether the willingness to act collectively is at hand in certain situations. Individualization is frequently seen as a major obstacle preventing people from acting jointly; it is likely to have some negative impact on collective struggles, but it is unlikely to render all of them impossible.

Even if there is a strong and long-lasting individualization process in modern societies, we should still not exclude the possibility of a future revival of collectivism. The collectivist–individualist tension seems to be a general feature in employment relationships and it can hardly be done away with once and for all. History gives us many examples of how the emphasis has shifted from one side to the other in that tension and there is no reason why it would be otherwise in the future. Another aspect is, as mentioned in Chapter 4, that collective solutions are not only important for workers but also have certain advantages for employers, for example by helping them avoid a 'race to the top' in terms of wages and other employment and working conditions.

The question of social integration

In concluding this section, I want to touch upon the question of social integration in a world with far-reaching individualization. To begin, the notion of an 'individualized society' almost seems like a contradiction in terms. How can society that is by definition a matter of social relations be individualized? Will it then not break down and dissolve? The proponents of the individualization thesis do not think that society will cease to exist, but they have difficulty explaining what it will be like. As previously noted, Beck and Beck-Gernsheim (2000: xxii, 11) sometimes use the term 'institutionalized individualism' to describe their position; it means that the individual has to live an independent life, 'outside the old bonds of family, tribe, religion, origin and class', and this has to be done 'within the new guidelines and rules which the state, the job market, the bureaucracy etc. lay down'.

However, as hinted previously, the two authors provide an analysis that must be described as ambiguous. They accuse the social sciences of a 'collective bias', which refers to its alleged 'institutionalized rejection of individualism' (Beck and Beck-Gernsheim 2002: xxii). When the individual is disembedded without being re-embedded, the theoretical collectivism of sociology must be ended. We may then wonder from where the above-mentioned 'new guidelines and rules' will come, but in that respect, Beck and Beck-Gernsheim provide little assistance. Yet, they ask a relevant question on the relationship between society and the individual and they also try to provide a first, tentative answer:

'But does this not mean that everyone just revolves around themselves, forgetting how much they rely on others for the assertion of their own push-and-shove freedom? Certainly the stereotype in people's heads is that individualization breeds a me-first society, but, as we will try to show, this is a false, one-sided picture ... There are also signs that point towards an ethic of "altruistic individualism". Anyone who wants to live a life of their own must also be socially sensitive to a very high degree'(Beck and Beck-Gernsheim 2002: xxii).

This quotation from Beck and Beck-Gernsheim offers little help for us to decide whether individualized society is a 'me-first society'; it only suggests that we will discover tendencies of altruism too. Now, some further attempt is made to answer the question of how individualized societies can be kept together and the answer is twofold; first, there must be 'a clear understanding' of the situation and, second, people must 'be successfully mobilized and motivated for the challenges present at the center of their lives (unemployment, destruction of nature etc.)' (Beck and Beck-Gernsheim 2002: 18). If issues such as that of unemployment were just individual problems, people would not have to be mobilized to deal with them; in other words, it appears that the authors are looking for some new collectivism. They also claim that 'society must be reinvented', when 'the old sociality is "evaporating"', but integration requires that 'no attempt is made to arrest and push back the breakout of individuals' (Beck and Beck-Gernsheim 2002: 18). This idea of how a new social integration can be developed appears to be little short of wishful thinking.

It remains an unanswered question how society can be sufficiently integrated if individualization approaches or goes beyond a critical point. Durkheim has probably better than anyone else analyzed the forces behind this issue, although his solution is not – to say the least – all that convincing. For my part, the question of integration in society is less of a problem, as I am less convinced than certain other observers about the direction and speed in which and with which history is moving. There are many conditions in society – social relations, structures and processes – that will form obstacles to the advance of individualization. If the latter process is as victorious in history as some believe, these conditions will eventually have to yield, but in my view we are far from such a situation. Collective identities and collective solutions still have a significant part to play in contemporary societies; not least, this can be observed in the labor market.

The social dimension of employment relationships

A crucial question in relation to the individualization thesis is what role the social dimension is actually supposed to have. The discussion on social integration above indicates that proponents of the individualization thesis do not come up with very satisfactory answers. In this section, the aim is to develop some ideas about the role of the social dimension in employment relationships or, rather, about the mixture of collective and individual elements. As a starter, a few remarks are made concerning the collective character of work in modern society. In this connection I also comment on a specific phenomenon that is quite common at workplaces today: teamworking. The development of work teams and project groups might seem to be the opposite of individualization, but, as we shall see, this is not the whole truth; still, the collective elements present cannot be neglected. Next, I return to a sociological tradition to which researchers (except for a small number of specialists) have not paid so much attention in the last decades, namely social comparison theory. A main assumption in this kind of analysis is that people tend to compare themselves with others, both to be guided in evaluative and normative matters and to assess whether their working and living conditions can be considered fair. As a final theme, I consider the trend toward professionalization of occupations. It is a phenomenon that evidently combines the individualism of career occupations with collective efforts to defend or obtain professional status for certain categories.

Work as collective effort

In classical sociology, not least in the work by Marx and Durkheim, it is maintained that an essential characteristic of modern industrial society is the need for cooperation between people. The general idea is that, to a higher degree than ever before, work becomes a collective effort; the increasing division of labor makes different sectors of society and different categories of individuals more interdependent. The buildings, plants, machines, bridges, ships, airplanes, and other artifacts that abound in modern societies cannot be produced without the cooperation of many workers with diverse skills. Factory work implies that large numbers of workers are gathered in the same place and each of them has a specific function in a common effort to produce goods of various kinds. Advanced healthcare is a parallel within the service sector; several occupational groups, doctors, nurses, physical therapists, etc. – all of them specialized with respect to knowledge and skills – cooperate to treat patients. To use Marxist terminology, these examples illustrate the socialization of the forces of production.

It can be asked whether this interdependence has changed with the substitution of service production for industrial production and with the arrival of the new information and communication technology. Generally, the answer must be in the negative. One part of it is that industrial production continues to be an essential activity, even though the proportion of industrial workers has declined in the advanced capitalist world. There are still large factories all over this world and manufacturing is a growing industry in several developing countries. Another issue is whether service work can be described mainly as individual labor or collective labor. Obviously, the type of services that sometimes are characterized as a 'game between persons' is to a large extent supplied by solo employees. Doctors, nurses, dentists, psychologists, social workers, financial counselors, salespersons, waitresses, etc., all meet their patients, clients, and customers on an individual basis, but far from every encounter is of that kind. Much of the work in hospitals, homes for the elderly, daycare centers, banks, department stores, and restaurants – just to mention a few examples – is clearly a matter of cooperation of work teams. What we see is a mixture of individual and collective features in work situations.

An example of this mix is work with the new information technology. With the arrival of the personal computer a great deal of work has become individualized; it can be done or, rather, has to be done by the individual at his/her computer. However, keeping up and developing the information systems require a great deal of cooperation between those who have specialized knowledge about these matters and it must be emphasized that communication between people has become easier. In a given business, it may very well happen that the individuals at one workplace become more independent in relation to one another, while at the same time the interdependence across workplaces increases. In other words, work is still characterized by both individual and collective features, although the ways in which they are combined have changed.

It would definitely be unwarranted to argue that the collective nature of work in contemporary societies is on its way out. Without question, some activities in the service as well as other sectors are individualized – and it appears likely that they are on the increase – but from this we cannot conclude that work will generally cease to be a collective effort by many. The interdependence of various activities in society rather seems to be stronger today than a number of decades ago. Moreover, by and large, the work done at each workplace remains very much a matter of joint achievement and it provides a basis for common solutions to employment relationship issues and for collective action among workers. Actually, it is possible to have both increasing interdependence and increasing individualization;

this is one of the principal lessons from Durkheim's analysis of the division of labor.

One aspect to be brought up in this context is team-working, which is a common way of organizing work in contemporary working life. The concept itself is used in somewhat different ways. In one sense, it does not require that specific groups are set up to handle certain tasks; the meaning is simply that people cooperate ('at this workplace we all work together as a team'). Such a notion means recognition of the collective character of work activities but also of the collective atmosphere at the workplace. Nevertheless, the probably most common use of the word is that it refers to especially organized groups. These groups may be of two types: those that collaborate more or less permanently and those that are designed for specific purposes (project teams).

Team-working is reported to have become more common over the last decades, although it is hard to draw any firm conclusions on this, as there is a great deal of variation across countries, industries and workplaces (cf. Blyton and Turnbull 2004: 268–70; Cully *et al.* 1999: 42–4). For quite some time now, this way of organizing things has been very popular in management discourse, which – given the trendy character of that kind of discourse – should not be confused with its dissemination in the real world. It still appears that teamwork and project teams are widespread phenomena of high significance for the functioning of working life. The question to be raised is then whether and how team-working fits in with the individualization thesis. I do not want to make any far-reaching generalizations in this respect, but some tentative observations will be supplied. On the one hand, it seems that work teams are often very tight units, with members who are dedicated to achieving certain goals and to working closely together. On the other hand, there may be more room in them for individualism and individualized solutions than in a traditional work organization, among other things because they are often put together only for specific tasks and composed so as to make the best out of individual competences. A team may have very much to benefit from being composed of individuals with a variety of qualifications and characteristics, given that a successful combination can be achieved.

Both in general work teams and in specific project teams, individuals can be expected to be quite dependent upon the group, its way of functioning and its values and norms. A common premise is that team members view work tasks as a responsibility for the group as a whole. Dominant individuals may, nonetheless, have a disproportionate impact on the group; it even occurs that they do most of the work in order to get it done their way or – to put it in more positive terms – make the joint assignment succeed. However, we can then question whether the notion of team-working is relevant any longer, but nor does individualization look like an appropriate notion; most of all the situation described seems to be a matter of other members acting less as individuals, since they give in to a self-appointed leader. In conclusion, team-working represents a mixture of collectivism and individualism, but the major point to be made here is that collectivism is an indispensable element in it; otherwise we could not talk about teams.

Social comparisons

Another perspective with relevance for the collective–individual dimension of employment relationships is the social comparison approach. The underlying idea is that people tend to make comparisons with one another and this also happens with respect to employment and working conditions. As an example we can think of individualized pay systems – that are indeed common and can be considered an aspect of individualization – and discuss some of their possible consequences. If such systems are fully developed, wages and salaries do not depend upon collective bargaining at all; the remunerations employees receive are then an affair only between them and the employer. Individualized pay systems are frequently based on the principle that the financial rewards should be positively and closely correlated with performances, although it is not always obvious how these are to be gauged. It may then be asked if employees compare their wages or salaries with those of their colleagues and, if so, what consequences follow. To throw some light upon these questions, it is convenient to turn to social comparison or reference 'group' theory.

Before going into the subject matter, a few remarks are made with regard to the label reference 'group' theory. This label is primarily associated with the work by Robert Merton (and his collaborator Alice Rossi). A central dividing line goes between groups that have a normative function – by defining the values and norms to be adhered to – and groups that serve as objects of comparisons (Merton 1964: Chs. 8–9). The entity referred to may be a group, a collective, a social category, or an individual (the model individual). It thus seems somewhat misleading to use reference 'group' theory as a general label for this approach, but it is an established term (cf. Merton 1964: 284; see also Hyman and Brough 1975: 40 n.10). This was now a long time ago and today it may be possible just to talk about reference theory. There are numerous issues to be dealt with in relation to it – many of which are discussed by Merton and Rossi themselves – but I leave that aside here; my point of departure is merely that this perspective can be fruitful when we want to examine certain issues connected with the individualization thesis.

Under the assumption that employees, at least to some extent, compare wages with one another, we can consider some possible consequences of individualized wage systems at the workplace. Let us imagine a worker who, after negotiations with the employer, gets a substantial pay rise and whose immediate reaction is one of great satisfaction. However, when, after a while, he/she gets to know that several of her closest colleagues have got even better deals, her initial satisfaction instantly turns into dissatisfaction. One interpretation of the outcome is that the employer has made a more positive evaluation of the colleagues' performances. This is not the only possible interpretation – as we shall see in a moment – but it may appear reasonable and, judging from his/her dissatisfaction, the worker is not happy with that assessment. As the theory teaches us, people do not just compare themselves with anybody but with significant others; the individual's reaction in this example suggests that his/her colleagues make up a relevant reference category. Social comparisons are likely to be particularly sensible if they involve workmates on the same hierarchical level and with the same or similar education and experience.

At the bottom of the worker's dissatisfaction is the double function of the wage. On the one hand, the wage gives purchasing power and, on the other hand, it is a symbol of what the employee is worth. From the angle of purchasing power only, an individual is generally likely to regard more money in the wallet as a positive thing. In contrast, as a symbol of value, a large wage increase appears as a negative experience for the individual, above all if others receive more (as in the example above). Under such circumstances, getting more money for consumption does not supply much consolation, as the gap to the colleagues indicates that they have a larger value for the employer and this is likely to become known also by others.

As mentioned above, the individual can make interpretations other than that the employer by giving others a higher raise in pay considers them more valuable. One possibility is that the outcome is a matter of favoritism; the employer does not really judge the colleagues' performances as better but has nevertheless rewarded them – due to personal preferences or other factors – more than they, properly, would deserve. This does not necessarily, however, lead to any improvement as regards the first individual's satisfaction; what is preferable may be a matter of taste: having an employer who unjustly considers others to be worth more or having an employer who does not make such an assessment but still gives them more. Even if favoritism – or the suspicion that there is favoritism – would be better for the individual, it may be just as bad for the workplace atmosphere. Another interpretation is that the colleagues have been more militant in their demands and that the employer has given in to their militancy. It is not clear whether this would be a better alternative for the dissatisfied worker, but it might be subjectively advantageous to explain the outcome in terms of either one's own lacking militancy or the weakness of the employer, or both. Yet, the feeling of not being able to look after his/her own interests may have a destructive effect upon the worker's self-confidence and self-respect.

Individualized wage systems can thus instigate dissatisfaction and irritation, which is not to say that they always – or even often – do so. It is an empirical question to what extent this occurs, but when it happens, we may expect some damaging impact on workers' motivation. Of course, those who have benefited from the system, or from the way it is applied, may feel more motivated, unless they have a bad conscience about it. There is also some risk that the whole atmosphere at a workplace is negatively affected. If workers who are not among the best in terms of performance (supposing we can decide that) nonetheless come out among the best in terms of payment, the whole incentive structure may be at stake. Equity issues are by definition social in character and they play, and will continue to play, an important part in workplace relations.

The entire problem can perhaps be disposed of if wage levels are kept secret. In many workplaces this is also more or less the case and workers simply do not talk about their wages or are even urged by their employer not to do so. An atmosphere or rules of that kind may thus eliminate or reduce the risk that people become dissatisfied, but it is not always easy to keep secrets and they may leak out, perhaps with such effects as those mentioned above. It can be questioned whether a situation in which social comparisons regarding individualized remunerations would cease to exist completely is a credible scenario; at least it would require repressive measures or self-censorship. We must keep in mind that wage levels are not the only objects for assessment; there are all kinds of other working conditions that can be compared: work tasks, workplace facilities, training opportunities, work schedules, etc. Individualized pay systems will probably spread the culture of wage secrecy, but all social comparisons will hardly vanish. It appears unlikely that the process of individualization would entirely do away with the tendency among people to contrast themselves with others, given that there are many dimensions along which this can be done. Comparisons seem to be a general condition of social life and will probably continue to be so, as long as people live and work together.

The drive toward professionalization

Workers have obviously been able to form trade unions and thus to some extent overcome their internal divisions, although this has not been done once and for all. There are continuous processes implying disaggregation and fragmentation of interests and collective organization. The tension between collective and individual aspects of employment relationships has never been overcome and within the framework of the present type of labor market we cannot expect that it ever will. Especially in one context it appears that collectivism is on the upswing and that is among incumbents or potential incumbents of professional occupations.

Professional jobs are generally associated with a considerable degree of individualism. To be a doctor, a lawyer, or to have some other kind of professional occupation requires long academic education, based on theoretical knowledge (see, e.g., Abbott 1988; Freidson 1986, 1994, 2001; Larson 1977; MacDonald 1995). In return, the jobholder is given ample discretion in defining how to carry out the work; the underlying assumption is that he/she is the expert and must therefore be allowed to decide what is best to do in various situations. In general, these occupations also mean intellectually stimulating work assignments, relatively high incomes, good career opportunities, and other advantages. Professionals tend to have individualistic leanings, related to the role of individual achievement in their lives. Their attitudes are to a large extent shaped by the effort it takes to obtain an academic degree and once the education is finished there is competition for attractive positions as well as for remunerations and resources; individual credentials and qualifications will thus continue to play a vital part.

The proportion of professionals tends to grow in society, on the one hand, because of an expansion among the already established professions and, on the other hand, because incumbents of certain other occupations struggle to reach professional status. Without going into concrete details, I present some ideas regarding the collective efforts to defend the interests of professionals and to make certain occupational categories become recognized as professionals. In both cases, the main actors consist of occupational associations and trade unions. Although these two kinds of organizations usually cooperate, they also differ from one another in terms of goals and strategies; the latter are generally more focused on wage and salary issues, working hours, and other working conditions, while the former tend to concentrate on the education required, authorization issues, and job contents.

Professional associations and trade unions are oriented toward defending the status of particular occupations, while organizations striving for professionalization want certain other occupations to obtain professional status. In the first case it is a matter of trying to keep a monopoly in the labor market for people with a specialized, longer academic education and recognized credentials, and in the second instance the aim is to establish a similar monopoly for some other categories, which at bottom means achieving collective mobility. Efforts to reach professional status may be described as usurpation – to use Frank Parkin's (1979: Ch. 5) term – but, at least if they take place within a new vocational branch, they do not have to include such strategies at all.

Organizational endeavors to defend or reach professional status are by definition collective, but this should not ignore the fact that professional organizations favor a great deal of individualism in employment relationships, for example individualized pay systems. Thus we encounter a mixture of collectivism and individualism; both are important, but in order to protect the professional monopoly or to enhance a process of professionalization some kind of joint action is necessary. Action is then often directed toward exerting influence on how jobs, and the appurtenant educational requirements, are to be defined and who can be a candidate for them. If employers neglect that their employees have the education generally demanded for a given job, we can expect professional associations or trade unions to react. In such a situation, these organizations are not likely to treat employment relationships as an issue between the employer and the individual only.

To conclude, efforts among organizations to promote professional interests or to obtain professional status for certain occupations represent something other than the struggles of traditional trade unions. All these endeavors, however, presuppose collectivism, which is simply part and parcel of every attempt to mobilize people for a common purpose. Professional associations have their own way of combining individualism and collectivism; they develop specific mixtures in this respect. Because professions and professionalization appear to become increasingly important elements in contemporary societies, we can expect them to have a considerable impact in the future. In a nutshell, this means individualism in certain respects but simultaneously a quantity of collectivism in others.

Pulling together

The issue dealt with in this chapter is the individual–collective character of employment relationships. Ideally these relationships can be a matter, on the one hand, between the employer and the individual worker and, on the other hand, between the employer and a collective of workers, but in real life there is often a mixture of different ways of regulation. Also employers may act collectively, but it seems that employees are more interested in joint regulation. Generally, collectivism represents a way for the subordinate actors in the labor market to gain power in relation to the dominant actors. Workers simply use the strength springing from their numbers to get employers to make concessions, whereas employers more easily get their will through if they negotiate with workers individually. This does not mean that employers are completely uninterested in collective arrangements or that subordinate employees always strive for such solutions. The two main parties' aims in these respects are more complex, but they tend to lean toward individual and collective settlements respectively. Usually, it is more difficult for actors to act jointly than individually, as it requires that they find common denominators and are able to unite around them. To close up in relation to employers, workers must overcome all kinds of dividing factors; this is rarely an easy task and history is full of examples of how workforce divisions have undermined common efforts. Yet, to some extent employees have been able to form strong collective organizations and to impose regulation of employment relationships with broad coverage.

A salient thesis in present-day sociology is that individualization is on the move. I do not deny that this thesis is correct – actually I think that some version of it is correct – but the justification for it is often unconvincingly argued in the literature. The discussions on individualization are rarely based on very robust empirical evidence and when empirical statements are made we have to establish whether or not they are reliable. Still, this criticism should not make us go too far by throwing the baby out with the bathwater; we must seriously pay attention to various developments of de-collectivization and individualization, but avoid carrying things to an excess.

The individual–collective dimension will continue to be relevant in analyses of employment relationships. It basically follows from the essential structure in the labor market, according to which employers own or control the resources necessary for the production of goods and services and the non-propertied are more or less obliged to hire out their labor power. The relationship stemming from this structure is to a great degree asymmetrical to the advantage of employers, which gives workers a motive to organize, thereby restricting their vulnerability and reducing the insecurities involved. Although the emphasis can switch from one epoch to another, the individual–collective dimension will remain significant.

There are many important factors that do not seem to be yielding. Work in contemporary societies is basically a collective effort and, as long as this is the case, large numbers of people have good reason to find collective solutions to their situation. As pointed out above, Durkheim has argued that increasing specialization and differentiation will create more space for individualism and that modern society will be more organically integrated. Even with increasing individualism, the collective features in working life are striking and they are to a large extent likely to prevail. This holds not only as regards the overriding societal division of labor but also at the workplace level. The popular use of team-working in principle represents a collective way of organization, although it may leave plenty of scope for individuality.

Social comparisons are another important feature of social life, including working life, and also individualized workers are likely to compare themselves with one another or other significant reference categories. It is often by comparing their own situation with that of others that workers start thinking in terms of injustices; in other words, this also entails a potential for action. Normally, in order to do something collectively, people must believe that injustices are possible to remedy; only if individuals find that they are disadvantaged because of the same reasons can we expect them to take joint action. In that way, social comparisons provide some prerequisites for collectivism and they are likely to occur even in situations characterized by far-reaching individualism.

The contradictions of the present trend toward individualization become very clear when we consider efforts to defend the professional status of certain occupations and to extend it to others. Professions are associated with a sizable degree of individualism due to the role played by educational achievements, competition over positions, remunerations, and resources, and a rather strong career orientation among jobholders. At the same time, every struggle to defend and expand the professional status of occupations is by definition a collective struggle. The social strata at issue tend to grow in numbers and they are likely to make up an increasingly more important element in society. In this context, the important thing is that professions represent a specific combination of individual and collective features.

Even though times are now in favor of individualism, collectivism has not totally evaporated; it is still there, although it seems to have a weaker position than for a long time. Presently, there is little reason to herald a comeback for workers' joint mustering of strength, but we should perhaps not be all that sure. Under all circumstances, collectivism will continue to play a role also in a more individualized world and the tension between the two dimensions will exist also in the future.

8
Labor Market Flexibility

During the last few decades, labor market flexibility has been a widely and intensely debated issue. The discussion has often conveyed the impression that everything is more in flux than ever before and it is assumed that actors in the labor market must constantly be prepared to make adjustments of various kinds. The story goes something like the following. Everybody – employers and employees alike – must be ready for change in different ways. Firms confront increasing pressures from market competition, because their products must be in demand and possible to sell at prices by an ample margin above costs. As a result, they have to be oriented toward developing products that fit in with specialized consumer preferences. To be competitive also requires continuous renewal of technology and organizational solutions; it is not enough to be responsive to consumer demands, but there must also be an aim to look after costs, find the best buy of machinery and raw materials, streamline the production process, improve the coordination of activities, and downsize the workforce to a minimum, that is, make production lean, on time, etc. There are thus unceasing demands for adjustment and flexibility represents the ethos of a new era; that is the message.

Employees will indeed be affected by these developments. They are supposed not only to change jobs once in a while but also to be willing to switch from one occupation to another, which in turn means acquiring new skills. It has become common to think about lifelong employment as something that belongs to the past. Restrictive employment protection legislation is being looked upon in the same way and deregulation is consequently on the agenda. Individualized and performance-related wage systems are favored and workers must be prepared for all kinds of adjustment, for example to alter their working hours in accordance with the operative needs of their employing organization. Although many demands are likely to be rejected by those concerned, flexibility stands for possibilities and openings; even the word itself has positive connotations. At any rate, we can expect to find tensions regarding flexibility issues; the adjustments that are required can be positive for employees, but they are sometimes very unfavorable. It must be kept in mind that the consequences vary substantially across social categories, which makes it relevant to identify winners and losers respectively and to ask if the same categories of people always or mostly come out on the winning side or the losing side.

The discussion entails another peculiar ambiguity. On the one hand, some observers tell us that the contemporary labor market is already flexible and will never again become what it used to be. On the other hand, there are also those who claim that the labor market still contains too much rigidity, which they suggest must be done away with in order to stimulate economic growth and lower unemployment. The first statement can perhaps be interpreted as a conscious or unconscious application of the self-fulfilling prophecy, implying that real consequences will follow from a definition of a situation as real (Merton 1964: 421–2). Thus, telling everybody that the labor market is flexible might be a means of promoting flexibility. There are, however, limits to this, particularly if it is simultaneously argued that the labor market is in many ways characterized by rigidity.

One problem in these discussions is that the concept of flexibility is often not clearly defined or not defined at all. Conceptual vagueness always helps people put forward badly argued and contradictory statements, as they can then more easily escape counter-arguments. Yet, there have actually been quite a few attempts to specify the notion of flexibility; it is not the lack of such attempts that is the problem, but rather the difficulty to create a useful and common terminology that can be accepted as the best way of describing the phenomena to be examined. Behind this difficulty lies the fact that the issues are to a large extent controversial. Therefore, in this chapter I first discuss the concept of flexibility. Some flexibility typologies are also presented and I suggest a typology of my own.

Having made certain clarifications as to the concept of flexibility and having distinguished some of its principal forms, I take up a number of issues associated with these forms. The current interaction between employers and employees embraces many different demands for adjustments and the consequences for the actors involved vary a great deal. Various solutions are sometimes functional alternatives to one another, but they can also be combined. As a matter of fact, we often find combinations of adjustments or what I refer to as 'flexibility mixes' and their role is touched upon. Finally, I briefly return to the question why flexibility or, rather, specific forms of it have come to the forefront in the public debate over the last decades.

The concept of labor market flexibility

Social scientists frequently start their discussions about flexibility by suggesting that the concept has a range of different, unclarified meanings and then go on to provide their own definition. Today it cannot reasonably be argued that we lack worked-out definitions of the crucial concept; if we still discover conceptual confusion, it is not because no one has tried to provide clarity, but rather because researchers have not been successful in doing so or at least not been able to make others adopt their solutions.

Looking for the simplest possible concept of flexibility, we can turn to an article by Danièle Meulders and Luc Wilkin. These two authors have formulated a straightforward definition, according to which flexibility stands for actors' 'capacity to adjust according to change' (Meulders and Wilkin 1987: 5). It is a useful point of departure for the discussion, although, unquestionably, the concept proposed needs to be elaborated further, as several other aspects must also be considered. In the following, a number of specifications will be added.

As suggested above, flexibility has a positive ring to it. With some irony, we may ask who can be against flexibility and who wants to be regarded as 'inflexible' or even 'rigid' (see, e.g., Karlsson and Eriksson 2000: 14; Standing 1999: 49). The concept often has an explicit positive value load, but sometimes this is hidden and needs to be revealed. A crucial issue is always on whose terms flexibility is supposed to take place or whose perspective we take as our point of departure. Guy Standing (1999: 81) has got it right in pointing out that when somebody 'calls on workers or on employers to be flexible, it usually means that he wants them to make concessions'. In other words, flexibility is often shorthand for some actors' demands that others adjust to their will.

We may prefer to work with value-neutral concepts, but the positive connotations of the term flexibility are difficult to eliminate or avoid. One way of dealing with this problem is to adopt the solution presented by the Swedish sociologist Dan Jonsson (2005), who simply suggests that the concept of flexibility be reserved for desirable variability. His definition requires that at least someone wishes to see a given kind of variation become implemented but not that everybody makes the same assessment. I soon go somewhat further into the specificities of Jonsson's conceptual proposal. Before that I take up another issue, namely whether flexibility should be taken to refer to actual or potential adjustments.

Potential and actual adjustment

In Meulders and Wilkin's (1987: 5) definition it is presupposed that changes occur to which actors may or must adapt and the focus lies on their capacity to do so; hence, flexibility is about potential rather than actual adjustment. In addition, potentiality implies that it is not enough to consider actors' capacities, but that their willingness also needs to be taken into account. It does not help very much if an employer or a worker has the ability to do something, if he/she does not want to do it and has the power to resist or refrain from doing it. Even with respect to the flexibility of systems (see further below), it may be relevant to distinguish between potential and actual adjustments, but 'willingness' then becomes an irrelevant dimension, as systems are not actors and have no will.

An elementary example can illustrate the difference between potential and actual flexibility and some of the difficulties involved. Let us imagine a man who is employed and is both willing and able to switch to another job if changes in the labor market would make such a move necessary. Since these changes have not occurred, there has been no motive for him to do anything. In fact, he has stayed in the same job for many years; his position has been secure, nothing clearly better – worth leaving for – has appeared, and his desire for a general change in life has not been strong enough to trigger a move. How should we then characterize this individual? Can he be considered flexible or not in terms of employment? He is willing, or at least not unwilling, and able to take on something else; he has the potential, but it has never been carried into action.

We find almost exactly the same discussion regarding the concept of mobility, probably because, to a considerable extent, it covers the same phenomena; mobility may also refer to both potential and actual changes. Herbert Parnes (1954: 13) has pointed out that this concept can have three different meanings. The first has to do with a worker's capacity or ability to move 'from one job to another, or into and out of employment, or into and out of the labor force', the second alludes to 'their willingness or propensity to make such moves', and the third refers to 'their actual movement'. Evidently, the first two meanings, that is, the individual's capacity and willingness to move, can be put into the category of potential mobility. The author's conclusion is that no matter what conceptual solution researchers prefer, when it comes to measuring mobility, they must very much rely on data on actual movements (Parnes 1954: 20). It is added that the usefulness of data is increased if we can identify voluntary quits, because forced job shifts have little to do with positive motivation. We should also draw attention to the studies in which people are asked about their propensities to be mobile (cf. Parnes 1968: 483).

These conclusions on mobility also apply to the concept of flexibility. Researchers who have tried to measure flexibility empirically have often ended up with data on actual rather than potential adjustments. A main reason is the difficulty to determine whether individuals are ready to adjust when things change, in particular when we want to have such information about large numbers of people in the labor market. Still, there are many studies on people's readiness to move to another place of residence, accept a pay cut, etc. (see, e.g., van den Berg, Furåker and Johansson 1997). The limitation with such data is that they only capture individuals' own statements about what they would do in a hypothetical situation and that there may be a considerable gap between declarations and actions. This is often as far as we can get, but we should not treat these data as uninteresting; even if respondents exaggerate their readiness to do certain things, it would be surprising if response patterns were entirely uncorrelated with people's actual behavior.

It is worth noting that certain 'objective' data reflect potential rather than actual adjustment; as an example information on temporary employment can be mentioned (see, e.g., Felstead and Jewson 1999a). Knowing the proportion of temporary employees at a workplace does not in itself tell us if there will be adjustments in the size of the workforce. What this kind of information can tell us is with what easiness the employer can lay off people; if there are quite a few employees on short-term contracts, the potential for large, rapid downsizing is greater. It is, however, rather common that temporary workers get their contracts prolonged and this means that no change takes place. Very much the same can be said about part-time work, another type of non-standard employment that is often considered to be an indicator of flexibility. In particular, many women work part-time, due to family obligations, and they may do so year after year. These employment relations do not necessarily involve more change than others (cf. Hakim 1996: 68; Rubery, Horrell and Burchell 1994: 213–14).

The overriding question in this section is whether or not potential or actual adjustment is the best basis for the flexibility concept. Although we should have the ambition to take potential adjustments as the point of departure, in concrete research it is not always feasible to get the desired relevant information and our strivings for the best possible result should not be allowed to become the enemy of the good by making us keep away from the second best. It is a fairly common problem in labor market flexibility studies that there are no data available on potential but only on actual adjustments. This is not always easy to do anything about, but by collecting many different types of data and by putting together various pieces of information we can make the picture more detailed and richer.

A conceptual scheme

In the terminology used by Jonsson (2005), flexibility means desirable variability, which in turn has reference to the potential of an actor to generate desirable variation: change or diversity. Change is variation from one point in time to another (diachronic aspect), whereas diversity stands for a set of responses that the actor can apply at a given point in time (synchronic aspect). The distinction can be illustrated in the following way. A worker who participates in a training program will acquire new skills and the transformation that takes place from the start to the end of the program can be characterized as change. If he/she at the latter point in time has the capability of carrying out a number of different work tasks – that is, is multi-skilled – the notion of diversity is relevant. Instead of 'desirable variability', I prefer to use the somewhat simpler expression 'desirable varia-

Table 8.1 Relationships between flexibility, inflexibility, stability, and instability

Variation	Yes	No
Desirable	Flexibility	Stability
Undesirable	Instability	Inflexibility

tion'; the former notion emphasizes the potential of an actor to generate change or diversity, but that is probably understood anyway.

Jonsson presents a scheme with four interrelated concepts – flexibility, instability, stability, and inflexibility – and they are all useful. As mentioned above, with respect to flexibility, I prefer 'variation' instead of 'variability' and this will have consequences also for the other three concepts. Accordingly, I present a slightly modified version of Jonsson's conceptual scheme (see Table 8.1).

The ideas behind the scheme can be described as follows. Variation does not have to be desirable but is sometimes undesirable, which makes it relevant to identify a 'mirror' concept of flexibility, that is, instability, which thus stands for undesirable variation. For example, the owner of a manufacturing firm may wish to have working time flexibility so that employees work shorter hours in periods when the firm is producing below full capacity. From the workers' point of view this can be very undesirable, simply because it means instability in terms of income.

Additionally, we should make a distinction between variation and non-variation and also the latter state of affairs can be characterized as either desirable or undesirable. As a consequence, we get two further concepts: stability and inflexibility. Stability means desirable non-variation and can be exemplified by a firm in which the employer has the ambition to make the already contracted workers stay in their jobs, since this is considered, for the time being, to be the best solution for developing the activities of the firm. If, at the same workplace, the employees or at least some of them instead would like to have some immediate job rotation or rejuvenation, they would perhaps describe the situation in terms of inflexbility.

Units of analysis

There is a further aspect to be considered, namely the unit to be chosen for the analysis. We have already seen that flexibility can mean very different things for various categories of actors. Employers and workers, or groups of workers, are therefore now and then at variance with one another on flexibility issues. We might add that the first-mentioned category is often short for the employing organization, but there is sometimes a good point in keeping the two analytically distinct. The employer is one actor in the organization, the principal to use the principal-agent terminology, and in that sense merely a part of it. What is good for the one is not necessarily always good for the other, although we tend to think of it in that way and although this can also be true.

Furthermore, the objects of study do not have to be actors. As Jonsson (2005) has pointed out, we may as well be interested in analyzing the flexibility of systems, for example production systems and the labor market as a whole. Nevertheless, only actors can alter systems, which we can see and illustrate by analyzing various suggestions that labor market flexibility needs to be increased; those behind these proposals are indeed likely to have some actor in mind. One common opinion is that employment protection statutory rules should be alleviated and the addressee is the legislative assembly or rather the political parties. Demands for more flexibility in the labor market as a system may, however, be meant directly for workers or jobseekers and the assumption is then that these individual actors should adopt another attitude and be prepared to make adjustments.

To make one more comment, systems are not actors, but this does not prevent us from talking about desired and undesired variation and non-variation. For example, if legislated employment protection is weakened, this is likely to be a positive type of change for some actors but a negative change for others and we may then be interested in identifying who are the winners and who are the losers. In other words, even if the system level is chosen as the unit of analysis, the consequences for different actors should not be overlooked.

Types of flexibility

It is easier to find typologies of flexibility than systematically elaborated definitions of it in the literature. For example, in various publications John Atkinson (1984: 28; 1987: 89–91; see also Atkinson and Meager 1986: 3–4) has suggested that we distinguish between three or four types: (a) functional flexibility ('so that employees can be redeployed quickly and smoothly between activities and tasks'); (b) numerical flexibility ('so that headcount can be quickly and easily increased or decreased in line with even short term changes in the level of demand for labour'); (c) financial or pay flexibility ('so that pay and other employment costs reflect the state of supply and demand in the external labour market' but it also includes 'a shift to new pay and remuneration systems that facilitate either numerical or functional flexibility'); and (d) distancing ('displacement of employment contracts by commercial contracts, as exemplified by subcontracting').

Meulders and Wilkin (1987: 6–9) have presented a similar typology but with a somewhat different set of categories. Their first two types, wage and numerical flexibility, are basically the same as (c) and (b) in Atkinson's scheme (although Atkinson uses the term 'financial or pay flexibility' for the first category mentioned). The third type suggested by Meulders and

Wilkin covers technical-organizational aspects and, on the whole, it corresponds to Atkinson's functional flexibility but may be somewhat wider, as it explicitly includes also the combination of 'new techniques of organisation and diversified equipment into an overall structure' (Meulders and Wilkin 1987: 8). Finally, the authors introduce the category of working time flexibility. It refers to how working hours and work schedules are adapted to various demands. In fact, this category is partly included in Atkinson's definition of numerical flexibility that covers adjustments in the amount of work carried out due to changing demands.

Researchers commonly stick to these three or four types or some variants of them, but some have added a few other categories. Standing (2002: 33) has presented the longest list with seven flexibility categories that I have hitherto encountered; besides the four most common types already mentioned his inventory includes 'organizational', 'job structure', and 'labor force' flexibility. We may even come up with further suggestions, although there is then a risk that the categories will overlap one another, which they to some extent appear to do already in Standing's typology.

The classification I suggest contains five categories: (a) employment flexibility; (b) work process flexibility; (c) working time flexibility; (d) workplace or spatial flexibility; and (e) wage flexibility. With the exception of category (d), these are all relatively close to those presented by Atkinson, Meulders and Wilkin, and others. Taken as a whole, my typology does not deviate that much from those mentioned above, but there are some differences that are detailed below. The following scheme is related to five basic dimensions of the employer–employee relationship: employment itself, the work process, working time, the workplace, and the financial remunerations.

Employment flexibility, which is my first category, refers to the employment relationship itself. It is arguably a better term than numerical flexibility, although the latter is very close and refers to the most commonly debated question in this connection, that is, whether or how fast employers can adjust the size of their workforce in accordance with what they consider necessary. Yet, the term employment flexibility is broader and therefore, as will become clear below, more adequate. The second category, work process flexibility, is about the potential of employers and workers to make adjustments regarding the organization of work tasks – and the skills related to them – as well as with respect to work intensity. Including the latter aspect implies an obvious difference compared with many other typologies. My third category, working time flexibility, is a matter of both the number of working hours and the allocation of work over the day, the week, or some other relevant period of time. It covers not only changes in terms of hours worked but also rearrangements of work schedules in adjustment to fluid circumstances. Fourth, I identify workplace or spatial flexibility that refers to such things as whether employees have to change workplaces and to what extent they can decide where to carry out their work. The final flexibility type is wage flexibility, which stands for adjustments in pay systems and in individuals' pay levels.

Issues of flexibility

In this section I discuss a number of issues associated with the five types of labor market flexibility defined above. The debate on flexibility has too narrowly focused on a few aspects but neglected others and it is my aim to widen the perspective at least a little bit by taking up certain other, often disregarded, dimensions and complexities. In a given situation, there are frequently several different kinds of adjustments that can be implemented and to some extent they represent functional alternatives to one another. Approximately the same goal can be reached in different ways and the one and same measure is commonly associated with divergent consequences for various actors; we thus need to develop an awareness of the multiplicity of aspects involved.

Employment flexibility

As mentioned above, the discussion on employment flexibility is very much focused on whether and how quickly employers can adjust the number of employees in accordance with changing needs of the organization. However, this is only one aspect of a more complex set of issues. To begin, in respect of the perspective of the employer, we easily realize that it is costly to have more people employed than demanded to do the work at hand (it can also be costly to have too few workers). The employer can thus be expected to attempt to adapt the size of the workforce, up or down, as needs are shifting. Among other things, this can be accomplished through voluntary quits, simply because such exits are often quite common at workplaces; some leave for other jobs, some become students, some retire, and so on. In order to reduce the workforce the employer can then just discontinue the positions that become vacant, but in times of rapid change this may not be enough; instead workers will have to be laid off. Especially for profit-oriented firms, it can be an urgent issue of how fast downsizing can take place and it is thus important what kind of employment protection workers have through legislation and negotiated agreements. Using the terminology presented above, employers are likely to place restrictive such rules under the category of inflexibility.

Employment protection legislation has been very much on the agenda over the last decades. One reason is that restrictions are supposed to make employers hesitant to hire workers, since it may be too costly to dismiss them again quickly if necessary. Thus, while legislation aims at protecting the already employed, it may also be an obstacle to new recruitment, resulting in lower employment and higher unemployment. In a comparison including a large number of OECD member states, the United States was shown to have weakest employment protection in the late 1990s (as well as in the late 1980s), with the United Kingdom not so far behind, whereas rules were particularly strict in southern European countries (OECD 1999: 66–7). The principal conclusion in the study is, though, that overall unemployment levels cannot be explained by the severity in employment security legislation (OECD 1999: 88). However, it appears that strict rules may have certain effects on the demography of unemployment, so that prime-age men proportionately less often become unemployed compared to youths and women.

We should also look more closely at the specific rules in employment protection legislation. Even when, on the whole, these rules are strict, it may be relatively easy to sign temporary contracts and this can be a compensatory mechanism for employers. In contrast, in countries with generally weak legislation, employers do not have that much to gain from the use of time-limited employment. It is therefore by no means surprising that a much lower proportion of workers are on temporary contracts in the United States compared to southern Europe where employment protection is clearly stricter (Hudson 2002: 40–2).

Employers share the need to have a workforce sized after the activities to be done, but it makes a difference whether they are profit-oriented and operate in a competitive market or not. If profit-oriented and subject to competitive pressures, they are often confronted with the choice of having to downsize the number of staff or ending up with a deficit that eventually may lead to bankruptcy. Also government agencies or institutions sometimes run into financial problems, but their problems tend to emerge more slowly and the political process to deal with them is slower. It thus takes more time to adjust the size of the workforce to a level that can be afforded within the limits of public budgets and that corresponds to actual needs. The call for employment flexibility can be similar no matter whether employers operate in the market or not, but the pressure is normally much more intense in the market.

In case the demand for labor is rapidly declining, downsizing is likely to be the solution for the employer but not always. A change for the better may come too quickly for that; it happens that recessions last only for a brief period of time and that the business cycle instead soon turns upward. Workers who have been laid off may then be needed again, but once they are gone it can be difficult to get them back or to recruit others. What at some point in time looked like flexibility – a variation desired by the employer – has thus become instability – to use the terminology suggested above. In particular, the work organization will meet with problems, if individuals with job-specific skills – that take a long time to acquire – are lost. One strategy for the employer to handle this problem is labor hoarding, that is, to keep workers over a recession so that no delay will occur in speeding up production when demand increases. In such a case, flexibility is a matter of keeping a desirable diversity, that is, of maintaining a repertoire of possibilities instead of making adjustments first in one direction and then in another. Diversity is needed to create stability and this illustrates one of my main points here, namely that flexibility and stability often go hand in hand.

With respect to downsizing, the employee perspective is normally very different; there is hardly any reason for workers to be happy about such measures, although the consequences may vary substantially across the workforce. For people who are about to leave their job anyway – for another job, to become pensioners, to start further education, and so on – it is likely to be more or less of no consequence. However, even if an employee is on his/her way out, it may be positive for him/her to keep a range of options open as long as possible and to avoid the negative consequences associated with being sacked. Others, who need to have a job for years to come, may experience it as a dramatic event to be forced out of work, particularly if they are not that young and do not have overwhelming prospects of finding alternative employment. While for the employer downsizing may be a necessary change, it commonly represents instability for workers.

At times, employers want to increase their workforce quickly and under such circumstances it is desirable that workers are available and respond to their demands. One way of ensuring this is to overbid other employers in terms of pay and benefits, thereby attracting workers from other workplaces. Overbids are above all likely to occur in superheated labor markets, that is, when it is difficult to find workers, although – in a given case – it may only be a matter of recruiting people with unique skills. We can thus expect that employers do not always have the same view about what norms should apply in the market. What is flexibility for one of them can sometimes be instability for another and attempts to recruit workers with generous offers may be met by counter-bids.

Two sources for recruitment are the unemployed and those who are outside of the labor force. In these cases, employers face another set of circumstances that affect employment flexibility. The incentive to take a job may not be very strong among potential recruits, if the unemployment benefits or other types of social benefits match the pay offered; to use another terminology, benefits are likely to affect jobseekers' reservation wage, that is, the lowest pay at which they will take a job. If the reservation wage exceeds what the employer can come up with, the chances for recruitment will be relatively small. At the same time, we also need to take other aspects into account, such as the fact that benefits will eventually be exhausted and that the individual may then have little choice. In addition, having a job is associated with remunerations other than pecuniary remunerations only.

As discussed in Chapter 5, family obligations can be obstacles in relation to demands for labor. Although housewives may be interested in finding a job, it is not always possible to recruit them, unless the employer can provide part-time employment and work schedules that fit their situation. The crucial dimension thus appears to be working time flexibility (see further below), which is an analytically separate category but linked to the prospects of recruiting new workers. One facility that can be vital in a situation such as that mentioned is childcare; accordingly, the lack of it may be a key element of inflexibility in the system, insofar as parents or at least one of them, usually the woman, cannot be available for the labor market.

In another situation, an employer needs to recruit people quickly but wants to employ them only for a short period, when the organization's activities peak, for example during the tourist or harvest season. The important and often decisive thing is then to what extent and under what conditions it is possible to hire people on a temporary basis. Employers can be expected to favor as much freedom as possible in this respect, but the conditions for such contracts can be narrowly regulated through legislation and collective agreements. A relatively new development, to which I will return shortly, is the expansion of temporary work agencies.

A functional alternative to hiring more people or even to keeping the already employed is outsourcing. It can be a matter of side activities to an organization's principal business, such as cleaning and restaurant services. Whatever is demanded is then instead bought in the market, perhaps through a long-term contract. Outsourcing is not a new phenomenon, but it has met with considerable interest in recent decades (see, e.g., Milgate 2001; Reilly and Tamkin 1996). The main advantage for the employer is that no employment relationship has to be established with those who carry out the work, which is a way of avoiding burdensome and costly obligations.

For workers, employment flexibility usually means something different to employers' interpretations. It may indeed be a very negative experience to be laid off involuntarily. The fact that this can happen at short notice suggests instability and insecurity. However, workers, for their part, may consider it very important to be able to leave a job quickly and thus not be bound by long-term contracts. If this kind of employment flexibility is denied or limited, an individual may remain longer than desired in a job that he/she – for one reason or another – does not want to be in. Now, the clauses of a contract do not have to be symmetric for the two parties involved, but the notice period to be observed may be longer for one of them; this may partly be a question of the power relations between the two sides.

If, during a given period, large numbers of employees at a workplace quit their jobs, it may lead to significant problems for the employer. High turnover is normally expensive both in terms of direct recruitment costs and the time it takes for newcomers to learn the job and adapt themselves to it. Likewise, with an insufficient number of employees who have longer experience at the workplace, many different problems can arise in the production process, in relation to customers, etc. Voluntary turnover is a kind of employment flexibility reflecting the will of workers and high turnover rates can represent a substantial degree of instability for employers. In such a situation the latter may try to promote stability, for example by offering gratification and benefit systems to keep at least a core workforce. This reminds us of the discussion in Chapter 3 on why and how internal labor markets are established and we thus see a connection between such labor markets and the issues of employment flexibility and stability. It should be repeated that in the recent debates on labor market flexibility employers' need for a stable workforce has often been greatly underestimated.

Temporary work agencies

In a short time, temporary work agencies have become an increasingly important element in modern labor markets. Their role has sometimes been widely exaggerated, but their share of the labor market has no doubt grown in many countries in recent years (see, e.g., Storrie 2002: 27–8; Bergström and Storrie 2003). The business concept of temporary work agencies is that they hire people for the purpose of offering them to other employers, thereby providing flexible manpower resources. It might be considered the ideal solution for employers who need to fill their vacancies quickly and who just want to keep the newcomers for a limited period of time or are unsure of what they want to do in a long-term perspective.

The question is then what employment in temporary work agencies means to workers. To provide an answer one has to look at existing employment contracts, which is an empirical task beyond the purpose of this book. Let me make the observation that these contracts are very different across countries and across agencies. Theoretically, however, being employed by a temporary work agency does not necessarily mean that workers have a very insecure or unstable position. They may stay with an employer for a while and then switch to another without any detrimental effects on their basic employment security, which all the time is with the agency. It thus depends upon this relationship whether or not agency workers have reasonable employment protection.

Temporary work agencies might represent a clever solution to some of the controversial flexibility issues. Employers are given the chance to adjust the size of their workforce according to short-term changes and to have precisely the personnel they need, but this does not have to leave workers without employment security. In principle, workers might be as secure with the agency as they would with any other employer. There are certain other advantages for secondary employers; hiring people from an agency can, for example, be a convenient way for regular recruitment. After a while, when the qualities and skills of a temporary employee have become known, it may very well happen that he/she is offered a permanent job. The secondary employers will thus weigh flexibility against the advantages of recruiting an individual who has already been tried out at the workplace and proved to stand the test. For the temporary employee it implies a chance to get a permanent job.

In real life, however, employment in temporary work agencies is associated with certain obvious drawbacks for workers. A crucial issue is of course what happens with the wage in a period when the demand for their services is low. Will the employees-for-rent be paid anyway or who will bear the costs? The main mechanism to provide an approximately full-time wage is that the secondary employers who use the services pay a relatively high price, but it seems that wages are mostly rather low (Storrie 2002: 54–7). As we might expect, in reality employees in temporary work agencies do not fare very well, although it need not have to be that way. One particular problem is that wages are usually positively correlated with seniority, whereas the whole idea with this solution is that workers should not stay that long with an employer. A related issue is that extra wage remunerations such as bonuses and social insurance schemes are often also tied to seniority.

Another very important aspect to consider is the relationship between the personnel hired through temporary work agencies and the ordinary workforce. Numerous problems can arise, of which I will mention a few. Agency workers may not get the most attractive work tasks, because existing employees are in an advantageous position to influence how various tasks are to be distributed and they may be inclined to keep the 'better' tasks for themselves. There are sometimes also difficulties for temps to do what the permanent staff does, because they are not expected to stay very long. It is then less convenient to engage them in, for example, work activities that require long-term relationships with customers or clients; such tasks have to be left to those who are employed on a permanent basis. Finally, it must be emphasized that agency workers have two employers, the agency and the secondary employer, and this is likely to create double loyalties that can be problematic in many different ways.

Work process flexibility

My next flexibility category is aimed at describing desired variation regarding the work process itself and two dimensions are then important. The first has to do with how work tasks are defined, combined, divided, and coordinated and the second has reference to work intensity. Obviously, the two dimensions are often interrelated.

Work tasks

There are many different reasons why, once in a while, the work process must be altered: expansion and contraction of existing activities, rationalization of production and administrative structures, introduction of new technology and new technical equipment, and so on. Changes often have considerable consequences for the nature of jobs as well as for their composition. The capacity to make adjustments in these respects depends very much on the interaction between employers and employers, not least with respect to how they handle issues of training and education.

When work task restructuring takes place, workers frequently have to acquire new skills. A crucial aspect is then to what extent they are willing and able to learn the things required. To take a well-known example, when personal computers, a couple of decades ago, started to invade one workplace after another, many employees had to face a completely different job situation. Some had very few years of employment left and did not therefore consider it worthwhile to learn how to handle the new equipment. We have no reason to assume that they would not have been able to learn, but their motivation was limited. In general, training and education may provide opportunities for individual development and career, but the attraction of such opportunities is of course limited when the employee has only a relatively short time left to retirement. Moreover, even if workers have acquired the skill diversity demanded by employers, it does not follow that they can be moved back and forth between different tasks; they may be very reluctant to accept that kind of instability. It seems reasonable to treat these problems in terms of a tension between desirable and non-desirable job rotation or work task switches.

Employers' demands for work task flexibility thus require some minimum degree of worker participation, because if workers are unwilling to make adjustments, no viable reorganization can be carried out. If a firm is under pressure from the market to install new machinery, this can be done provided that workers are prepared to go through the designated training. In case they do not, the employer may start thinking of the possibility to lay off old employees and begin to recruit new employees; in other words, the situation may be handled through employment flexibility in substitution of work task flexibility.

As seen in the above, there is a significant link between work task flexibility and education and training. Provided that people should be able to switch between jobs or between work tasks several times during a lifetime, they must have the chance to learn new things and to acquire new skills. Recurrent education, competence development, and lifelong learning have become catchwords for this (see, e.g., Edwards 1997; Field and Leicester 2000). Adjustment in these terms may imply instability for workers, but it no doubt often means flexibility in the positive sense of the word suggested here. Taking on an education can be a challenge for the individual and it may eventually lead to many positive consequences in terms of career, income, and personal development.

Work intensity

Work intensity flexibility represents yet another dimension of work process flexibility. The requirements on job incumbents as to how intensely and fast they should work sometimes vary quite a lot across the day, the week, the season, etc. A crucial demand from the employer may be that workers must speed up on certain occasions. For example, grocery stores are often crowded during rush hours when everybody is on the way home after work; restaurants generally receive most of their guests at lunchtime and in the evening; and most shops in the West have a peak during the weeks before and after Christmas. The pressure upon employees to be speedy and on the alert in what they are doing – as well as the possibility of being slower and more relaxed – can thus be expected to vary with such peaks.

A functional alternative to work intensity flexibility is to recruit extra personnel when there is a peak in an organization's activities, for example during rush hours in supermarkets and restaurants. One reason for choosing this solution is the risk that workers are completely exhausted if work intensity is too high. Employers may prefer not to empty all reserves but instead rely on having more people in the organization during certain periods of time. The variations in the amount of work are by the way not entirely predictable and the management often needs to have some fallback to keep a reasonable freedom of action.

From an employee perspective, work intensity flexibility can have some advantages, but it is also related to many problems. It may not be a big deal to have some variation in speed, but peaks are often associated with stress and other health problems. One issue that has recently been discussed is whether work has generally become more intense than it used to be (see, e.g., Burchell, Lapido and Wilkinson 2002). As discussed in the next section, work intensity flexibility is closely related to working time flexibility, but analytically the two are separate. Working time flexibility is a matter of how many hours people work and when they do it, while work intensity is about the workload and speed during these hours.

Working time flexibility

Flexibility in terms of working time refers to desirable variation regarding hours and schedules. Adjustment in the number of working hours is sometimes treated as numerical flexibility, because it may be used as a functional alternative to adapt the amount of work done at the workplace. A firm may, for example, introduce a four-day week or a 30-hour week during a recession instead of sacking people. But we should not confuse the two solutions and one reason is that the consequences for employees of shorter working hours and layoffs respectively are very different. Employees cannot generally be expected to be happy with lowering their input to a four-day week – it represents instability with respect to income – but it is as a rule more severe for them to lose their jobs. The following discussion is divided into two parts. Flexibility will be dealt with in terms of hours worked and work schedules respectively.

Hours worked

To get a suitable amount of work done, the employer may want to go beyond what is normal or agreed upon and make the personnel adjust to longer or shorter hours. Proposals in these directions can be related to fluctuations and changes in demand for goods and services or the need to utilize investments in machinery day and night, including weekends. Sometimes when employers want to get more work done than usual, they can command or try to persuade the existing personnel to work overtime instead of recruiting new workers and this is accordingly a functional alternative to employment flexibility. At least, if there is no permanent expansion and the already employed are willing and able to accept it, overtime may be a convenient alternative. One aspect to be taken into account is the problem of knowing how long the need for longer hours will last. Difficulties to find suitable workers as well as recruitment and training costs are other important factors. There may thus be several reasons for employers to rely on the existing employees to put in extra hours, particularly if the response among them is positive to such demands.

Many workers may regard overtime or longer hours as relatively advantageous, in any case if it is optional and their income can be increased substantially, perhaps in excess of what the regular overtime tariffs will bring in. In contrast to this, for people with, for example, heavy family obligations or severe health problems, it may be difficult or even impossible to cope with to the demands for extra hours put forward by an employer.

Work schedules

Working time flexibility is not only a matter of the number of hours worked. Both employers and employees may want to have adjustments in how work is distributed across the day, the week, the year, etc. This can be illustrated by firms within the retail trade, for which it is crucial to have employees to work more at times when there are many prospective buyers in the shopping malls and the stores and less when there are few of them. Within the processing industries, employers frequently need to keep production going also at night, as any interruption may be very costly, and consequently they have to employ shift workers. Numerous other institutions – hospitals, police departments, fire departments, and so on – are required to have personnel working or on duty at night.

When workers are interested in work schedule flexibility, we can expect to find other factors behind. For example, they sometimes wish to adjust their schedule to handle childcare problems. The important thing for them can be to have the opportunity to start working later than usual in the morning and work longer in the afternoon, or vice versa, since that

perhaps aids to ease the family's childcare situation. It may even be a positive thing for one or both of the parents to be able to work during weekends, because this allows them to take turns with the caring responsibilities.

Workplace or spatial flexibility

Another type of flexibility has to do with where the work is done. In many
jobs, employees are required to carry out their work in different places.
Some stay within the local area but switch workplaces during the day, from
one day to another, or less often. Others are supposed to travel long or
short distances, which may include being away from home overnight. The
work tasks can be carried out during the travel (e.g., pilots, flight attendants, train personnel), or at the destination (e.g., traveling salesmen,
mobile repairmen, journalists). There is a great deal of variation across
occupational categories in all of these respects and, without going into
detail, we can note that many jobs are associated with unconditional
requirements for workplace flexibility. From a workers' perspective, it is
easy to identify both positive and negative consequences of work-related
traveling and workplace shifts. On the one hand, these types of spatial
flexibility may be stimulating, offering new experiences and challenges, but
on the other hand they are sometimes also associated with long hours, late
evenings, heavy workload, and stress.

Teleworking and homeworking represent a specific type of workplace
flexibility (cf., e.g., Felstead and Jewson 1999a, 2000). Such arrangements
have become more common with the use of the new information technology, although they are perhaps not as widely implemented as many had
expected. They imply that people do not have to be present at the workplace but can stay at home or be somewhere else. There are varying consequences for both employers and employees with these arrangements. One
conceivable advantage for employers is the lower need for office and other
kinds of space when employees work at home. However, there can be extra
costs for portable computers and the like and the absence of daily face-to-
face contacts may be a negative aspect, among other things, because it
makes continuous monitoring of the work process difficult or even impossible to sustain. For employees, the main advantage is probably that they
get more freedom to decide not only where but above all when to carry out
their duties; in other words, spatial flexibility also leads to working time
flexibility. Work is thus to a large extent organized on employees' conditions, but the lack of daily contacts with colleagues is probably often a
drawback for them.

On the level of the labor market as a whole, spatial flexibility is a matter
of jobseekers moving from one place of residence to another or of jobs
being moved from one place to another. In both cases, mobility can be
encouraged through government subsidies or other kinds of government
intervention. How to handle labor market mismatch with high unemploy-

ment in certain regions and plenty of vacancies in other regions is an important issue in many countries.

Wage flexibility

The final flexibility type to be discussed is wage flexibility, which refers to adjustments with respect to pay systems or pay levels. There are two aspects to be dealt with; the first of these has to do with the issue of recruitment and the possibility of attracting workers and the second with the relationship between performance and pay.

Recruitment

The potential for recruiting workers is dependent on the supply and demand in the labor market. To secure their needs, employers sometimes find it necessary to increase their offers of pecuniary remuneration above what is normal. Jobseekers, on their part, may appreciate that they are attractive in the labor market and welcome employment with good pay. It does not have to be a problem if a new entrant gets a higher wage than his/her colleagues had when they were recruited, but it is another thing if he/she gets more at the time of his/her entry. Expressing it differently, there is an embedded equity issue, possibly best analyzed in terms of social comparison theory, as discussed in Chapter 7. If the employer's decision is regarded as unfair, it may reduce motivation among existing employees.

We can also consider the opposite situation of a surplus of jobseekers willing to accept a low wage to get a job. With high unemployment and weak social protection, people are likely or forced to take whatever they can get. A generous welfare state and strong unions can, however, modify the situation, for example by means of high unemployment benefits and legislation or collective agreements identifying minimum wage levels for different kinds of work. If jobseekers' reservation wage surpasses what employers think they can afford, vacancies run the risk of remaining unfilled or at least of not being filled very quickly. Thus, when employers complain about inflexibility or rigidity in these respects, they are often focused on and critical of some type of union or government intervention. It may also happen that already employed workers have to accept lower payment or delay an agreed-upon wage increase to keep their jobs (cf. Hyman 1999: 104). Wage flexibility is thus used as a functional alternative to downsizing or shorter working hours. From a worker perspective, such a solution may be considered the best possible alternative, but it obviously represents – to use the terminology suggested – instability in terms of income.

There has been a great deal of discussion about the assumption that wage flexibility and wage dispersion are positively related to employment growth. Much of this debate in the 1980s and the 1990s was concentrated on the differences between the flexible United States and the rigid Europe

202 *Sociological Perspectives on Labor Markets*

(OECD 1994, Part II: Ch. 5; Freeman and Katz 1994; Esping-Andersen 1999: 125–8). It has, however, been rather difficult to determine any unambiguous causal relationship between the two variables, when other factors are taken into consideration.

Performance

The second aspect of wage flexibility has to do with remunerations of worker performances. Generally, employers are likely to support wage systems that encourage better performance. The assumption is that if workers are paid the same no matter what they actually do, they cannot be expected to do their best; accordingly, individualized wage systems are favored.

Workers and unions often take a skeptical stand to individualized wage systems because they tend to perceive them as mechanisms to increase competition among themselves. In the event that competition is intensified, solidarity is likely to be affected, with negative consequences for union or other collective efforts to promote employees' interests. Individualized wage systems may also imply income instability, insofar as remunerations are tied to performance. A crucial issue is of course measurement of performance, because what people do in their jobs is not all that easy to assess and, additionally, connected with questions of equity. There is much literature on the relationship between equity and efficiency with different authors taking different positions (cf., e.g., Kenworthy 2004; Okun 1975; van den Berg, Furåker and Johansson 1997: Ch. 4). Some argue that there is a tradeoff between the two factors and others that the former is supportive of the latter. Another aspect of individualized pay schemes is that they are open to favoritism and other kinds of 'unfair' treatment.

To recall the discussion in Chapter 7, one way of making everybody comfortable with individualized pay schemes is to keep individual wages or salaries secret. If workers are ignorant of how much their colleagues earn, they have nothing to be unhappy about. It is also a matter of common practice in certain workplace cultures that pay levels are secret or, rather, that people just do not speak about them; they are looked upon as a business exclusively between the employer and the individual worker. This means that social comparisons are made impossible, but information may leak and, by the way, rumors may be more or less true; consequently, this solution is no guarantee that everybody is happy.

Flexibility mixes and conflicting interests

It is common that employers want to see various kinds of adjustment on the part of workers and workers may want to have (other) adjustments made by the employer. Demands for flexibility are thus subject to struggle at the workplace level but also more generally in society at large.

Adaptation that fits the other party's interests may imply conflicts between employers and workers, but we should not think of flexibility issues as always controversial. There are numerous situations in which all actors involved easily agree upon what is needed and in which they are also willing to behave accordingly. Moreover, flexibility is not only a source of conflict between employers and employees, but different categories of workers also disagree among themselves on the consequences of required or proposed adjustments. Employers, on their side, compete with one another and they may disagree over flexibility-related phenomena such as recruitment and wage policies.

A main conclusion from the discussion in this chapter is that there are many flexibility issues and they are often closely intertwined. The potential of employing organizations and workers to adjust to changing circumstances usually includes a wide range of options. With the notion of flexibility mixes we have a label for the fact that different types of adjustments can be combined for the purpose of accomplishing to the same or approximately the same outcome. Jonsson's four concepts – flexibility, inflexibility, stability, and instability – help us see the complexities of various solutions.

In the recent discussions on labor market flexibility only certain forms have been given emphasis; actually, the debate has very much focused on employers' demands for adjustments in the size of the workforce, working hours, work schedules, wage levels, and wage systems. The spotlight has then been directed to the 'rigidities' created by employment protection legislation, welfare state benefits, and union activity. Although employers are often neither united nor consistent in their demands, they generally try to push back worker-friendly government regulation, union influence, and other forms of collective pressures and instead put forward demands for larger wage differentials, more fixed-term contracts, and further variations in working hours.

Why, then, have certain employers' demands for adjustments by workers become so predominant? For a general answer we might return to what has happened with the balance of power in the labor market, as discussed in Chapter 6. The shift in power relations has above all occurred within the capitalist sector, but it has also had repercussions in the public sector. A crucial aspect is the development of market competition, which is in turn related to the new information technology and to the process of economic globalization. Several other factors, which have made the power shift possible, such as the decline of the traditional working class and of trade union influence, must also be taken into account. If resistance is weak or growing weaker, employers are more likely to get their demands through and they may also become bolder in formulating their claims regarding the terms of employment.

As mentioned in Chapter 6, some authors are critical of the idea of globalization as well as the notion of competitiveness. It is also often claimed that these discourses are taken as an excuse for flexibility demands. In that vein, for Standing (1999: 73; emphasis in original), for example, it is 'the *idea* of globalisation' – 'partly ideological' – that is linked to 'demands for *more* labour market flexibility'. In other words, it is not globalization in itself but the belief in it that matters, and this belief is taken to function as a justification for requiring certain adjustments among workers. To my mind, such a point of departure is too vague, unless it is shown how this 'partly ideological' idea has risen. Although it may be true that the force of globalization has been exaggerated – and that some have evoked the threat of it to justify specific types of action – there is nonetheless also real globalization and competition and, accordingly, a genuine basis for calling for flexibility.

At all events, the real or alleged intensification of competition has made it easier for employers – or rather put pressure on them – to demand more labor market flexibility in many different respects, otherwise profitability cannot be sustained and in the long run firms will not survive without making enough profit. It is likely that employers tend to exaggerate the threat of having to close down production or move it to other countries, but real competition is nevertheless in operation. Still, even if worker resistance has become weakened, employers do not dominate completely. One reason why they have not been totally successful is that their demands meet with resistance from governments, unions, and workers.

Furthermore, employers do not always agree on what is the best solution and there are sometimes rather divergent interests among them. We should also emphasize that they are to a high degree interested in stability. In order to be profitable, firms need to have a stable workforce or at least a core workforce on which they can rely; thus, for example, weak employment protection legislation may not be the most urgent claim. Whereas some employers have been very eager to demand that all kinds of regulation be reformed, others feel that union or government influence is not a big issue. It is also important that different flexibility mixes can be used to obtain similar outcomes; the pragmatists usually find some mix that works.

9
Unemployment, Marginalization, and Employment Prospects

In this chapter, I address a range of issues related to the fact that large population segments are being excluded from the labor market in advanced capitalist countries. Although, for a long period, the standard of living has successively increased for the citizens in these countries, the problem of providing sufficient numbers of jobs has not been solved and, with capitalism, it will hardly be solved once and for all. Sizable proportions of the population are left outside working life as unemployed, marginalized, or excluded; the expectations in terms of jobs and income that people may have are only partly met by the economic system. We shall thus turn to the relationships between individuals and the labor market, not implying employment.

Some observers do not simply make the observation that demand for labor power is too low, but they see no reason why things should improve, neither in the short term nor in the long term; they rather expect deteriorating opportunities for people to earn a living through paid employment. It is frequently suggested that non-employment is growing, a process that is sometimes referred to as the emergence of a 'two-third society' or as a 'Brazilianization' process. These conceptions represent a pessimistic perspective concerning the future, although, in a way, an optimistic interpretation is also possible. The marginalized categories are assumed to increase in numbers and to become more or less permanently excluded. In addition, it is sometimes suggested that new social dividing lines are being drawn between those who have (secure) jobs and those who do not.

Taking the process of marginalization to be inevitable, some authors conclude that wage-work or even work-based society will come to an end or, to be more accurate, that we need to dispose of the manner in which work is organized in the existing socioeconomic order. Seemingly paradoxically the deterioration of present labor markets is supposed to pave the way for a desired change. One of the more influential authors advocating the end of wage-work, André Gorz, has accordingly described himself as a 'pessimistic optimist'. He, and some other intellectuals, do not stop at predicting or hoping for a specific kind of change; they are also engaged in suggesting reforms that will further the desired future (see, e.g., Gorz 1985, 1999; Offe 1996; Standing 1999, 2002; Van Parijs 1992). Such suggestions should perhaps be taken more seriously than predictions that are often mere guesswork. The most significant proposal in this context is that of a citizenship or basic income and, as this idea seems to be gaining ground among certain intellectuals, it may be important to pay attention to it.

This chapter, first, provides some conceptual clarification with respect to unemployment and marginalization, and, second, will touch upon some issues related to these phenomena. Third, I will comment on the two rather similar scenarios of the two-third society and Brazilianization; my aim is to examine the assumptions on which these scenarios are based and to establish if they have anything analytically valuable to contribute. Fourth, I turn to the 'end-of-work' thesis, which goes one step further to argue that the era of wage-work is over or has entered into its terminal phase. This thesis does not seem to be derived from serious analysis but rather represents utopian and wishful thinking. A fifth discussion deals with the idea of a citizenship income that is a key proposal both by end-of-work proponents and by some authors who more modestly believe that full employment belongs to the past. Finally, I ask whether contemporary advanced societies really tend to run into increasing difficulties as regards employment developments. My general answer is that the demand for labor is not likely to diminish dramatically or at least that it does not have to be that way. Although unemployment and marginalization will continue to haunt the populations, I doubt that paid work is on its way out and I develop my reasons for taking that position.

Unemployment and marginalization

Insofar as people do not get a sufficient foothold in working life, we can describe their situation by means of such labels as unemployment, marginalization, and exclusion. These labels are commonly applied more or less interchangeably and, as they are not all that clear, we shall take a look at some of the conceptual solutions available. In my view, there is no immediate reason to prefer one ahead of another notion, although in this chapter I above all refer to unemployment and marginalization. When involved in empirical research, the most important thing is to define distinct concepts that fit the purpose of a given study and that can help us make sense of existing data. This is not my task here, but I nonetheless try to bring about some conceptual clarification.

As discussed in Chapter 2, unemployment simply refers to a situation when a non-employed individual offers his/her labor power in the market but finds no one who wants to hire it. Although the language is slightly different, this concept is fundamentally in line with the definitions used in the national labor force surveys, carried out on a regular basis in the developed capitalist countries. To express it simply, people who are not employed during a given period, but who actively search for a job, are classified as unemployed. The category just defined can be referred to as 'open' unemployment to distinguish it from other, hidden dimensions that are also identified in the labor force surveys.

There are importantly two such hidden dimensions. The first covers partial unemployment or underemployment. Despite much variation in the definitions across national labor force surveys, underemployment generally means that an individual has a part-time job but would like to and be able to work more and, additionally, the reason for his/her shorter working hours should be difficulties in getting full-time employment (OECD 1995: 65, 84–5). Accordingly, for example, having problems to find childcare is in principle not enough to qualify for underemployment status, as it is another kind of issue. Because we cannot know whether an individual – even if he/she has given such an answer – would actually take on more work if he/she got the chance, the data on underemployment must be treated cautiously. However, insofar as the question is asked repeatedly, year after year, in the same way, we can follow whether patterns change over time and, above all, whether they are cyclical or show some long-term tendency to increase or decrease. An important aspect is whether the composition of the underemployed – in terms of age, gender, marital status, etc. – undergoes change. For the purpose of determining the value of the data, we can also benefit from examining to what extent patterns are consistent with other kinds of information available.

The second hidden dimension of unemployment is found with the concept of discouraged worker, referring to – again with some cross-national variation – individuals who are not employed and do not seek employment, but who declare themselves to be able and willing to take an upcoming job (OECD 1995: 45–7). The reason why these individuals do not actively search for work, or have given up searching, is their negative assessment of the likelihood of becoming successful. The question in the labor force surveys is hypothetical and consequently, again, we must be careful – or conservative perhaps – with the data. After inspection of cross-national differences, it has been concluded that not all discouraged workers are 'close' to the labor market (OECD 1995: 64). However, the above remarks concerning survey questions asked repeatedly in the same way can also be applied in this case.

A further issue is how to classify participants in labor market policy programs and as with other classifications there are different solutions in the national labor force surveys. Labor market policy measures are primarily arranged for people who have difficulties in finding steady employment and who are therefore jobless or run the risk of becoming unemployed. At the same time, we must also be aware of the differences between programs as regards their role in the labor market (Furåker 2002: 131–2). Some of them are typically related to business cycles; they are set up or expanded in recessions and limited or closed down in boom periods. Others are organized to provide long-term support for certain categories, for example disabled people who have difficulties in the labor market even when demand for labor is high. In some countries there are rather ambitious programs – sheltered workshops, subsidies to employers, etc. – to provide employment for these categories.

Marginality is sometimes referred to as unemployment – including its various above-mentioned dimensions – plus atypical or non-standard employment, which means that part-timers and temporary workers are also included. In a book chapter, co-authored with Ulrich Mückenberger and Ilona Ostner, Claus Offe (1996: 203) goes one step further, when – with Germany in mind – he argues that 'the areas at the margins of the employment system, where the connection between wage labor and subsistence is uncertain, is beginning to grow' and that people are facing increasing difficulties to find 'professional, continuous, full-time productive activity within enterprises', all of which compels them to accept 'part-time and/or discontinuous and/or undervalued and/or unprotected employment'. With these formulations the author incorporates not only part-timers and people with discontinuous or unprotected employment, but also incumbents of jobs that are undervalued and that are not professional. This is definitely a considerable step beyond the common notion of treating workers in atypical jobs as marginalized.

The question is of course – as always in definitional matters – in what are we interested. With regard to marginality, we must, among other things, be aware that all kinds of work besides permanent, full-time jobs are not problematic for the individual. For example, having small children at home may indeed be difficult to combine with paid work and, under such circumstances, a part-time job is perhaps the best and even a fairly stable compromise for an individual (cf., e.g., Hakim 1996: 65–74; Rubery, Horrell and Burchell 1994: 213–14). Thus, if anything, people sometimes have a choice between part-time work and no work at all. An analogous argument can be made with respect to temporary employment. It may very well fit the needs of a student to have a temporary job, as the purpose is no more than to earn some extra money for a limited period of time. Yet, it can hardly be denied that having a job without 'normal' employment conditions implies a marginal position relative to the labor market; the point is rather that further specifications are valuable when we want to make overall judgments of the situation.

Another possibility is to conceptualize marginality in the way Gino Germani has done. He takes it to mean lack of participation by individuals or groups in contexts where they are expected to participate (Germani 1980: 49). This concept is not restricted to the labor market but can be applied for in principle any phenomena. If we concentrate on the labor market, its implications can easily be seen; individuals who are expected to have employment but cannot find a job should be classified as having a marginal position. Interpreted in that way, the concept seems to be quite close to that of unemployment, but there is one obvious difference: Marginality in Germani's analysis is based on socially defined norms rather than on non-employed individuals' search activities.

We may then raise the question of whether people in atypical employment would be counted as marginalized under Germani's definition. The answer is yes, if expectations are unambiguous that citizens should have standard contracts. As indicated above, it may very well be the norm that women with small children should work part-time at most. Germani has a good sociological point in defining marginality the way he does, but the concept is associated with considerable difficulties when we want to find useful operationalizations. To continue with the example above from another angle, women who stay at home with their children will not be classified as marginalized, except when there is normative pressure upon them to find at least part-time employment. The problem is how to determine whether the pressure is strong or clear enough to justify the label marginality. Norms are frequently contradictory and they may vary across population segments, not least concerning whether or to what extent mothers with small children should be gainfully employed.

As can be seen from the form of the word, the concept of marginalization – in contrast to marginality – refers to a process. Accordingly, time is an important factor; marginalization in the labor market indicates a process through which an individual becomes increasingly more cut off from work, perhaps ending up as totally excluded. The concept can thus be used to grasp developments at the workplace leading to – as described in Chapter 5 – labor power's loss of use value. A worker whose health is deteriorating may first get somewhat lighter tasks, eventually another job, then shorter working hours, and finally an early retirement pension. We can also employ the marginalization concept to describe how an already jobless individual is likely to meet with growing difficulties to find employment. In such a situation, a number of mechanisms are in operation, expanding the gap between the individual and the labor market; for example, his/her skills are not updated, his/her work contacts are likely to become weaker, and he/she may become engaged in activities outside the labor market.

Probably the most important aspect of marginalization is that the disadvantages of a marginal position are likely to accumulate with time. We do not expect short-term unemployment to cause great problems for the individual, at least not if there are unemployment benefits, support from the family, or other sources of income available. However, when the period during which the individual has no job is stretched out, although he/she still wants to find employment, his/her experiences are likely to become more cumbersome. There may not only be financial difficulties but also a range of other problems such as loss of contacts with previous workmates, stigmatization, and psychological distress. Concepts such as marginalization and marginality furnish us with tools that can possibly help us discover some of the fundamental mechanisms and processes behind such social disadvantages and failing living conditions.

Actually, the notion of marginality is sometimes taken one step further to include the effects of being outside what is 'normal' in society; in other words, it covers consequences in terms of standard of living, social relations, and life styles. Also the concept of 'social exclusion' – sometimes used interchangeably with 'labor market exclusion' – by and large has this kind of wide meaning (see, e.g., Mayes, Berghman and Salais 2001; Muffels, Tsakloglou and Mayes 2002). To be without a steady job is one thing, but to be socially excluded is not limited to the individual's position in the labor market; it stands for something more than just being out of employment. There are many different versions of the concept, but it commonly depicts a situation in which people do not have the resources and living conditions that are considered 'normal' in a given society. It is then a matter of multidimensional and accumulative deprivation; social exclusion refers not only to lack of employment and income but also to inadequate education, poor housing, weak social participation, insufficient social integration, powerlessness, etc. Another aspect is the neighborhood dimension of the concept, which means that it goes beyond the individual also to include lacking community resources.

Evidently, the concept of social exclusion is rather close to two other concepts, on the one hand, that of poverty and, on the other hand, that of underclass (in addition to the references above, see, e.g., Crompton 1998: 188–99; Morris 1994; Mingione 1996; Wilson 1993). With respect to poverty, a major issue is whether it should be treated as an absolute or a relative category. Moreover, it may be taken to include lifestyles and subcultures, which is frequently also the case with the concept of underclass. Both poverty and underclass are commonly used when the life situation of Blacks, Chicanos, and other groups in the big cities in North America and elsewhere are being studied. It would take us too far to go into the details of the concepts and the issues involved in these studies and I will instead make another theoretical point.

The crucial analytical issue in the discussion above is that we actually have two different concepts. One type is aimed at capturing individuals' problems to find (steady) employment in the labor market and the other additionally includes the consequences of these problems. It is not, however, satisfactory to include both the determinants and the consequences in the one and same concept, since such an operation will obscure the causal mechanisms conceivably involved (cf. Whelan and Whelan 1995). Departing from the assumption that unemployment and marginalization in the labor market are likely to be important explanatory factors behind poverty and other social problems, separate concepts must be used for the two sets of phenomena; otherwise their interrelationship cannot be determined, for example as to whether unemployment leads to poverty or whether growing up in a poor neighborhood increases the likelihood of becoming unemployed. These questions are in any event difficult to answer, but if we merge the basic concepts into one concept it will definitely be impossible.

To cope with this problem, it is enough to make a distinction between labor market exclusion and social exclusion, where the former notion more narrowly covers the fact that people are outside employment and the latter has a wider signification involving social isolation, lack of integration, etc. With its distinct meaning of being 'outside', labor market exclusion is a more clear-cut concept than marginalization. Although the attraction of having distinct concepts cannot be denied, there is a limitation in this case insofar as people may not be really (or permanently) excluded but move back and forth between casual jobs and unemployment or non-employment. When the situation is characterized by some flux and fluidity – and this is commonly the way it is – marginalization must be considered a more adequate notion.

In studying people's problematic relationship to the labor market we need suitable concepts and for that purpose both unemployment and marginalization do well. These notions can be more or less narrowly defined; open unemployment is a possible starting point, but we can thereafter add the dimensions of hidden unemployment as well as miscellaneous categories of casual or precarious employment. Labor market exclusion can also be a practicable concept, although – as pointed out above – its applicability is somewhat more limited. If we want to go further and examine the possible consequences of unemployment, marginalization, and labor market exclusion on standards of living and ways of life, concepts such as poverty and social exclusion can be made use of.

Issues of unemployment and marginalization

Numerous studies have verified that unemployment is associated with many disadvantages (see, e.g., Alm 2001; Gallie and Paugam 2000; Strandh 2000). Inability to find a job correlates negatively not only with people's incomes and standard of living but sometimes also with their physical health, mental well-being, social participation, etc., although neither the primary direction of the causal relationship nor the consequences of unemployment are all that clear. A similar picture is found also when marginality is taken to refer to people in non-standard or atypical forms of employment. Compared to standard jobs, temporary and part-time jobs are associated with certain negative characteristics such as job insecurity, relatively small chances for training and promotion, and low levels of pay and benefits (see, e.g., Gallie *et al.* 1998: 152–85; Gallie and Paugam 2000: 356–61; OECD 1998: Ch. 1).

Paid work is a crucial factor behind the standard of living that people enjoy in modern societies. This can help us understand why it is, with a few exceptions, a norm for healthy, working-age people to engage in gainful employment. Failure to live up to this norm – that in one way or another can be said to characterize the unemployed, marginalized, and excluded – is accompanied by certain social-psychological consequences; it carries stigma and stigmatization. The situation of the unemployed and the marginalized is frequently explained in terms of their personal shortcomings (see, e.g., Furnham 1982; Komarovsky 1973; Gallie 1994). As a consequence, unless they have some excuse conceived as legitimate, the individuals concerned are likely to be looked down upon by their peers.

Stigmatization has to do with the norms that prevail in society. Erving Goffman (1963: 5), who is perhaps more than anyone else associated with the concept of stigma, makes a distinction between 'normals' and 'undesired differentness' and argues that normals develop some kind theory to help them explain why persons with a stigma are inferior and what dangers they represent. Unemployment is one example of 'differentness' and to some extent the unemployed can be expected to adopt these theories themselves. Internalizing stigmas means a risk for having feelings of shame, which is a painful experience connected with psychological distress (see, e.g., Eales 1989; Scheff 1990, 1997; Rantakeisu, Starrin and Hagquist 1997). The experience of stigma seems to vary substantially across nations and the variation is partly explained by the relationship between the unemployed or the marginalized categories and the remaining population (Paugam and Russell 2000: 261–3). In the event that it is common among wage earners now and then to become unemployed or marginalized it is likely that stigmatization will be weaker than if these problems hit only a more limited category.

A main observation regarding the mechanisms of stigmatization is that there is no simple way of avoiding them. The standard of living in developed societies cannot be sustained without large numbers of people carrying out work day after day and, as long as this is the case, there will be certain norms about who is to do it. These norms in turn supply the prerequisites for stigmatization to take place. My conclusion in this respect is very different from that of Offe, one of the most well-known critics of work-centered types of sociological analysis. Already many years ago, he postulated a decline of the work ethic in modern capitalist societies. To him, the explanation behind this alleged development could be sought in the 'decentring of work relative to other spheres of life' and its 'confinement to the margins of biography' (Offe 1985: 141). Although there may have been various changes in the norms regarding paid work, we have little evidence in support of the thesis that everything is very different today compared to some decades ago. The issue of stigmatization can actually be taken as a test of which norms are important in society. From this point of view, it seems that – with some cross-national variation and with certain exceptions (when being a student, having personal assets, etc.) – the normal for able and working-age individuals is even now to have paid employment.

There are many negative features related to unemployment, marginalization, and exclusion and, consequently, we should carefully follow how the labor market changes in these dimensions. One task is to study the size of the social categories in question and the answer is obviously dependent upon how they are defined. We should also find out what changes take place. Is unemployment, marginalization, and exclusion on the increase and, if so, how fast is it happening? The crucial issue is whether it will soon become significantly larger than today or whether it moves up and down; again, the answer is dependent upon the definitions employed. Likewise, we need to examine the permanency of the division between people in jobs or standard jobs and the marginalized population. It makes a great difference whether those who have become marginalized also stay that way for a longer period of time. To be at the margins of the labor market is usually not a big issue for people, if, after a short while, they are able to move on to steady employment (cf. Esping-Andersen 1993). Quite the reverse holds for those who remain in precariousness month after month or even year after year.

No matter how important they are, the questions raised above can only be answered in empirical terms and they will therefore not be further dealt with in this book; it is a task that would require another type of analysis. Nevertheless I turn to two illustrations of how the present situation in modern societies is described and in both cases it is assumed that we are moving toward larger marginalization and exclusion. The two scenarios are presented under the labels of two-third society and Brazilianization respectively. Certainly, these labels are merely metaphors, but as such they have some influence on or even shape the way we look at the development of contemporary capitalism.

The notions of 'two-third society' and 'Brazilianization'

Commenting on what is happening with the labor markets in the rich capitalist world, some authors emphasize the difficulties for sizable segments of the population to support themselves through regular employment. It is a rather widespread view that these problems tend to grow and, in addition, that the marginalized categories will be more permanently excluded from the labor market. Also, these assumptions sometimes lead to the conclusion that a new main dividing line might develop in society, between people in regular jobs and the marginalized or excluded. Various metaphors are suggested to describe this kind of scenario. One term that is used in the literature is 'two-third society' and another is 'Brazilianization'. I will provide some comments on each.

The German author Peter Glotz (1984: 167–76; 1985: 37–40, 43–9) originally coined the expression two-third society or, in German, *Zweidrittelgesellschaft*. It is used to describe a society, in which most citizens are able to live in quite good social and economic circumstances, but where about one third of the population is more or less left outside of the common way of life. A large minority will run into hardship, mainly because of difficulties in finding steady employment; therefore they cannot sustain a normal standard of living and normal living conditions in other respects. Apparently, Glotz never had the ambition to elaborate the notion of two-third society any further; for him it is primarily a metaphor for a state of affairs that might be the outcome when the political right is in power and that left politics should try to counteract. It is easy to endorse the ambition to avoid a division of the population as suggested; yet, we need to scrutinize the concept of a two-third society, its connotations, and its possible role in the public debate.

Actually there does not have to be a growth in marginalization in order for us to talk about a two-third society; using a wide definition, we may even come to the conclusion that, at least in some countries, it is already here. We must draw attention to certain alarming developments; whereas unemployment – our fundamental indicator – was kept relatively low in most advanced capitalist nations for some time after World War II, after the mid-1970s it has generally risen substantially (Korpi 2002). Unfortunately, there are no strong signs that figures will come down to their previous levels and it is therefore easy to adopt a pessimistic view. One important thing to observe is, however, that unemployment rates fluctuate with business cycles and even if, in the main, they are clearly higher now than in the 1950s and 1960s, they continue to vary with economic development; in other words, there is no linear deterioration.

No matter what answer we come up with regarding the size of the marginalized population, the idea of a two-third society is confusing. Taken literally, the assumption of an unfolding numerical logic is absurd and mystifying. In sociological analysis, numbers cannot be attributed the status that they seem to be bestowed in this case; to presuppose that two categories, defined as the outcome of a social process, would end up in given proportions simply does not make sense. A crucial weakness is that the fractions are selected *a priori*; why should the relevant dividing line be drawn at two thirds and not at, for example, three fourths or one fifth? It would make more sense to base the numbers upon a given empirical picture. At best, therefore, the whole idea of a two-third society is simply a metaphor for a society with a large proportion of marginalized individuals.

We must also return to the issue of the permanency or long-term character of marginality. The image of the two-third society is that the marginalized would stay in their position for a longer period. With respect to the key category of unemployment, however, that picture must be modified and we can expect this to hold also for the other categories. There is often a great deal of turnover among the unemployed and quite a few of them do find jobs (OECD 1995: 19–34). Although long-term unemployment is a reality for some categories, turnover must be taken into account in studying marginalization and labor market exclusion; otherwise the concepts run the risk of losing their meaning. To be out of work for a shorter period is indeed something different than to be lastingly excluded from employment.

Another problem with the two-third society model is the way it depicts social contradictions. The division into marginalized and non-marginalized categories suggests a new main dividing line in society. With the assumption that two thirds are winners and one third are losers, the majority camp consists of both highly privileged categories and ordinary white- and blue-collar workers, side by side, in opposition to a minority of the marginalized and the excluded (Svallfors 2004: 203–10). To assume that this division represents a focal point for the ongoing social and political struggles must be considered a misrepresentation of the major mechanisms generating conflicts in society. Although there may be some tension between those who have a (steady) job and those who do not, we can hardly attribute that much weight to it. All of the struggles commonly regarded as central (such as that between labor and capital) have not suddenly been replaced by a conflict between marginalized and non-marginalized categories. It is a distortion of the distributive conflicts in society to treat ordinary workers as being on the same side as well-paid and privileged managers and top-level professionals. We should also recall that unemployment is a rather common experience among both blue-collar workers and white-collar workers; these categories often go in and out of unemployment. Ordinary employees have rather close social ties with the unemployed and the marginalized and especially if the latter two categories are supposed to include as many as one third of the total population we can be sure to find such a pattern.

Brazilianization is a similar concept to that of two-third society. The term itself does not suggest any specific proportions of the marginalized and the non-marginalized segments, but when presenting this scenario Ulrich Beck (2000: 1–2) points out that in Brazil less than half of the economically active population have a wage or a salary from full-time work; the majority have 'more precarious conditions', as they 'are travelling vendors, small retailers or craftworkers, offer all kinds of personal service, or shuttle back and forth between different fields of activity, forms of employment and training'. Moreover, taking Germany as an example, the author concludes that in the 1960s one tenth had such precarious conditions, in the 1970s it was one quarter and in the late 1990s one third, which to him suggests that 'in another ten years only half of the employees will hold a full-time job for a longer period of their lives, and the other half will, so to speak, work *á la brésilienne'* (Beck 2000: 2). In other words, also in this case we find that numbers have a more or less suggestive role to play.

Beck points out that the Brazilianization phenomenon has been typical of Latin America for a long time. With respect to Europe or, rather, 'the West', his assumption is that if governments and others continue to pursue policies oriented toward full employment, it will become a reality here also (Beck 2000: 141). This is indeed a strange and remarkable statement; the author apparently prefers that the efforts – not always that determined – to obtain full employment be given up. However, we are not presented with any reason why it would be so; no mechanism as to why policies are counter-productive is suggested. The only thing that Beck comes up with is that in order to avoid Brazilianization, a new type of citizenship must be created, requiring that people be integrated with the state and the market in a new way. How this integration will appear remains unclear, but it is probably supposed to have something to do with the proposal of a citizenship income.

The idea that Europe would follow in the footsteps of Latin America is not very convincing. In describing the increase of precarious employment in Germany, referred to above, Beck fails to account for the inflow of women into the labor market and into part-time jobs; as a matter of fact, women's entrance to the labor market is very much due to the possibility of getting part-time work. Within the framework of the existing gender roles, this solution often represents the only feasible compromise between family obligations and gainful employment; in large measure part-time jobs exist because of women's situations. In contrast, the Latin American picture is mainly related to the much greater class differences and the relatively much stronger power of employers. Even though there has been some power shift also in Europe to the advantage of employers, we are nonetheless far from being in a Latin American situation. We should perhaps never say 'never', but it seems very unlikely that, in a few years' time (before 2010), Germany or some other major country within the European Union would have a Brazilian type of labor market.

There is no doubt that – due to insufficient job opportunities – large population segments in the advanced capitalist countries can be classified not only as unemployed but also as marginalized and excluded. Actually, this is one of the most urgent problems that the labor markets in these countries face. The size of the problem varies with business cycles, but to some degree the evidence at hand can be interpreted to be in line with what the two-third-society and Brazilianization labels are meant to describe. Yet, this does not imply that these labels have any explanatory power; instead, there is a risk that we are left with a distorted image of what is awaiting in modern welfare capitalism, including how social conflicts will develop. We should take the problems of unemployment, marginalization, and exclusion most seriously but stay away from misleading metaphors.

The end of wage-work?

Some authors, who believe that unemployment, marginalization, and exclusion tend to increase, envisage the end of wage-work society. They do not assume that people will stop working but only that wage-work, as we know it, will or should come to an end. Gorz (1999: 55) has been careful to make precisely this distinction; according to him, what is disappearing is the kind of work that is subject to transactions in the labor market, 'the monetarily exchangeable work or commodity labour which was invented and forcibly imposed by manufacturing capitalism from the end of the eighteenth century onwards'. Of course, this is a drastic argument with far-reaching implications and as such highly questionable.

In the literature, there is also a focus on the political goal of full employment. Thus, Beck (2000: 38) does not believe that 'work society will run out of work'; it is instead 'the end of full employment which is at issue'. Whereas the first decades after World War II – a period classified as the 'first modernity' – was characterized, among other things, by full employment, the 'second modernity' of today indicates a decline of paid work (Beck 2000: 18). The conclusion is that full employment cannot be sustained and that the present system therefore cannot solve the social and economic problems, as was once promised.

Also Offe has repeatedly expressed the idea that the prospects for full employment are not very promising. A couple of decades ago, he argued that we were witnessing the decline of work-centered society and, as a consequence, work ceases to be a key sociological category. Based on, at best, fragmentary evidence, the general conclusion is formulated in unambiguous terms: 'A highly developed industrial capitalist society guided by a highly developed welfare state evidently tends to exclude increasing portions of social labour power from participating in the sphere of wage labour' (Offe 1985: 147). We thus have to expect marginalization and exclusion to grow and the goal of full employment must be considered futile. In the text referred to above, written together with Mückenberger and Ostner, Offe (1996: 208–9) emphasizes the illusory character of traditional strategies for full employment – be they 'more growth through more market' or 'growth through state intervention' – and the three authors even argue that these strategies are 'economically undesirable', 'ecologically indefensible', and 'socially unacceptable'. The idea is instead to have a basic income for all citizens guaranteed by the state; I come back to that issue below.

A relevant question is whether we are dealing with forecasts of the end of wage-work or full employment or rather with hopes for it; actually, the latter alternative often seems to be the most adequate answer. Looking at the period since the early 1970s, we discover that the proportion of the adult population in employment has decreased in some countries, but in others there is little change or it is even the opposite (Wilson 2004: 56–9). It must be added that the proportions of working women have increased everywhere, whereas the male figures have declined. What is particularly noteworthy is the development in North America, where the employment rates for the total population have increased substantially. Ironically enough, when the American author Jeremy Rifkin (1995) ten years ago proclaimed the 'end of work', more Americans than ever before were gainfully employed (Wilson 2004: 1).

There is no doubt that the whole idea of the end of work society is very much a matter of wishful and utopian thinking. This will become even clearer shortly, when I turn to the reforms that quite a few authors suggest to further what they regard as a desirable state of affairs. Nobody can reasonably argue that thinking relies on robust sociological analysis and paying closer attention to it would be to attribute an undeserved importance to it. My intention is therefore to be brief on the issues involved, but two things need to be done. The first is to comment on some of the basic assumptions in this type of reasoning. The second is to provide a general assessment of the concrete proposals that many of the authors in question tend to support, above all the idea of a basic income for all citizens. There is also another idea that has been commonly advocated, shortening of working hours (including partition of jobs as one method), but it seems to have lost most of its steam in a decade or two. Today it appears to be the idea of a citizenship income that is gaining support and quite a few intellectuals endorse it; we should listen to the discussion, as the proposal, if carried out, will have significant effects on labor markets.

The explanations as to why we should expect the end of work-centered society usually refer to the development of productivity under capitalism. For Gorz (1985), a crucial source of inspiration is Karl Marx's idea that liberation can take place only through the abolition of work, that is, when the 'realm of necessity' is left for the 'realm of freedom'. By technological innovation and increased productivity, capitalism will bring about a reduction in the amount of necessary labor and in that way make human emancipation possible. Gorz provides a rather elaborate account of how less and less effort is required to produce various necessities, but he is not so interested in factors that may result in new needs for goods and services and consequently increase the demand for labor power. I return to this latter issue in the end of the chapter. Rifkin (1995: Ch. 1, 10) presents a similar view as Gorz; he suggests that technological change leads to a decrease in the number of jobs and in his view the service sector cannot make up for this, as it is also being rationalized. Thus, the advanced capitalist societies will provide too few jobs for everybody to find employment.

Many authors do not believe that work-based society will end in an acceptable way by itself; the process is therefore assumed to need some assistance and two kinds of positive reforms appear in the discussions how to make the desired vision come true. One of them has to do with working hours; it is suggested that they should be reduced and that people should have better opportunities to choose their own hours. If one believes that wage-based society is coming to an end anyway, the first part of this seems like a redundant proposal. Nevertheless, we encounter the idea that something must be done to avoid that some individuals work very much and others not at all. Gorz (1999: 94) argues that working hours must be reduced to balance 'a decreasing quantity of work' and 'an expanding workforce' and Beck (2000: 60) arrives at the same conclusion saying that we must avoid 'new class divisions between the some with too much work and the others with none'. It is somewhat unexpected to see the word 'class' in a new guise, in the light of the latter author's eagerness to dismiss it as a 'zombie' or living-dead sociological category (cf. Chapter 7), although it is probably no more than a word in this context. Returning to the working time issue, we should observe that both Gorz and Beck have definite reservations as to the desirability of a reduction in working hours, in the event that it would be allowed to create larger gaps between different categories of people.

Shorter working hours are nonetheless often supposed to increase the number of permanent jobs and accordingly to reduce unemployment. It has not been proved, however, that this kind of measure will lead to the preferred outcome. In countries such as France and Germany, where the method has been implemented, the results are not very encouraging (Anxo and Lundström 1998; Hunt 1996; Wilson 2004: 156). We should, in addition, observe that Gorz (1999: 94) emphasizes the advantages with expanding people's opportunities to choose their own hours. Obviously, there may be some contradiction between the two goals, at least if *longer* hours are also allowed to be an option. There are in fact people who want to work more, even among full-timers (Bielenski, Bosch and Wagner 2002; Lilja and Hämäläinen 2001).

Working time reforms and the proposal concerning a citizenship income have to be carried out by governments. One problem is whether people will support these ideas and commit themselves to make them materialize. With respect to working time reductions, some support has been mobilized among unions and social democratic parties, but the idea of a citizenship income does not have a great support outside of the generally small green parties in Europe and certain other groups. It must be emphasized that there is a typical pattern here; utopian ideas are often not connected with any subject to carry out the reforms suggested. Gorz (1982) long ago bid adieu to the proletariat and, to my knowledge, he has found no other actor to take its place as a possible motor of change.

Having no clear idea about how desired changes are to be brought about, utopian thinking often ends up assuming that they will just happen. It is, for example, suggested that if people merely have a basic income they will carry out all kinds of socially useful work in the informal sector, providing care for children and for the elderly, etc. However, in the literature we find some reservations as to whether all of those in need of care would really obtain sufficient assistance in this way. In my opinion, it would be a huge step backward if people who are unable to get by without certain types of help would have to rely on the benevolence of individuals. There is even among basic income supporters some distrust that the so applauded spontaneity of the informal sector will be enough to ensure all individuals the services they need. As a consequence, many years ago, Gorz (1985: 40–4) proposed a very different solution that a basic income must be associated with compulsory work. We may indeed doubt that this is a suitable way of supplying personnel to caring activities and the like, since compulsory work can be expected to have a negative impact on motivation and caregivers definitely need to be motivated in order to do their best in treating patients and clients. Gorz (1999: 84–93) obviously later abandoned the idea for moral and philosophical reasons.

The advocates of the end-of-wage-work thesis are generally enthusiastic about the informal sector, in which unpaid, voluntary and spontaneous work is carried out, and this predilection colors their arguments and conclusions. Typically, a woman who takes care of children in a nursery school and gets a salary is contrasted with another who stays at home to take care of her own children without being paid for it (Gorz 1999: 3). The first woman is engaged in an employment relationship, which is a matter of a work-for-wage exchange, whereas the second woman is not. This can of course be considered unfair and with a citizenship income for everybody it would not have to be economically disadvantageous to stay at home with one's children. However, the question is whether the argument is not directed against female labor force participation or perhaps rather the norm that even parents with small children should be able to have gainful employment, that is, the idea behind parental allowance systems. In all events, the issues of a gender-biased division of labor and informal sector work as a 'trap' for women are neglected.

We may push the issue one step further. If there is a political majority for it, the tasks of taking care of one's own children or elderly relatives might be turned into paid work, financed by the state or the local community. In glaring contrast to what many advocates of the end-of-wage-work thesis want to see, this kind of reform entails that more activities are drawn into the labor market. Although it will imply some loss of freedom for those concerned, a number of positive changes will also come about. People who perform the work get an employment contract, in turn connected with other benefits, and they are paid for their efforts. Another aspect is the liberating effect of 'defamilialization' that will appear unless the job is confined to a contracted individual's own family. The transfer of responsibilities to public authorities is in addition a way of securing that those who need certain services actually get them. My aim with this discussion is not to come up with any concrete proposal but only to visualize an alternative to the informal sector that is so cherished by advocates of the end-of-work thesis.

The proposal of a citizenship income

One of the most far-reaching proposed reforms in relation to the labor market is that of a citizenship or basic income. Those who believe that the end of wage-work is close at hand also tend to advocate some reform of that kind. As a matter of fact, there are several different proposals, but I do not intend to go into the technical details of any of them. I assume that the income would be for all citizens and that it would be large enough to survive on; on the basis of these assumptions, my aim is no more than to discuss some of the universal principles involved as well as some of the likely consequences.

To begin, the general public has mostly responded to the proposals of a citizenship income with silence; very few take these ideas seriously enough even to criticize them. If a firm proposal would make it all the way to the actual political agenda, we can be quite sure that it will encounter considerable resistance. Guy Standing (1999: 358; 2002: 204–19) has suggested that the major objections to a can be boiled down to three: moral, economic, and political. I take his arguments as a good example of a line of reasoning and the following discussion is therefore structured in the same way. The underlying assumption is that other authors, who are also in favor of the idea of a basic or citizenship income, have rather similar perspectives, although their proposals may differ regarding certain arguments and details (see, e.g., Gorz 1985; 1999; Offe 1996; Van Parijs 1992).

With respect to the moral objections, I prefer to be brief. People take different stands on moral issues and these stands are rarely that interesting when we want to describe and explain how things work or will work. There is, however, one point on which I would like to comment. Standing mentions that a main objection to the citizenship income has been that rights should be accompanied by obligations. In other words, the opponents call for reciprocity; if people receive a wage they should do something in return for it and not just receive the money. Standing's counter-argument is that there are many situations in which no reciprocity is demanded. For example, if a person has inherited a fortune and is therefore provided for during his/her remaining life, the issue of reciprocity is usually not brought up. The author even puts forward the idea that we might have a social inheritance principle, implying that everybody would have a part of what the previous generations have left behind. It is a sympathetic but very different idea that must not have anything to do with a citizenship income. The reciprocity dimension cannot be left in this way; it will keep its significance and its political bearings should least of all be underestimated.

To continue to the economic aspect, there are two different problems to take into account. First, we have the issue of the direct costs for a citizenship income, that is, the price tag of these benefits minus the costs of other benefits and their administration that can be eliminated. We do not know what benefit level Standing has in mind, as he does not tell us, but he is apparently convinced that there will be no problems at all and this is a common attitude among other proponents of the idea. Nevertheless, assuming that the citizenship income would be something like a guaranteed pension for a single individual, if provided for everybody the costs would definitely amount to substantial figures. Unquestionably, certain government expenditures can be reduced but far from all of them. Standing (1999: 363; 2002: 211–12) apparently also recognizes this, although he does not explain his argument. We can think of many different motives why other social benefits must be kept; for example we may find it reasonable that disabled individuals' extra needs be covered. Another issue is, of course, what will happen with all of those systems – the parental insurance, the unemployment insurance, etc. – that today have higher levels of compensation than the citizenship income would entail.

An income provided for all citizens would undoubtedly lead to large costs in the usually very tight public sector budgets, although each individual would not receive much to get by on. At the same time, unless people continue to work as usual, tax incomes will be lowered, which in turn squeezes the room for the basic income. One option is then to cut the amount of money for everybody or for certain categories such as children and married couples. At some point, however, the sum will not be sufficient to live on and accordingly it will not liberate the individual from the necessity of finding gainful employment. Another proposal is that the citizenship income should be introduced successively, but even so it may become rather expensive and also a reform that is carried out stepwise must be evaluated in terms of what the full-scale solution will be in the end.

The second economic issue to be considered is that the citizenship income will have an impact upon the supply of labor and upon wages. To do firm calculations in these respects would require econometric modeling of a detailed proposal, which is far beyond the aim and scope of this book. Yet, as the possible effects on the supply of labor power to the market are likely to be very crucial, it is important to think through the arguments at least a little. According to Standing, the recruitment of workers to jobs will be no problem whatsoever; people may be even more willing to take low-paid jobs when they have a basic income to start with. This reasoning is indeed both peculiar and amazing and it is difficult to see it as anything but the ideas of an unworldly dreamer. On the one hand, Standing argues that people would no more have to carry out work that is negative (monotonous, hard, dirty, or whatever), because the economic pressure upon them is taken away; but on the other hand he does not want to admit that there might be a supply problem. He simply fantasizes that jobs will be improved so that people will become interested in taking them.

To avoid all misunderstanding, I do not deny that many jobs need to be greatly improved, although this is not always easy to accomplish. Leaving the issue of pay aside, we must ask to what extent it is possible to make all jobs attractive. It may happen that a citizenship income would lead to some improvement to facilitate the recruitment of workers, but it is hard to envisage any radical change in a situation when the whole economy would be in great difficulties. Moreover, the question still remains why people, if they are already provided for, should spend 40 hours a week (or somewhat less perhaps) on activities that do not engage them that much. In the event that they are interested in doing some work, they may be happy with – let us say – half-time jobs; in other words, it must be concluded that a considerable labor shortage will emerge. We can also turn the argument around. If nothing will happen in respect of the supply of labor, it seems that the basic income does not mean anything at all, and what is then the point of it?

In my opinion, there is a considerable risk that numerous vacancies will not be filled unless substantially higher pay or other improvements are offered. The only ways to counteract labor shortages are to raise wages and to make jobs better. There is one important complication with wage increases; they will most likely be accompanied by rising inflation, which in turn reduces the value of the citizenship income. Standing (1999: 363; 2002: 212–13) does not comment on this problem; he is simply happy to posit that wage flexibility can be increased with a citizenship income. This apparently implies larger wage differentials and it is somewhat surprising that he, suddenly, regards such a change as something positive, as his whole argument for the rest is oriented toward the goal of accomplishing more equality.

One aspect that must be considered is that people do not work for economic reasons alone. As I have pointed out several times in this book, there are other motives, for example that jobs are interesting, allow human creativity to develop, furnish social contacts, and provide individuals with a significant identity. The question is how important these motives are in a situation when it would be legitimate not to have a job but to still be supported. If large numbers of people are outside of the labor market simultaneously, they can more easily get together, organize common activities, and thus fulfill their different non-economic needs without having a job. This makes a great difference when compared to a situation with more or less isolated unemployed individuals who may be missing contacts with their workmates. We must accordingly ask how values and norms would develop under such new circumstances. I am not convinced that gainful employment would continue to be a very strong preference.

To ensure that the supply of labor is sufficient, the gap between income from employment and the citizenship income probably has to be large. This means either that the latter must be kept very low, which makes it difficult to survive on, or that the former would have to be allowed to rise clearly above the present level. In cases of large wage increases, inflationary effects can be expected to hit the economy and, as a consequence, the purchasing power of the citizenship income will be weakened, which, if it goes far enough, could undermine the whole reform. In other words, we end up with a vicious circle and a typical 'Catch-22' situation.

Some comments should also be made concerning Standing's discussion on the political difficulties to win support for a citizenship income. In his view, the political objections must be considered the main obstacle to the implementation of the supposedly desirable reform. The resistance is blamed on politicians and others who are stuck with the ideas behind the traditional social insurance system. In this connection, the author asks whether a citizenship income may be 'too radical' for people to accept and therefore he proposes a step-wise introduction (Standing 1999: 364, 2002: 215). He completely ignores the fact that large segments of the population may distrust this kind of reform and regard it as a dangerous experiment threatening their standard of living, if everybody is just being supported without having to do anything at all in return.

There is another most remarkable and astonishing omission in Standing's argument. Globalization and global labor flexibility are key issues for him – one of the two books that I refer to here actually has the title *Global Labour Flexibility* (Standing 1999) – but that aspect is not even mentioned in his discussion. It is indeed unlikely that all developed countries simultaneously would provide an unconditional income for everybody and we may therefore ask what would happen in the event that one country alone would introduce this measure. A whole range of questions needs to be thought through in relation to such a step. 'Socialism in one country' was once highly contested and it seems that 'a citizenship income in one country' would most likely be so too.

In conclusion, the idea of a citizenship income is, as I see it, very much out of touch with reality. Economically it will cost too much – most of all perhaps because can be expected to have a negative impact on the supply of labor – and politically it is unrealistic, not least because the moral issue of reciprocity is also a political issue. Nevertheless, in response to the objection that people will use a citizenship income to do no more than necessary, Standing (1999: 365) writes, 'if one is optimistic about human aspirations and behaviour, freedom of choice will lead to more skill acquisition and more creative and productive endeavour, rather than "loafing"'. This quotation is very telling with regard to the author's whole outlook and let me simply conclude that it can hardly be enough just to be optimistic.

Employment prospects

On the question whether jobs will become fewer and fewer, and thus whether increasingly larger segments of the population will become marginalized, I offer some arguments. Capitalism has typically – due to the fact that market competition puts pressure upon firms to rationalize – reduced the time needed to produce goods and accordingly, all other things being equal, the demand for labor. However, our conclusions about what will happen with jobs cannot be based merely on this observation; there are several other factors that point in the opposite direction.

Increased productivity is followed by increased consumption; in modern societies, people generally have more money than ever before, buy more of the same, replace things more frequently, and buy a larger variety of products. For example, think about the clothes that people wear. The number of garments owned by average European or North American citizens is today much larger than it used to be a century or half a century ago and the turnover of these items is more rapid, partly due to the increased role of fashion. We find a similar picture for numerous other things that people possess. All of this in turn makes it necessary to increase production and, as a consequence, new jobs are created. In short, there are two tendencies with contrary effects on employment; on the one hand, capitalist production is constantly being rationalized, but, on the other hand, it is also expanded by the introduction of more and new goods to be consumed. The latter aspect requires that sufficiently large segments of consumers have sufficient purchasing power to buy the products and this requirement has evidently been fulfilled through the development of modern capitalism.

Still – needless to say – there is some limit to material production and although we have not yet reached that limit, production cannot continue to increase forever. Let us, however, return to another aspect – treated mainly in Chapter 6 – namely the production of services. Notwithstanding the difficulties in using the service concept, industries such as healthcare and education have come to play a much greater role in modern societies during recent decades. Furthermore, new activities – related to entertainment, culture, hobbies, sports, tourism, and the like – emerge as increasingly important. With respect to many services, including healthcare, education, culture, and sports, it is difficult to identify a point where demand would cease; people's needs are perhaps not insatiable, but we cannot really see their limits.

A crucial argument to be brought forward is that services often cannot be rationalized to the same extent as material production. Whereas the number of hours it takes on average to manufacture a car has been drastically reduced since the first Ford left the assembly line, no such change has occurred, or even can occur, with respect to, for example, childcare. In the latter case one hour simply means the same today as before. If we assume that wages as well as facilities stay intact, the only thing that can be done for the purpose of making childcare less expensive is to have larger groups of children, fewer nurses, or fewer hours open. These cost-reducing measures, however, all imply a change in the quality of the service – less staff per child and less availability – rather than rationalization in the true sense of the term.

In this context, what is usually called Baumol's (1967) disease – referring to the growing imbalance between production of goods and production of services due to differences in prospects for rationalization– can be considered not a disease but a cure. With an increasing proportion of the gainfully employed engaged in service production, the tendency toward a decrease in the number of jobs is counteracted. This is not to say that there will always or even often be a balance between the two sectors, but it is at least possible. A fundamental dimension is price relations; rationalization of material production makes goods relatively less expensive in comparison with those services that cannot be rationalized to the same degree. As a result people may choose to take care of various activities themselves and it has even been suggested that we are headed toward a 'self-service' society (Gershuny 1978). The production of cheap goods obviously helps in that process; for example, buying a washing machine and wash at home may be a good deal compared to paying a laundry for doing it. There is some point in this argument, but the service sector has nevertheless expanded.

Another aspect is that wages and salaries in certain parts of the service sector may decline relative to those in manufacturing, which will aid in keeping down the price of services and in keeping up the demand for service workers. Thus, wage flexibility – in this case taken to mean adjustments of wages across jobs – is a mechanism that can contribute to counteracting the effects of diverging productivity developments. Given that it goes far enough, it can have a significant impact on tertiary sector employment. Moreover, many otherwise very costly services (such as certain kinds of healthcare and education) are often supplied for free or at subsidized fees by governments. As a result, public sector employment is a balancing factor in the labor market. Governments may also subsidize private organizations that carry out socially important activities and by doing this they also help preserve or expand the number of jobs in these organizations. Without wage flexibility and subsidies, however, services will become more expensive relative to goods, but there is yet one other mechanism of adjustment to be mentioned. To some extent people can be expected to adapt to new price relations; at least in a longer perspective, they are likely to get accustomed to a situation where services are on the whole relatively more costly than they used to be.

My conclusion on unemployment, marginalization, and exclusion in the developed capitalist societies is that these phenomena should indeed be taken seriously. One of the main drawbacks with capitalism is its incessant failure to provide jobs for everybody. Political parties, unions, and other organizations interested in avoiding mass unemployment and marginalization of large segments of the population must therefore continue their struggle for full employment. They are not likely to be fully successful in reaching this goal, but if they are strong enough something will be accomplished. It is difficult to see any reason of principle why this struggle should be impossible; people's needs are almost insatiable and there is consequently plenty of work to be done. Unemployment, marginalization, and labor market exclusion are not 'natural' nor necessary phenomena, but only the consequences of the way in which production is organized in society – or even the way in which society itself is organized – and this can be changed or modified. The disaster scenarios provided by some authors no doubt sow pessimism, but to become aware that they are little more than bizarre ideas about the future can perhaps help us regain positive spirits.

10
Labor Market Continuity and Change

In this book, I have tried to elaborate several concepts that can make up the basic theoretical building bricks for a sociological analysis of the labor market, particularly in advanced capitalist societies. First and foremost, the concept of labor market has been defined as a 'hiring fair' for labor power, the human capacity for work. It is an arena that involves two major types of actors: those who offer and those who hire labor power; the latter actors have a need to get some work done and the resources to pay for it, while the former join in above all to earn a living. With regard to the human laboring faculties, we can distinguish three main dimensions: biological capabilities, qualifications, and motivation. If an individual offers his/her capacities for work in the market and finds someone willing to hire it, an employment contract can be established between the two parties. The job to be done consists of a number of work tasks, commonly assembled into what we call occupations. If the individual, however, does not find an employer willing to use his/her capacity for work, he/she must be classified as unemployed.

The hiring of labor power is connected not only with the capitalist but also with other sectors in modern societies; thus the role of public sector as well as other kinds of non-capitalist employment must be taken into account. In the discussion of these issues, I have suggested that we utilize some version of the traditional Marxist concept of mode of production. Moreover, in overhauling the arsenal of analytical tools, I have found that we can make use of Fred Block's concept of marketness. In my interpretation, this notion is taken to stand for – to put it very simply – dependence on mechanisms of prices, supply and demand, including the integration with other markets.

Commodification and decommodification are two other concepts that I have attempted to elaborate. With regard to the labor market, these twin concepts are basically applied to refer to processes by which labor power becomes or ceases to be a commodity or, to include also gradual changes, get a larger or smaller commodity role. They are relevant to put into prac-

228

tice, for example when we want to assess the consequences of welfare state benefits for people's readiness to find and accept employment. I have also aimed at showing that commodification and decommodification can be helpful concepts in the study of other labor market-related social phenomena and processes such as the role of the family and the transitions between self-employment and wage-work.

In approaching concrete matters, we must move beyond the most abstract concept of the labor market and look for subcategories. Geographic and occupational divisions endow the labor market with specific structural features and the same can be said with respect to sector, class, gender, age, ethnicity, etc. Rather sturdy and durable structures have been developed, but they are of course possible to alter and, across time, actually also undergo change. The relevant actors – such as jobseekers/workers, employers, employees' organizations, employers' organizations, and the state – must adjust to or try to transgress or transform the ways in which the labor market is structured. Once submarkets are identified, we also have a basis for analyzing individuals' mobility between them.

As has been conveyed in several of the previous chapters, there are many authors who suggest that the labor markets of advanced capitalism are subjected to rather great transformations. It has become almost a fashion to paint a picture according to which existing socioeconomic conditions and structures are breaking down and being replaced quicker than ever before. In this conception, everything is in a constant state of flux and very little will stay the way it used to be. Since we live in the midst of these processes, however, our understanding of what is really happening is assumed to be limited. Only particularly sharp-eyed viewers are able to describe the width and depth of the transformations that are now taking place.

The picture of rapid, comprehensive, and irreversible change is strongly underpinned by the development of new information and communication technologies that has no doubt been overwhelming and will certainly continue to have an immense impact on social and economic activities. It has meant a spectacular acceleration of numerous processes within the spheres of production, distribution, and life in general, and it has made things possible that many of us could not even think of just a few decades ago. Increasing possibilities for mobility of capital, products, and people are other significant components in the scenario of far-reaching change. We should still not forget the need for cautiousness and critical reflection, because we must avoid the unwarranted conclusion that social relations and structures are transformed at the same speed and to the same extent.

Social forecasting has generally not been a very successful business, but apparently many observers of present-day labor markets think that they know not only what is going on but also what will happen in the future and they feel obliged to tell us. As noted in several of the previous chapters, some of them are – to put it mildly – carried away in their predictions about the coming decades. Their most sweeping prophecies about wide-ranging change are not based on serious and scrupulous examination of existing realities and developments but impressionistic at their best and mere speculation at their worst. We must be conscious of this and therefore think more critically about ongoing social and economic processes, how they should be explained, and what consequences they may have at present and in the future.

In my view, there are two remedies for the tendency to exaggerate social change, namely the two tools that are assigned a key role in the introductory chapter of this book: theory and empirical investigation. The latter is perhaps most important, as it can tell us whether or not statements and predictions about reality are correct. We should not, however, underestimate the value of careful theoretical analysis, keeping in mind that useful theories must have reference to reality. By discovering ill-founded or contradictory assumptions, conceptual ambiguities, and inconsistencies in theoretical reasoning we can dispose of many ideas that simply do not hold and therefore should not be entertained.

These words of caution are not meant to deny that social conditions and structures change; they unquestionably do. One of the most important points of criticism raised some time ago against structural-functionalist sociology emphasized its difficulties in dealing with social change. Once profoundly influenced by that assessment, I reject any view of society – or any other organization – that treats it as being static. Nevertheless, it must be kept in mind that there is not only change but also continuity in the ways human life is organized. Looking back, it can be admitted that the criticism against structural functionalism sometimes went too far; the questions this theoretical perspective raised about the reproduction of social patterns and of society as a whole were not irrelevant and ought not to be played down. Actually, continuity and change are just two sides of the same coin and we have to deal with them both, insofar as we want to give a full picture of our objects of study.

The final pages in this book focus on certain issues related to labor market continuity and change. They also summarize some of the main arguments that have been dealt with in the previous chapters. As a starting point, I provide a simple classification of three types of possible labor market change and this categorization will thereafter be used to structure the discussion. My aim is to examine whether these three types can be identified in the developed capitalist world or whether they are at least in sight. This also gives me an opportunity to touch upon possible explanations of why certain changes have taken place, while others have not occurred or are not even likely to occur. I find it important to spell out some arguments that can help us understand why labor markets are in many ways relatively stable. The idea is to counterbalance some of the existing literature that is too narrowly focused on change.

Three types of change

For the purpose of providing us with an analytical point of departure, I want to make a distinction between three types of change in the labor market. The first refers to transformations of the labor market as such – that do away with the labor market in its present form – and the other two changes apply to within the existing systems. An example of the former kind would be a socialist transformation in which labor power ceases to be subject to the hiring activities characteristic of a capitalist system but is instead allocated through other mechanisms: administrative or political decisions. It should, however, be pointed out that also really existing socialism had labor markets, although these systems were typically characterized by a lower degree of marketness.

The first category of change also covers the end-of-wage-work perspective *á la* André Gorz and others, despite the fact that it is very unclear what would then come instead of the labor market. Furthermore, it appears that 'the-end-of-employment-as-we-knew-it' scenario, as suggested by Robert Reich, at least partly belongs to this category. This approach seems to be built on the assumption that self-employment will become much more common in the not too distant future and that traditional employment relations will therefore to a large extent be done away with.

The other two types of change in my scheme imply that the basic structure of the labor market remains intact; changes are simply supposed to occur within the framework of that structure. The first of the two subtypes has to do with the composition of jobs and of jobholders. For example, as mentioned previously, the labor markets in developed capitalist countries have gone through a transformation toward more service employment and less manufacturing employment. An increasingly smaller proportion of all workers are made up by the male-dominated industrial proletariat, whereas, at the same time, we find a substantial expansion of the service sector that has recruited large numbers of women. There has also been a redistribution of employment across countries due to processes of internationalization and globalization. We have witnessed a huge influx of immigrants to certain countries and it has in turn altered the composition of the workforce. All of these changes – that are indeed very important – refer to the division of labor in society, but we should not underestimate their effects on power relationships that are in focus in the final type of transformation to be discussed.

My third category of labor market change covers shifts in the balance of power between employers and workers and within each of the two categories. One or another kind of actor thus gets a stronger influence on employment contracts and the various conditions involved in employment relationships. Throughout the capitalist world, the major trends over the last few decades seem to be indisputable. Employers have generally strengthened their power in relation to workers, especially those in peripheral positions, while, at the same time, certain other categories of workers, primarily the strata referred to as professional-managerial employees, tend not only to grow as a proportion of the total workforce but also to become a more important social force.

Accounting for continuity and change

We need to consider both continuity and change in respect of labor markets, particularly as the contemporary literature has often dealt more with the latter than with the former. This selective treatment of the subject might very well be justified; important changes have no doubt taken place and there may be good reasons to pay special attention to them. Nonetheless, everything does not change and we must also account for structures and mechanisms that survive. I begin by dealing with the first category in my classification above, focusing on why transformations that would overrun the present labor market system are rather unlikely to occur.

Considering continuity

The labor market is a crucial institution for capitalism; the latter can hardly function without it. To say this, one does not have to be dedicated either to Marxist or to structural-functionalist theory (despite certain crucial differences, the two perspectives show some striking resemblances), but it possibly helps to be familiar with that kind of thinking. Capitalist profit-making is more than anything else based on production of goods and services and the labor market is simply a way of supplying workers to production. There is no such thing – and will never be – as automated industries in which no labor at all is required. Production processes may no longer need that many manual workers of the traditional variety, but the kind of activity is not the issue here. In Karl Marx's words, it does not matter whether the capitalists invest their money in a sausage factory or an educational institution; the overriding purpose is anyway to make profit (cf. Chapter 6). Owners of capital can certainly bring in profits from speculation and other financial transactions, but at least some of them will have to hire workers to produce goods and services and this production must generate a surplus or otherwise firms – and ultimately the whole system – will run into difficulties.

Furthermore, capitalism is without any doubt the dominant mode of production in our epoch –particularly after the breakdown of Soviet-type state socialism – and for the time being there is no sign at all of any significant change in that respect. It is indeed unlikely that this prevailing socioeconomic system would be abandoned in the foreseeable future, although it does not have to last forever. The idea put forward by Franco Fukuyama about the end of history – that the present type of liberal capitalism predominant in the West is the end station – cannot be taken literally, but as long as capitalism continues to dominate or at least play a major role, labor markets 'as we know them', to paraphrase Robert Reich, will hardly be done away with.

As has been emphasized throughout this book, there is also a public sector labor market that despite large cross-national differences is sizable in the economically developed countries. Public sector employment relationships are not all that different from those in the capitalist arena, but they are generally not subject to demands for profit and they are characterized by a lower degree of marketness. In many countries, government employment has gone through a good deal of retrenchment, downsizing, and privatization in recent years, although reforms have often been smaller than sometimes reported. Anyhow, at present we do not find much reason to anticipate any larger public sector growth. If, however, this were to occur, we can no doubt expect to see significant effects on the labor market, but the system in itself would not have to be altered.

Actually, there is a continuous and rather fierce battle going on in many countries as to whether various activities should be organized through the private or the public sector. In the 1980s, I argued that this would be one of the most significant developments to take place in the years to come (Furåker 1987) and it seems today that my prediction was well-founded. A number of political-ideological arguments – which essentially and schematically have to do with, on the one hand, efficiency and freedom of choice and, on the other hand, equality and equity among citizens – are provided for the two solutions respectively. Both models presuppose a labor market, although, again, the private sector alternative brings with it stronger dependence on market mechanisms. Thus, no matter whether work is organized through the private sector or the public sector, wage-work can be expected to stay on and recruitment of employees will take place through the labor market. Both spheres represent continuity with respect to the existing system and the implication is that labor power remains a commodity.

The commodity status of labor power is, as stressed throughout the book, affected by many different factors and it may be more or less undermined by various counteracting forces. A shift toward self-employment can be mentioned as one example of this. Among individuals who start a business of their own, demanding full-time commitment, there is no need to worry about finding a job with an employer. In many developed countries no more than about one tenth of the gainfully employed are self-employed; in other words, it might indeed require a very dramatic shift toward self-employment before it would be meaningful to talk about even the beginning of 'the end of employment as we knew it'. According to my judgment, such a development is quite unlikely, although there may undoubtedly be an increase, and even a considerable increase, of the proportion of people running their own businesses. Still, the effect on the existing labor market

234 Sociological Perspectives on Labor Markets

must be expected to become relatively limited, but regular employment contracts may begin to look more like the contracts that consultants have.

There is another factor that might have a substantial impact upon the commodity status of labor power, namely the introduction of a citizenship or a basic income. Depending on how such a reform would be arranged – in terms of income levels and rules – at least in the worst case scenario, the labor market might be strongly affected by a failing supply of labor power. With an arrangement worthy of the name of a citizenship income, it is indeed difficult to maintain the incentives for paid work and, in my view, this kind of reform would generate more problems than it can solve, if it can solve any problem at all. We may be critical of the present system of wage-work, but there is no point in replacing it with something worse. For one thing, to maintain the standard of living, people must continue to work – actually a great deal – and they must get paid for it. With a decreasing ratio between the population of working age and those above and below that age, it is crucial that all of those who have the capacities and possibilities for it contribute in the production of goods and services. In order for all the necessary work to get done, it is essential with a strong norm saying that, in principle, everybody who can make a contribution should do so. This can be seen as an implication of being a member of society, if conceived of in terms of both rights and obligations. The joint efforts of large numbers of people in working life must be considered the key societal asset for creating a decent standard of living and a worthy life for the whole population and it requires that work and not just citizenship be remunerated. Evidently, the political prospects for a citizenship income are not that great, but, because quite a few intellectuals are supportive and make propaganda for it, we must disclose its unrealistic features to ensure that it will not be tried as an experiment.

Capitalism is likely to survive in the foreseeable future and at the present moment no other option is on the agenda. Consequently, as it is an integrated part of capitalism, the labor market is here to stay. From this perspective, it does not matter whether the public sector will grow or not, although an expansion of it would have repercussions on the degree of the marketness of the labor market. The whole idea of the end of wage-work emanates out of the blue or, rather, from wishful thinking, but there may very well be an increase in both self-employment and marginalization. It is indeed unlikely that an expansion of self-employment would be large enough to undermine the existence of the labor market, although it may lead to certain changes in its way of functioning. There may also be an increase of the marginalized population, but we should then expect that – due to the power and vigor of political democracy – some restraining measures will be taken; to what degree they will be successful is another story.

Another important conclusion is that the basic struggle between employers and workers will continue. It is generated from the fundamental structure of capitalist and other labor markets and we have no reason to believe that it will disappear. To make this point, it is better to rely more on Marxist than on structural-functionalist theory, as one of the main drawbacks of the latter perspective is its limited ability to deal with contrasting interests. Quite another issue is whether and how concrete conflicts will develop and in that respect, following a Weberian line of reasoning, we cannot take for granted that the potential of workers' collective resistance will unfold. There have been numerous attempts to weaken the basis for collective action among workers and to make employment relationships more individual; some of them have been successful but far from all. However, even a shift in the power relations between the parties would not eliminate the tensions that go with the labor market as a structure.

Considering change as to jobs and jobholders

A significant change emphasized in this book is the rapid employment decrease over recent decades in the traditional manufacturing industries. This process is due to capitalist rationalization based on competition and on scientific and technological developments and is a reminder of a prior decline within agriculture. It has occurred despite two factors that tend to increase the consumption of goods: higher living standards and the development of new products. Gradually lower proportions of the populations are now directly working with the production of goods and the extraction of raw materials. Instead services – here taken in the broad meaning of everyday language – have become more important in modern societies. Post-industrial theory has called attention to this development, but it sometimes fails to recognize that industrial production still plays a fundamental role; even if industrial employment has declined, it maintains a major or even the prime position in the advanced capitalist economies.

The decline of industrial production is thus accompanied by a growth in the service sector. This development must be accounted for, but we should be wary of too far-reaching redefinitions of the socioeconomic structure that is still mainly capitalist, despite the interpretations put forward by certain theorists. Regarding this issue, Manuel Castells has provided a forceful correction to many other accounts by maintaining that what he calls 'informationalism' is fundamentally capitalist in nature. It is important that we do not lose sight of this perspective in analyzing the development of labor markets. Actually, owners of capital have increasingly geared into the production of services, as the production of goods has been rationalized, and one reason is that the possibilities of making profits in the service sector have expanded. However, public sector services, organized on the basis of political democracy, have to a large extent been developed to fulfill needs that otherwise would not be met.

We should also call attention to the processes of globalization and internationalization, connected with communication technologies and the dissemination of information. These processes include the removal of obstacles for investments and trade as well as for individual mobility across national borders and consequently both jobs and workers have been redistributed across countries. The advanced capitalist world has lost industrial jobs but had an expansion with respect to services. It accordingly shows a relative decline in the size of the industrial blue-collar working class and an expansion of the proportion of certain categories of white-collar workers, particularly of professional-managerial categories. The latter categories are often highly educated and education has thus become an increasingly significant institution in society. The character of manufacturing work has also changed in many ways with the development and spread of new information and communication technologies. We should additionally observe that international migration is extensive and that the prerequisites for a further expansion of it have improved substantially in the last few decades, even though there are still many obstacles to overcome. In my view, it is likely that we will see a great increase of migration flows in the not too distant future.

Another aspect, related to the expansion of services, is the increased proportion of women entering the labor market. This process has been facilitated by the fact that modern families generally have fewer children than families had a number of decades ago. Many service jobs also have work tasks with which women have some affinity – healthcare and childcare are typical examples. The advanced capitalist countries have had several decades with a more or less steady growth of female employment and in almost all of them – despite great cross-national variation – a clear majority of working-age women are today gainfully employed, although often only on a part-time basis. This change has taken place while at the same time male employment rates have fallen off; yet, the male figures continue to be higher. Moreover, men and women tend to cluster in partly different occupations and industries and many of these patterns seem to be very persistent. For many occupations a development toward a more balanced composition is visible, but for others not much at all has happened. Men on average earn more and they are over-represented on the higher levels of work organization hierarchies. Despite some significant change, much of the traditional gender patterns are thus reproduced in the labor market; there is in fact both continuity and change.

Considering change in power relations

During the last few decades, there have been certain changes in the balance of power in the labor market. Employers have gained power relative to their actual and potential employees and this is reflected in the decline of union membership, in the deregulation of government control of labor markets, in the cuts in welfare state provisions, and in the privatization of public activities. As a result, in many ways workers are more vulnerable today than they have been for a long time.

One reason for the changes in the balance of power is that the manufacturing blue-collar workers – who represent the most important counterforce to capitalist hegemony – have become relatively fewer, at least in the advanced capitalist nations. This is a result of technological progress and rationalization and of the simultaneous expansion of services. However, also service workers may resist capitalist domination, but on the whole they have so far been less inclined or able to do so. To some extent this can be explained by the fact that many workplaces in the service sector are small – shops, restaurants, etc. – and that workers in small units tend to be less willing to organize and form a counterforce to employers, because their relationship is closer with those who hire their labor power.

The decline in the relative size of the industrial proletariat is accompanied by an expansion of the new middle class and above all the professional-managerial strata. These social categories are either more directly tied to the employer side or retain an in-between position in social struggles. We should keep away from two interpretations of this development, often trotted out in books and articles. First, it does not mean that class has become insignificant but only that certain changes have occurred in the class structure. Second, it does not imply that blue-collar workers have ceased to resist capitalist domination; they continue to do so, although from a generally weaker position. The important overall conclusion is that the expansion of the new middle class, and in particular the professional-managerial categories, represents a significant element in the shifting balance of power in society.

Another important factor is the development of competition in the capitalist markets and it is connected with two other interrelated factors – new technology and globalization. With intensified competition, employers come under growing pressures to make adjustments in terms of employment, the work process, working hours and schedules, and wages. These pressures are thus translated into demands on workers, who frequently have to comply or accept that their jobs disappear. Workers are generally on the defensive, knowing that if adjustments are not made, they run the risk of ending up in unemployment. Furthermore, pressures for flexibility have been converted into political demands; governments have been pushed to weaken employment protection legislation, cut down on social benefits, lower taxes, and deregulate and privatize various activities controlled by public agencies.

The discussion on globalization and internationalization is still fundamentally divided as to how far the changes have actually gone and what impact they have on national policies, union influence and the like. The view that globalization has almost completely eliminated the possibilities for self-determination among nation-states is strongly exaggerated, but we should recognize that the scope for such self-determination has been pushed back. Capitalist firms tend to become more loosely tied to their national

238 Sociological Perspectives on Labor Markets

origin and they are increasingly less inhibited by national borders. What economic globalization mainly does is to put firms under additional pressure to be competitive and the necessity of being competitive is in turn, to a considerable degree, translated into demands on workers to make various kinds of adjustment. This is an important explanation as to why, over recent decades, we have seen so much focus on labor market flexibility.

To the extent that employers have been successful in their demands for adjustment on the part of workers, they have extended the scope for market mechanisms to operate in the labor market. It has then become more unusual that outcomes are determined by factors other than price-related factors, for example union and government interventions. In other words, the degree of marketness in the system of hiring labor power is augmented. A shift in power relations for the benefit of employers is something that makes labor markets develop in the direction of the ideal 'free' market, although the final destination is still far away. Yet, I want to stress that employers have not been all that successful. It is true that some significant deregulation of labor market and workplace legislation has taken place, that many public monopolies have been privatized, that the influence of trade unions has diminished substantially in many industries and countries, and so on, but the opposite side still prevails. Not even all governments that are eager to express their pro-business attitudes fully embrace neo-liberal ideology but to some extent provide resistance to employer demands. Unions continue to struggle for their members and there are numerous other forms of collective resistance.

Much of the development described here does not fit very well with the predictions that Marxist theory once formulated. The industrial working class has declined in size and with the expansion of services the collective strength of workers has been weakened, despite the fact that part of the service sector employment has a similar character. We can recall Weber's skeptical attitude as to whether those in a common class situation would unite and act jointly to advance their interests; history is obviously a more open affair than the traditional Marxist scheme presupposes. One point with the latter is, though, that it keeps us aware of the fundamental conflicts in the capitalist system. In a similar spirit, the power resources theory, elaborated by Walter Korpi and others, is a fruitful tool to understand the development that has taken place over recent decades, but it needs to be supplemented in certain respects. We should develop a theory of how competition affects the power resources of the actors in the labor market and how resources outside the political sphere affect political processes and decisions.

Too much of 'end-of' theses

In concluding this book, I want to pay attention to the fact that 'end-of' theses abound in the literature on contemporary labor markets. It is all too common that books and articles proclaim the end of industrial society, the nation-state, class, unions, collective action by and large, 'employment as we knew it', standard forms of employment, wage-work in general, and so on. These statements and predictions have not been proved or, rather, they have proved to be false. In fact, all the phenomena mentioned remain essential factors in the labor market and it does not seem likely that they will disappear in the foreseeable future. We may indeed be surprised that so loosely anchored and even incorrect proclamations and forecasts have been able successfully to break through in the public debate; it is a task of its own to study how this has been possible.

At any rate, there is an urgent need to counteract the influence of the 'end-of' theses on our interpretations of the contemporary world and various perspectives calling attention to the basic mechanisms and conflicts of capitalism may provide an effective therapy for leanings toward these ideas. In that way we can avoid illusions about the evaporation of fundamental capitalist relations into the sky, as the prerequisites for conflicts in the labor market are still at hand. From this contrary, down-to-earth perspective, it is a secondary aspect whether we live in a service, information, knowledge, or globalized society or whatever label is applied to characterize the present situation.

The fact that unions and other kinds of collective resistance have been weakened does not mean the end of unions, class, the nation-state, or collective action. Actually, the contradiction between employers and workers in the capitalist system will not cease to exist only because one of the parties has – perhaps temporarily – become weakened. In other words, it is a much better prediction for the future that we will witness new labor disputes, strikes, lockouts, boycotts, etc. than to assume that all of this is over. Even more importantly, there will also be an incessant stream of struggles that do not come out in the open in the way that strikes and similar events do. Less spectacular negotiations will continue to take place and they are all manifestations of the same underlying tensions.

Employers, workers, employers' associations, trade unions, political parties, and governments will continue to be engaged in struggles over the conditions of employment relations. This prediction is rooted in a theoretical perspective that directs our attention to the fundamental structure of the labor market; it is the division into those who hire and those who hire out labor power that will continue to fuel the battles to come. We should of course not gloss over the question of whether workers will be able to keep up resistance, as there are many factors counteracting their capacities to do so. During several decades, the relative size of the traditional working class has declined, while the professional-managerial element of the workforce has expanded. The latter strata of higher-level white-collar employees have a rather individualistic outlook; they tend to distinguish themselves from ordinary workers and find their own, less universally defined but nevertheless common solutions. This development – in combination with certain difficulties associated with globalization and global competition – has changed the balance of power in the labor market. Today broad collective solutions are thus on the defensive, but this does not have to keep on forever; the tide may turn again.

References

Abbot, A. (1988) *The System of Professions. An Essay on the Division of Expert Labor*, Chicago and London: University of Chicago Press.

Åberg, R. (2002) 'Överutbildning – ett arbetsmarknadspolitiskt problem?', 41–61, in K. Abrahamsson *et al.* (eds) *Utbildning, kompetens och arbete*, Lund: Studentlitteratur.

Ackers, P., C. Smith and P. Smith (eds) (1996) *The New Workplace and Trade Unionism*, London: Routledge.

Alestalo, M., S. Bislev and B. Furåker (1991) 'Welfare State Employment in Scandinavia', 36–58, in J.E. Kolberg (ed.) *The Welfare State as Employer*, Armonk, NY: M.E. Sharpe.

Alm, S. (2001) *The Resurgence of Mass Unemployment. Studies on Social Consequences of Joblessness in Sweden in the 1990s*, Stockholm University: Swedish Institute for Social Research.

Althauser, R.P. and A.L. Kalleberg (1981) 'Firms, Occupations, and the Structure of Labor Markets: A Conceptual Analysis', 119–49, in I. Berg (ed.) *Sociological Perspectives on Labor Markets*, New York: Academic Press.

Althusser, L. (2001) *Lenin and Philosophy and Other Essays*, New York: Monthly Review Press.

Anxo, D. and S. Lundström (1998) *Arbetstidspolitik – ett europeiskt perspektiv*, Stockholm: Swedish Council for Working Life and Social Research.

Arnot, M. (2002) *Reproducing Gender. Essays on Educational Theory and Feminist Politics*, London and New York: Routledge.

Atkinson, A.B. and J. Micklewright (1991) 'Unemployment Compensation and Labor Market Transitions: A Critical Review', *Journal of Economic Literature* 29: 1679–1727.

Atkinson, A.B. and G.V. Mogensen (1993) *Welfare and Work Incentives*, Oxford: Clarendon Press.

Atkinson, J. (1984) 'Manpower Strategies for Flexible Organisations', *Personnel Management* (August): 28–31.

Atkinson, J. (1987) 'Flexibility or Fragmentation? The United Kingdom Labour Market in the Eighties', *Labour and Society* 12(1): 87–105.

Atkinson, J. and N. Meager (1986) *Changing Working Patterns: How Companies Achieve Flexibility to Meet New Needs*, London: National Economic Development Office.

Bacchi, C.L. (1996) *The Politics of Affirmative Action. 'Women', Equality and Category Politics*, London: Sage Publications.

Bachrach, P. and M.S. Baratz (1970) *Power and Poverty: Theory and Practice*, New York: Oxford University Press.

Bacon, N. and J. Storey (1996) 'Individualism and Collectivism and the Changing Role of Trade Unions', 41–76, in P. Ackers, C. Smith and P. Smith (eds) *The New Workplace and Trade Unionism*, London: Routledge.

Baran, P.A. and P.M.Sweezy (1968) *Monopoly Capital. An Essay on the American Economic and Social Order* (paperback edn), New York: Monthly Review Press.

Bauman, Z. (2002) 'Individually, Together', xiv–xix, in Beck and Beck-Gernsheim (2002).

Baumol, W. (1967) 'The Macroeconomics of Unbalanced Growth', *American Economic Review* 57: 415–26.

Beck, U. (1992) *Risk Society. Towards a New Modernity*, London: Sage Publications.

Beck, U. (2000) *The Brave New World of Work*, Cambridge: Polity Press.

Beck, U. and E. Beck-Gernsheim (eds) (2002) *Individualization*, London: Sage Publications.

Bell, D. (1976) *The Coming of Post-Industrial Society. A Venture in Social Forecasting*, 2nd edn, New York: Basic Books.

Bendix, R. (1963) *Work and Authority in Industry. Ideologies of Management in the Course of Industrialization*, New York and Evanston: Harper & Row.

Bergmann, B.R. (1996) *In Defense of Affirmative Action*, New York: Basic Books.

Bergström, O. and D. Storrie (eds) (2003) *Contingent Employment in Europe and the United States*, Cheltenham: Edward Elgar.

Bielenski, H., G. Bosch and A.Wagner (2002) *Working Time Preferences in Sixteen European Countries*, Dublin: European Foundation for the Improvement of Living and Working Conditions.

Blauner, R. (1964) *Alienation and Freedom. The Factory Worker and His Industry*, Chicago: University of Chicago Press.

Block, F. (1990) *Postindustrial Possibilities A Critique of Economic Discourse*, Berkeley and Los Angeles: University of California Press.

Blyton, P. and P. Turnbull (eds) (1992) *Reassessing Human Resource Management*, London: Sage Publications.

Blyton, P. and P. Turnbull (2004) *The Dynamics of Employee Relations*, 3rd edn, Basingstoke: Palgrave Macmillan.

Bowles, S. and H. Gintis (1976) *Schooling in Capitalist America. Educational Reform and the Contradictions of Economic Life*, New York: Basic Books.

Bradley, H. (1989) *Men's Work, Women's Work. A Sociological History of the Sexual Division of Labour in Employment*, Cambridge: Polity Press.

Braverman, H. (1974) *Labor and Monopoly Capital. The Degradation of Work in the Twentieth Century*, New York: Monthly Review Press.

Brochmann, G. and T. Hammar (eds) (1999) *Mechanisms of Immigration Control. A Comparative Analysis of European Regulation Policies*, Oxford and New York: Berg.

Brown, H.P. (1990) 'The Counter-Revolution of Our Time', *Industrial Relations* 29(1): 1–14.

Brown, R. (1965) *Social Psychology*, New York: The Free Press.

Burchell, B., D. Lapido and F. Wilkinson (eds) (2002) *Job Insecurity and Work Intensification*, London and New York: Routledge.

Cahn, S.M. (ed.) (1995) *The Affirmative Action Debate*, New York and London: Routledge.

Cain, C.G. (1976) 'The Challenge of Segmented Labor Market Theories to Orthodox Theory: A Survey', *Journal of Economic Literature* 14(4): 1215–57.

Calmfors, L. (1994) 'Active Labour Market Policy and Unemployment – A Framework for the Analysis of Crucial Design Features', *OECD Economic Studies* 22: 7–47.

Carroll, G.R. and K.U. Mayer (1986) 'Job-shift Patterns in the Federal Republic of Germany: The Effects of Social Class, Industrial Sector, and Organizational Size', *American Sociological Review* 51: 323–41.

Casey, C. (2002) *Critical Analysis of Organizations. Theory, Practice, Revitalization*, London: Sage Publications.

Castles, S. and M.J. Miller (2003) *The Age of Migration*, 3rd edn, Basingstoke: Palgrave.

Castells, M. (1996) *The Information Age: Economy, Culture and Society. The Rise of the Network Society*, vol. 1, Oxford: Blackwell.

Clark, C. (1951) *The Conditions of Economic Progress*, 2nd edn, London: Macmillan.

Cohen, G.A. (2000) *Karl Marx's Theory of History: A Defence*, expanded edn, Oxford: Oxford University Press.

Colgan, F. and S. Ledwith (1996) 'Sisters Organising – Women and Their Trade Unions', 152–85, in S. Ledwith and F. Colgan (eds) *Women in Organisations. Challenging Gender Politics*, Basingstoke and London: Macmillan.

Colgan, F. and S. Ledwith (eds) (2002) *Gender, Diversity and Trade Unions. International Perspectives*, London and New York: Routledge.

Crompton, R. (1998) *Class and Stratification. An Introduction to Current Debates*, 2nd edn, Cambridge: Polity Press.

Crompton, R. (ed.) (1999) *Restructuring Gender Relations and Employment. The Decline of the Male Breadwinner*, Oxford: Oxford University Press.

Crompton, R., F. Devine, M. Savage and J. Scott (eds) (2000) *Renewing Class Analysis*, Oxford: Blackwell Publishers.

Cully, M., S. Woodland, A. O'Reilly and G. Dix (1999) *Britain at Work. As Depicted by the 1998 Workplace Employee Relations Survey*, London: Routledge.

Dahl, R.A. (1985) *A Preface to Democratic Theory*, Chicago and London: Chicago University Press.

Dahl, R.A. (1961) *Who Governs?*, New Haven: Yale University Press.

Dahl, R.A. (1982) *Dilemmas of Pluralist Democracy. Autonomy vs. Control*, New Haven: Yale University Press.

Deery, S. and J. Walsh (1999) 'The Decline of Collectivism? A Comparative Study of White-Collar Employees in Britain and Australia', *British Journal of Industrial Relations* 33: 245–69.

Devine, F., M. Savage, J. Scott and R. Crompton (eds) (2005): *Rethinking Class. Culture, Identities and Lifestyle*, Basingstoke: Palgrave Macmillan.

Dicken, P. (2003) 'A New Geo-economy', 303–10, in D. Held and A. McGrew (2003a).

Doeringer, P.B. and M. Piore (1971) *Internal Labor Markets and Manpower Analysis*, Lexington, MA: Heath Lexington Books.

Donaldson, L. (1990) 'The Ethereal Hand: Organizational Economics and Management Theory', *Academy of Management Review* 15(3): 369–81.

Drew, E., R. Emerek and E. Mahon (eds) (1998) *Women, Work and the Family in Europe*, London and New York: Routledge.

Drucker, P.F. (1994) *Post-capitalist Society*, paperback edn, New York: HarperCollins.

Dryler, H. (1998) *Educational Choice in Sweden. Studies on the importance of Gender and Social Contexts*, Stockholm University: Swedish Institute for Social Research.

du Gay, P. (1996) *Consumption and Identity at Work*, London: Sage Publications.

du Gay, P. (1999) 'In the Name of "Globalization": Enterprising Up Nations, Organizations and Individuals', 78–93, in P. Leisink (ed.) *Globalization and Labour Relations*, Cheltenham: Edward Elgar.

Duncan, S. and R. Edwards (eds) (1997) *Single Mothers in an International Context: Mothers or Workers?*, London: UCL Press.

Duncan, S. and R. Edwards (1999) *Lone Mothers, Paid Work and Gendered Moral Rationalities*, Basingstoke and London: Macmillan.

Durkheim, É. (1964) *The Division of Labor in Society*, New York: Free Press.

Eales, M.J. (1989) 'Shame among Unemployed Men', *Social Science and Medicine* 28(8): 783–9.

Edwards, R. (1979) *Contested Terrain. The Transformation of the Workplace in the Twentieth Century*, New York: Basic Books.

Edwards, R. (1997) *Changing Places: Flexibility, Lifelong Learning, and a Learning Society*, Florence, KY: Routledge.

Edwards, R.C., M. Reich and D.M. Gordon (eds) (1975) *Labor Market Segmentation*, Lexington, MA: D.C. Heath.

Elfring, T. (1988) *Service Sector Employment in Advanced Economies. A Comparative Analysis of Its Implications for Economic Growth*, Aldershot and Brookfield: Avebury.

Ehrenreich, B. (2002) *Nickle and Dimed. On (Not) Getting By in America*, New York: Henry Hold.

Erikson, R. and J.H. Goldthorpe (1993) *The Constant Flux. A Study of Class Mobility in Industrial Societies*, Oxford: Clarendon Press.

Esping-Andersen, G. (1985) *Politics against Markets. The Social Democratic Road to Power*, Princeton, NJ: Princeton University Press.

Esping-Andersen, G. (1990) *The Three Worlds of Welfare Capitalism*, Princeton, NJ: Princeton University Press.

Esping-Andersen, G. (ed.) (1993) *Changing Classes. Stratification and Mobility in Post-industrial Societies*, London: Sage Publications.

Esping-Andersen, G. (1999) *Social Foundations of Postindustrial Economies*, Oxford: Oxford University Press.

Etzioni, A. (1964) *Modern Organizations*, Englewood Cliffs, NJ: Prentice-Hall.

Etzioni, A. (1975) *A Comparative Analysis of Complex Organizations. On Power, Involvement, and Their Correlates*, revised and enlarged edn, New York: Free Press.

European Commission (2002) *The Social Situation in the European Union 2002*, Luxembourg: Eurostat and European Commission.

Faist, T. (2000) *The Volume and Dynamics of International Migration and Transnational Social Spaces*, Oxford: Oxford University Press.

Felstead, A. and N. Jewson (eds) (1999a) *Global Trends in Flexible Labour*, London: Macmillan.

Felstead, A. and N. Jewson (1999b) 'Flexible Labour and Non-Standard Employment: An Agenda of Issues', 1–20, in Felstead and Jewson (1999a).

Felstead, A. and N. Jewson (2000) *In Work, at Home. Towards an Understanding of Homeworking*, London: Routledge.

Ferguson, K.E. (1984) *The Feminist Case against Bureaucracy*, Philadelphia: Temple University Press.

Fevre, R. (1992) *The Sociology of Labour Markets*, Hemel Hempstead: Harvester Wheatsheaf.

Field, J. and M. Leicester (eds) (2000) *Lifelong Learning. Education across the Lifespan*, Florence, KY: Routledge.

Fisher, A.G.B. (1935) *The Clash of Progress and Security*, London: Macmillan.

Fligstein, N. (2002) *The Architecture of Markets. An Economic Sociology of Twenty-First-Century Capitalist Societies*, 2nd printing, Princeton, NJ: Princeton University Press.

Freeman, R.B. and L.F. Katz (1994) 'Rising Wage Inequality: The United States vs. Other Advanced Countries', 29–62, in R.B. Freeman (ed.) *Working Under Different Rules*, New York: Russel Sage Foundation.

Freidson, E. (1986) *Professional Powers. A Study of the Institutionalization of Formal Knowledge*, Chicago: Chicago University Press.

Freidson, E. (1994) *Professionalism Reborn. Theory, Prophecy, and Policy*, Cambridge: Polity Press.

Freidson, E. (2001) *Professionalism. The Third Logic*, Chicago: University of Chicago Press.

Furåker, B. (1986) *Stat och arbetsmarknad. Studier i svensk rörlighetspolitik*, 3rd edn, Lund: Arkiv.

Furåker, B. (1987) *Stat och offentlig sektor*, Stockholm: Rabén & Sjögren.

Furåker, B. (2000) 'Offentligt och privat anställdas upplevelser av sitt arbete', *Arbetsmarknad & Arbetsliv* 6(1): 33–47.

Furåker, B. (2002) 'Is High Unemployment Due to Welfare State Protection? Lessons from the Swedish Experience', 123–42, in J.G. Andersen, J. Clasen, W. van Oorschot and K. Halvorsen (eds) *Europe's New State of Welfare. Unemployment, Employment Policies and Citizenship*, Bristol: Policy Press.

Furåker, B. (2003) 'Post-industrial Profiles. North American, Scandinavian and Other Western Labor Markets', in T.B. Boje and B. Furåker (eds) *Post-industrial Labour Markets. Profiles of North America and Scandinavia*, London: Routledge.

Furåker, B. and T. Berglund (2003) 'Are the Unions Still Needed? On Employees' Views of Their Relationship to Unions and Employers', *Journal of Economic and Industrial Democracy* 24(4): 573–94.

Furåker, B. and R. Lindqvist (2003) 'The Welfare State and Labour Market Policies', 77–95, in T.B. Boje and B. Furåker (eds) *Post-industrial Labour Markets. Profiles of North America and Scandinavia*, London: Routledge.

Furnham, A. (1982) 'Explanations for Unemployment in Britain', *European Journal of Social Psychology* 12(4): 335–52.

Galenson, W. (1994) *Trade Union Growth and Decline. An International Study*, Westport, CT: Praeger.

Gallie, D. (1994) 'Are the Unemployed an Underclass? Some Evidence from the Social Change and Economic Life Initiative', *Sociology* 28(2): 737–57.

Gallie, D. and S. Alm (2000) 'Unemployment, Gender, and Attitudes to Work', 109–33, in D. Gallie and S. Paugam (eds) *Welfare Regimes and the Experience of Unemployment in Europe*, Oxford: Oxford University Press.

Gallie, D. and S. Paugam (2000) 'The Experience of Unemployment in Europe: The Debate', 1–22, in D. Gallie and S. Paugam (eds) *Welfare Regimes and the Experience of Unemployment in Europe*, Oxford: Oxford University Press.

Gallie, D., M. White, Y. Cheng and M. Tomlinson (1998) *Restructuring the Employment Relationship*, Oxford: Oxford University Press.

Ganzeboom, H.B.G, D.J. Treiman and W.C. Ultee (1991) 'Comparative Intergenerational Stratification Research: Three Generations and Beyond', *Annual Review of Sociology* 17: 277–302.

Gellerman, S.W. (1963) *Motivation and Productivity*, New York: American Management Association.

Gellerman, S.W. (1998) *How People Work: Psychological Approaches to Management Problems*, Westport, CT: Quorum Books.

Germani, G. (1980) *Marginality*, New Brunswick, NJ: Transaction Books.

Gershuny, J. (1978) *After Industrial Society? The Emerging Self-service Economy*, London and Basingstoke: Macmillan.

Glotz, P. (1984) *Die Arbeit der Zuspitzung. Über die Organisation einer regierungsfähigen Linken*, Berlin: Siedler Verlag.

Glotz, P. (1985) *Manifest für eine Neue Europäische Linke*, Berlin: Siedler Verlag.

Goffman, E. (1963) *Stigma. Notes on the Management of Spoiled Identity*, Englewood Cliffs, NJ: Prentice-Hall.

Goldfield, M. (1987) *The Decline of Organized Labor in the United States*, Chicago: University of Chicago Press.

Goldthorpe, J.H. (1982) 'On the Service Class, Its Formation and Future', 162–85, in A. Giddens and G. Mackenzie (eds) *Social Class and the Division of Labour. Essays in Honour of Ilya Neustadt*, Cambridge: Cambridge University Press.

Goldthorpe, J.H. (in collaboration with C. Llewellyn and C. Payne) (1987) *Social Mobility and Class Structure in Modern Britain*, 2nd edn, Oxford: Clarendon Press.

Goldthorpe, J.H. (2000) *On Sociology. Numbers, Narratives, and the Integration of Research and Theory*, Oxford: Oxford University Press.

Goldthorpe, J.H., and K. Hope (1974) *The Social Grading of Occuaptions. A New Approach and Scale*, Oxford: Oxford University Press/Clarendon Press.

Goldthorpe, J.H., D. Lockwood, F. Bechhofer and J. Platt (1968) *The Affluent Worker: Industrial Attitudes and Behaviour*, Cambridge: Cambridge University Press.

Gordon, C. (1987) 'The Soul of the Citizen: Max Weber and Michel Foucault on Rationality and Government', 293–316, in S. Whimster and S. Lash (eds) *Max Weber, Rationality and Modernity*, London: Allen and Unwin.

Gordon, C. (1991) 'Governmental Rationality: an Introduction', 1–51, in G. Burchell, C. Gordon and P. Miller (eds) *The Foucault Effect: Studies in Governmentality*, Hemel Hempstead: Harvester Wheatsheaf.

Gordon, D.M. (1972) *Theories of Poverty and Unemployment. Orthodox, Radical, and Dual Labor Market Perspectives*, Lexington, MA: Lexington Books.

Gordon, D.M., R. Edwards and M. Reich (1982) *Segmented Work, Divided Workers: The Historical Transformation of Labor in the United States*, Cambridge: Cambridge University Press.

Gordon, M.M. (1963) *Social Class in American Sociology*, New York: McGraw-Hill.

Gorz, A. (1982) *Farewell to the Working Class: An Essay on Post-Industrial Socialism*, London: Pluto Press.

Gorz, A. (1985) *Paths to Paradise: On the Liberation from Work*, London: Pluto Press.

Gorz, A. (1999) *Reclaiming Work. Beyond the Wage-Based Society*, Cambridge: Polity Press.

Gouldner, A.W. (1954) *Patterns of Industrial Bureaucracy*, Glencoe, IL: Free Press.

Gouldner, A.W. (1979) *The Future of Intellectuals and the Rise of the New Class*, London and Basingstoke: Macmillan.

Gowan, P. (1999) *The Global Gamble. Washington's Faustian Bid for World Dominance*, London: Verso.

Granovetter, M. (1981) 'Toward a Sociological Theory of Income Differences', 11–47, in I. Berg (ed.) *Sociological Perspectives on Labor Markets*, New York: Academic Press.

Granovetter, M. (1995) *Getting a Job. A Study of Contacts and Careers*, 2nd edn, Chicago and London: University of Chicago Press.

Habermas, J. (1973) *Legitimationsprobleme im Spätkapitalismus*, Frankfurt am Main: Suhrkamp.

Hakim, C. (1996) *Key Issues in Women's Work. Female Heterogeneity and the Polarisation of Women's Employment*, London and Atlantic Highlands, NJ: Athlone Press.

Hall, J.H. (ed.) (1997) *Reworking Class*, Ithaca and London: Cornell University Press.

Hamermesh, D.S. (1979) 'Entitlement Effects, Unemployment Insurance and Unemployment Spells', *Economic Inquiry* 17(3): 317–32.

Hamermesh, D.S. (1980) 'Unemployment Insurance and Labor Supply', *International Economic Review* 21: 517–27.

Harrison, B. and B. Bluestone (1988) *The Great U-Turn. Corporate Restructuring and the Polarizing of America*, New York: Basic Books.

Hatt, P.K. (1950) 'Occupation and Social Stratification', *American Journal of Sociology* 55(6): 533–43.

Hedberg, M. (1967) *The Process of Labor Turnover*, Stockholm: Swedish Council for Personnel Administration.

Held, D. and A. McGrew (2002) *Globalization/Anti-Globalization*, Cambridge: Polity Press.

Held, D. and A. McGrew (eds) (2003a) *The Global Transformations Reader. An Introduction to the Globalization Debate*, 2nd edn, Cambridge: Polity Press.

Held, D. and A. McGrew (2003b) 'The Great Globalization Debate: An Introduction', 1–50, in Held and McGrew (2003a).

Held, D., A. McGrew, D. Goldblatt and J. Perraton (1999) *Global Transformations. Politics, Economics and Culture*, Stanford, CA: Stanford University Press.

Herod, A. (2001) *Labor Geographies. Workers and the Landscape of Capitalism*, New York: Guilford Press.

Hirschman, A.O. (1970) *Exit, Voice, and Loyalty. Responses to Decline in Firms, Organizations, and States*, Cambridge, MA: Harvard University Press.

Hirst, P. and G. Thompson (1999) *Globalization in Question: The International Economy and the Possibilities of Governance*, 2nd edn, Cambridge: Polity Press.

Hochschild, A.R. (1983) *The Managed Heart. Commercialization of Human Feeling*, Berkeley and Los Angeles: University of California Press.

Holmlund, B. (1984) *Labor Mobility. Studies of Labor Turnover and Migration in the Swedish Labor Market*, Stockholm: Research Institute of Industrial Economics (IUI).

Homans, G.C. (1951) *The Human Group*, London: Routledge & Kegan Paul.

Hudson, M. (2002) 'Flexibility and the Reorganization of Work', 39–60, in B. Burchell, D. Lapido and F. Wilkinson (eds) *Job Insecurity and Work Intensification*, London and New York: Routledge.

Huijgen, F. (in collaboration with J. Smith, M. Latta and A. Parent-Thirion) (2000) *Self-Employment: Choice or Necessity?*, Dublin: European Foundation for the Improvement of Living and Working Conditions.

Hunt, J. (1996) *Has Work-Sharing Worked in Germany?*, Cambridge, MA: National Bureau of Economic Research.

Hyman, R. (1992) 'Trade Unions and the Disaggregation of the Working Class', 150–68, in M. Regini (ed.) *The Future of Labour Movements*, London: Sage Publications.

Hyman, R. (1999) 'Imagined Solidarities: Can Trade Unions Resist Globalization?', 94–115, in P. Leisink (ed.) *Globalization and Labor Relations*, Cheltenham: Edward Elgar.

Hyman, R. and I. Brough (1975) *Social Values and Industrial Relations. A Study of Fairness and Equality*, Oxford: Blackwell.

Jacobs, J.A. (1983) 'Industrial Sector and Career Mobility Reconsidered', *American Sociological Review* 47: 415–21.

Jacobs, J.A. and R.L. Breiger (1994) 'Careers, Industries, and Occupations. Industrial Segmentation Reconsidered', 43–63, in G. Farkas and P. England (eds) *Industries, Firms, and Jobs. Sociological and Economic Approaches*, expanded edn, New York: Aldine de Gruyter.

Jensen, M.C. and W.H. Meckling (1976) 'Theory of the Firm: Managerial Behavior, Agency Costs and Ownership Structure', *Journal of Financial Economics* 3: 305–60.

Jonsson, D. (2005) *Flexibility, Stability and Related Concepts*, unpublished manuscript, Göteborg University: Department of Sociology.

Jonsson, J.O. (1999) 'Explaining Gender Differences in Educational Choice: An Empirical Assessment of a Rational Choice Model', *European Sociological Review* 15: 391–404.

Kalleberg, A.L. and A.B. Sørensen (1979) 'The Sociology of Labor Markets', *Annual Review of Sociology* 5: 351–79.

Kanter, R.M. (1990) *When Giants Learn to Dance. Mastering the Challenge of Strategy, Management, and Careers in the 1990s*, New York: Simon & Schuster.

Karlsson, J. Ch. (1983) 'Yrken', 168–88, in J. Ch. Karlsson (ed.) *Om lönearbete. En bok i arbetssociologi*, Stockholm: Norstedts.

Karlsson, J. Ch. and B. Eriksson (2000) *Flexibla arbetsplatser och arbetsvillkor. En empirisk prövning av en retorisk figur*, Lund: Arkiv.

Kelly, J. (1998) *Rethinking Industrial Relations. Mobilization, Collectivism and Long Waves*, London: Routledge.

Kelly, J. and J. Waddington (1995) 'New Prospects for British Labour', *Organization* 2 (3/4): 415–26.

Kenworthy, L. (2004) *Egalitarian Capitalism: Jobs, Incomes, and Growth in Affluent Countries*, New York: Russel Sage Foundation.

Kern, H. and M. Schumann (1990) *Das Ende der Arbeitsteilung? Rationalisierung in der industriellen Produktion*, 4th edn, München: G.H. Beck.

Kerr, C. (1977) *Labor Markets and Wage Determination. The Balkanization of Labor Markets and Other Essays*, Berkeley and Los Angeles: University of California Press.

Kerr, C., J.T. Dunlop, F.H. Harbison and C.A. Myers (1960) *Industrialism and Industrial Man. The Problems of Labor and Management in Economic Growth*, Cambridge, MA: Harvard University Press.

King, R. and G. Kendall (2004) *The State, Democracy and Civilization*, Basingstoke: Palgrave Macmillan.

Kjellberg, A. (2001) *Fackliga organisationer och medlemmar i dagens Sverige*, 2nd edn, Lund: Arkiv.

Kjellberg, A. (2002) 'Ett nytt fackligt landskap – i Sverige och utomlands' *Arkiv* 86–7: 44–96.

Kleinbeck, U., H.-H. Quast, H. Thierry and H. Häcker (eds) (1990) *Work Motivation*, Hillsdale, NJ: Lawrence Erlbaum.

Komarovsky, M. (1973) *The Unemployed Man and His Family. The Effect of Unemployment upon the Status of the Man in Fifty-nine Families*, New York: Octagon Books.

Konrád, G. and Szelényi, I. (1979) *The Intelligentsia on the Road to Class Power. A Sociological Study on the Role of the Intelligentsia in Socialism*, Brighton: Harvester Press.

Korpi, W. (1978) *The Working Class in Welfare Capitalism. Work, Unions and Politics in Sweden*, London: Routledge & Kegan Paul.

Korpi, W. (1983) *The Democratic Class Struggle*, London: Routledge & Kegan Paul.

Korpi, W. (2002) 'The Great Trough in Unemployment: A Long-term View of Unemployment, Inflation, Strikes, and the Profit/Wage Ratio', *Politics & Society* 30(3): 365–426.

Korpi, W. and J. Palme (2003) 'New Politics and Class Politics in the Context of Austerity and Globalization: Welfare State Regress in 18 Countries, 1975–95', *American Political Science Review* 97(3): 426–46.

Kumar, K. (1988) *The Rise of Modern Society. Aspects of the Social and Political Development of the West*, Oxford: Blackwell.

Larson, M.S. (1977) *The Rise of Professionalism. A Sociological Analysis*, Berkeley: University of California Press.

Lash, S. and B. Wynne (1992) 'Introduction', 1–8, in Beck (1992).

Legge, K. (1995) *Human Resource Management. Rhetorics and Realities*, Basingstoke: Palgrave.

Lewis, J. (ed.) (1997) *Lone Mothers in European Welfare Regimes: Shifting Policy Logics*, London: Jessica Kingley.

Lilja, R. and U. Hämäläinen (2001) *Working Time Preferences at Different Phases of Life*, Dublin: European Foundation for the Improvement of Living and Working Conditions.

Lincoln, J.R. and A.L. Kalleberg (1990) *Culture, Control, and Commitment. A Study of Work Organization and Work Attitudes in the United States and Japan*, Cambridge: Cambridge University Press.

Lipset, S.M. and R. Bendix (1959) *Social Mobility in Industrial Society*, Berkeley and Los Angeles: University of California Press.

Lister, R. (1994) '"She Has Other Duties" – Women, Citizenship and Social Security', 31–44, in S. Baldwin and J. Falkingham (eds) *Social Security and Social Change: New Challenges to the Beveridge Model*, New York: Harvester Wheatsheaf.

Lister, R. (2003) *Citizenship: Feminist Perspectives*, 2nd edn, London: Palgrave Macmillan.

Lødemel, I. and H. Trickey (eds) (2001a) *'An Offer You Can't Refuse'. Workfare in International Perspective*, Bristol: Policy Press.

Lødemel, I. and H. Trickey (2001b) 'A New Contract for Social Assistance', 1–39, in Lødemel and Trickey (2001a).

Lovering, J. (1994) 'Employers, the Sex-Typing of Jobs, and Economic Restructuring', 328–65, in A.M. Scott (ed.) *Gender Segregation and Social Change. Men and Women in Changing Labour Markets*, Oxford: Oxford University Press.

Lukes, S. (1974) *Power: A Radical View*, London: Macmillan.

Lysgaard, S. (1961) *Arbeiderkollektivet. En studie i de underordnedes sosiologi*, Oslo: Universitetsforlaget.

MacDonald, K.M. (1995) *The Sociology of Professions*, London: Sage Publications.

Machlup, F. (1962) *The Production and Distribution of Knowledge in the United States*, Princeton, NJ: Princeton University Press.

Magill, F.N. (ed.) (1995) *International Encyclopedia of Sociology* 1, London and Chicago: Fitzroy Dearborn Publishers.

March, J.G. and H.A. Simon (in collaboration with H. Guetzkow) (1958) *Organizations*, New York: John Wiley.

Marshall, G. (1997) *Repositioning Class. Social Inequality in Industrial Societies*, London: Sage Publications.

Marshall, G., A. Swift and S. Roberts (1997) *Against the Odds? Social Class and Social Justice in Industrial Societies*, Oxford: Clarendon Press.

Martin, B. (1993) *In the Public Interest? Privatisation and Public Sector Reform*, London: Zed Books.

Martin, J.P. (2000) 'What Works among Active Labour Market Policies: Evidence from OECD Countries' Experiences', *OECD Economic Studies* 30: 79–113.

Martin, J.P. and D. Grubb (2001) *What Works and for Whom: A Review of OECD Countries' Experiences with Active Labour Market Policies*, Uppsala: Office of Labour Market Policy Evaluation, Working Paper 2001: 14.

Marx, K. (1933) *Wage-Labour and Capital*, New York: International Publishers.

Marx, K. (1963) *Theories of Surplus-Value*, Part I, Moscow: Progress Publishers.

Marx, K. (1971) *A Contribution to the Critique of Political Economy*, London: Lawrence & Wishart.

Marx, K. (1976) *The Poverty of Philosophy*, 105–212, in K. Marx and F. Engels, *Collected Works* 6, London: Lawrence & Wishart.

Marx, K. (1996) *Capital. A Critique of Political Economy* (volume I), in K. Marx and F. Engels, *Collected Works* 35, London: Lawrence & Wishart.

Marx, K. (1998) *Capital. A Critique of Political Economy* (volume III), in K. Marx and F. Engels, *Collected Works* 37, London: Lawrence & Wishart.

Marx, K. and F. Engels (1998) *The Communist Manifesto*, London: Verso.

Maslow, A.H. (1970) *Motivation and Personality*, New York: McGraw-Hill.

Mayes, D.G., J. Berghman and R. Salais (eds) (2001) *Social Exclusion and European Policy*, Cheltenham: Edward Elgar.

McGregor, D. (1985) *The Human Side of Enterprise*, New York: Harper & Row.

Meager, N. (1992) 'Does Unemployment Lead to Self-Employment', *Small Business Economics* 4: 87–103.

Meager, N. (1994) 'Self-Employment Schemes for the Unemployed in the European Community. The Emergence of a New Institution and Its Evaluation', 183–242, in G. Schmid (ed.) *Labor Market Institutions in Europe. A Socioeconomic Evaluation of Performance*, New York: M.E. Sharpe.

Merton, R.K. (1964) *Social Theory and Social Structure*, revised and enlarged edn, Toronto: Collier-Macmillan.

Meulders, D. and L. Wilkin (1987) 'Labour Market Flexibility: Critical Introduction to the Analysis of a Concept', *Labour and Society* 12(1): 3–17.

Michels, R. (1962) *Political Parties. A Sociological Study of the Oligarchical Tendencies of Modern Democracy*, New York: Collier Books.

Milgate, M. (2001) *Alliances, Outsourcing, and the Lean Organization*, Westport, CT: Quorum Books.

Miliband, R. (1969) *The State in Capitalist Society*, New York: Basic Books.

Miliband, R. (1972) 'Reply to Nicos Poulantzas', 253–62, in R. Blackburn (ed.) *Ideology in Social Science. Readings in Critical Social Theory*, London: Fontana.

Miliband, R. (1973) 'Poulantzas and the Capitalist State', *New Left Review* 82: 83–92.

Mills, C.W. (1956) *White Collar. The American Middle Classes*, New York: Oxford University Press.

Mingione, E. (ed.) (1996) *Urban Poverty and the Underclass. A Reader*, Oxford: Blackwell.

Ministry of Finance, Denmark (1998) 'Availability Criteria in Selected OECD-Countries', Working Paper 6.

Momsen, J.H. (ed.) (1999) *Gender, Migration and Domestic Service*, London: Routledge.

Morris, L. (1994) *Dangerous Classes. The Underclass and Social Citizenship*, London and New York: Routledge.

Muffels, R.J.A., P. Tsakloglou and D.G. Mayes (eds) (2002) *Social Exclusion in European Welfare States*, Cheltenham: Edward Elgar.

Naisbitt, J. and P. Aburdene (1990) *Megatrends 2000: Ten New Directions for the 1990s*, New York: William Morrow.

Nickell, S. and R. Layard (1999) 'Labor Market Institutions and Economic Performance', 3029–84, in O. Ashenfelter and D. Card (eds) *Handbook of Labor Economics* 3C, Amsterdam: Elsevier.

Nielsen, K. and R. Ware (eds) (1997a) *Exploitation*, New Jersey: Humanities Press.

Nielsen, K. and R. Ware (1997b) 'Introduction. What Exploitation Comes to', in Nielsen and Ware (1997a).

Nolan, J. (2002) 'The Intensification of Everyday Life', 112–36, in Burchell, Lapido and Wilkinson (2002).

Noon, M. and P. Blyton (2002) *The Realities of Work*, 2nd edn, Basingstoke: Palgrave Macmillan.

Nordenmark, M. (1999) *Unemployment, Employment Commitment and Well-being*, Umeå University: Department of Sociology.

North, C.C. and P.K. Hatt (1949) 'Jobs and Occupations: A Popular Evaluation', 464–73, in L. Wilson and W.L. Kolb (eds) *Sociological Analysis. An Introductory Text and Case Book*, New York: Harcourt, Brace & Co.

Nozick, R. (1974) *Anarchy, State, and Utopia*, New York: Basic Books.

O'Connor, J. (1973) *The Fiscal Crisis of the State*, New York: St Martin's Press.

O'Connor, J.S. and G.M. Olsen (eds) (1998) *Power Resources Theory and the Welfare State. A Critical Approach*, Toronto: University of Toronto Press.

OECD (1994) *The OECD Jobs Study. Evidence and Explanations*, Part I-II, Paris.

OECD (1995) *Employment Outlook*, Paris.

OECD (1997) *Employment Outlook*, Paris.

OECD (1998) *Employment Outlook*, Paris.

OECD (1999) *Employment Outlook*, Paris.

OECD (2000) *Employment Outlook*, Paris.

OECD (2001) *Employment Outlook*, Paris.

Offe, C. (1984) *Contradictions of the Welfare State*, Cambridge, MA: MIT Press.

Offe, C. (1985) *Disorganized Capitalism. Contemporary Transformations of Work and Politics*, Cambridge: Polity Press.

Offe, C. (with U. Mückenberger and I. Ostner) (1996) 'A Basic Income Guaranteed by the State: A Need of the Moment in Social Policy', 201–21, in C. Offe *Modernity and the State. East, West*, Cambridge, MA: MIT Press.

Okun, A.M. (1975) *Equality and Efficiency. The Big Tradeoff*, Washington, D.C.: Brookings Institution.

Olson, M. (1965) *The Logic of Collective Action Public Goods and the Theory of Groups*, Cambridge, MA: Harvard University Press.

Ossowski, S. (1963) *Class Structure in the Social Consciousness*, London: Routledge & Kegan Paul.

Oxenstierna, S. (1990) *From Labour Shortage to Unemployment? The Soviet Labour Market in the 1980s*, Stockholm: Swedish Institute for Social Research.

Pakulski, J. and M. Waters (1996) *The Death of Class*, London: Sage Publications.

Parker, D. (ed.) (1998) *Privatisation in the European Union. Theory and Policy Perspectives*, London and New York: Routledge.

Parkin, F. (1979) *Marxism and Class Theory: A Bourgeois Critique*, London: Tavistock Publications.

Parnes, H.S. (1954) *Research on Labor Mobility. An Appraisal of Research Findings in the United States*, New York: Social Science Research Council.

Parnes, H.S. (1968) 'Markets and Mobility', 481–7, in D.L. Sills (ed.) *International Encyclopedia of the Social Sciences* 8, New York: Macmillan and Free Press.

Parreñas, R.S. (2001) *Servants of Globalization. Women, Migration and Domestic Work*, Stanford, CA: Stanford University Press.

Parsons, T. (1951) *The Social System*, Toronto: Collier-Macmillan.

Parsons, T. (1964) *Essays in Sociological Theory*, revised edn, New York: Free Press.

Parsons, T. and N.J. Smelser (1956) *Economy and Society. A Study in the Integration of Economic and Social Theory*, London: Routledge & Kegan Paul.

Paugam, S. and H. Russell (2000) 'The Effects of Employment Precarity and Unemployment on Social Isolation', 243–64, in D. Gallie and S. Paugam (eds) *Welfare Regimes and the Experience of Unemployment in Europe*, Oxford: Oxford University Press.

Perrow, C. (1986) *Complex Organizations: A Critical Essay*, 3rd edn, New York: McGraw-Hill.

Petras, J. and H. Veltmayer (2001) *Globalization Unmasked.Imperioaism in the 21st Century*, Halifax, NS: Fernwood Publishing.

Piore, M.J. (1975) 'Notes for a Theory of Labor Market Stratification', 125–50, in Edwards, Reich and Gordon (1975).

Piore, M.J. (1980) 'Dualism as a Response to Flux and Uncertainty', 23–54, in S. Berger and M.J. Piore (eds) *Dualism and Discontinuity in Industrial Societies*, Cambridge: Cambridge University Press.

Piore, M.J. and C.F. Sabel (1984) *The Second Industrial Divide: Possibilities for Prosperity*, New York: Basic Books.

Polanyi, K. (1957) *The Great Transformation. The Political and Economic Origins of Our Time*, Boston: Beacon Press.

Polsby, N.W. (1980) *Community Power and Political Theory: A Further Look at Problems of Evidence and Inference*, 2nd and enlarged edn, New Haven, CT: Yale University Press.

Poulantzas, N. (1972) 'The Problem of the Capitalist State', 238–53, in R. Blackburn (ed.) *Ideology in Social Science. Readings in Critical Social Theory*, London: Fontana.

Poulantzas, N. (1973a) 'On Social Classes', *New Left Review* 78: 27–54.

Poulantzas, N. (1973b) *Political Power and Social Classes*, London: New Left Books.

Poulantzas, N. (1978) *Classes in Contemporary Capitalism*, London: Verso.

Pringle, R. (1989) *Secretaries Talk. Sexuality, Power and Work*, London and New York: Verso.

Rantakeisu, U., B. Starrin and C. Hagquist (1997) 'Unemployment, Shame and Ill Health: An Exploratory Study', *Scandinavian Journal of Social Welfare* 6(1): 13–23.

Rees, M. (1973) *The Public Sector in the Mixed Economy*, London: Batsford.

Reich, R.B. (2002) *The Future of Success. Working and Living in the New Economy*, New York: Vintage Books.

Reilly, P. and P. Tamkin (1996) *Outsourcing: a Flexible Option for the Future?*, Brighton: Institute for Employment Studies.

Reiss, A.J. Jr (1961) *Occupations and Social Status*, New York: Free Press of Glencoe.

Reissert, B. and G. Schmid (1994) 'Unemployment Compensation and Active Labour Market Policy', 83–119, in G. Schmid (ed.) *Labor Market Institutions in Europe. A Socioeconomic Evaluation of Performance*, New York: M.E. Sharpe.

Rifkin, J. (1995) *End of Work: The Decline of the Global Labor Force and the Dawn of the Post-market Era*, New York: G.G. Putnam's Sons.

Robinson, P. (2000) 'Active Labour-market Policies: A Case of Evidence-based Policy-making?', *Oxford Review of Economic Policy* 16(1): 13–26.

Roemer, J.E. (1982) *A General Theory of Exploitation and Class*, Cambridge, MA: Harvard University Press.

Roethlisberger, F.J. and W.J. Dickson (1939) *Management and the Worker. An Account of a Research Program Conducted by the Western Electric Company, Hawthorne Works, Chicago*, Cambridge, MA: Harvard University Press.

Ross, S.A. (1974) 'On the Economic Theory of Agency and the Principle of Similarity', 215–37, in M.S. Balch, D. McFadden and S. Wu (eds) (1974) *Essays on Economic Behavior under Uncertainty*, New York: American Elsevier.

Rubery, J. *et al.* (1998) *Equal Pay in Europe? Closing the Gender Gap*, Basingstoke and London: Macmillan.

Rubery, J., S. Horrell and B. Burchell (1994), 'Part-time Work and Gender Inequality in the Labour Market', 205–34, in A.M. Scott (ed.) *Gender Segregation and Social Change*, Oxford: Oxford University Press.

Rubery, J., S. Smith, and C. Fagan (1999) *Women's Employment in Europe. Trends and Prospects*, London: Routledge.

Russel, H. and P. Barbieri (2000) 'Gender and the Experience of Unemployment', 307–33, in D. Gallie and S. Paugam (eds) *Welfare Regimes and the Experience of Unemployment in Europe*, Oxford: Oxford University Press.

Saunders, P. and C. Harris (1994) *Privatization and Popular Capitalism*, Buckingham: Open University Press.

Savage, M. (2000) *Class Analysis and Social Transformation*, Buckingham: Open University Press.

Savage, M. (2001) 'Class Identity in Contemporary Britain: The Demise of Collectivism?', 79–100, in G. van Gyes, H. de Witte and P. Pasture (eds) *Can Class*

Still Unite? The Differentiated Work Force, Class Solidarity and Trade Unions, Aldershot and Burlington: Ashgate.

Sayer, A. and R. Walker (1992) *The New Social Economy: Reworking the Division of Labour*, Oxford: Blackwell.

Scheff, T.J. (1990) *Microsociology: Discourse, Emotion, and Social Structure*, Chicago: University of Chicago Press.

Scheff, T.J. (1997) *Emotions, the Social Bond, and Human Reality: Part/Whole Analysis*, Cambridge: Cambridge University Press.

Schiller, H.I. (1996) *Information Inequality. The Deepening of Social Crises in America*, New York and London: Routledge.

Selznick, P. (1949) *TVA and the Grassroots. A Study in the Sociology of Formal Organizations*, Berkeley: University of California Publications in Culture and Society.

Sengenberger, W. (ed.) (1978) *Der gespaltene Arbeitsmarkt – Probleme der Arbeitsmarktsegmentation*, Frankfurt and New York: Campus Verlag.

Sengenberger, W. (1987) *Struktur und Funktionsweise von Arbeitsmärkten. Die Bundesrepublik Deutschland im internationalen Vergleich*, Frankfurt and New York: Campus Verlag.

Shragge, E. (ed.) (1997) *Workfare. Ideology for a New Under-Class*, Toronto: Garamond Press.

Singelmann, J. (1978) *From Agriculture to Services: The Transformation of Industrial Employment*, Beverly Hills, CA: Sage Publications.

Sjöberg, O. (2000) 'Unemployment and Unemployment Benefits in the OECD 1960–1990 – An Empirical Test of Neo-classical Economic Theory', *Work, Employment, and Society* 14(1): 51–76.

Skrentny, J.D. (1996) *The Ironies of Affirmative Action. Politics, Culture, and Justice in America*, Chicago: University of Chicago Press.

Stalker, P. (1994) *The Work of Strangers. A Survey of International Labour Migration*, Geneva: International Labour Office.

Standing, G. (1999) *Global Labour Flexibility. Seeking Distributive Justice*, London: Macmillan Press and New York: St Martin's Press.

Standing, G. (2002) *Beyond the New Paternalism. Basic Security as Equality*, London: Verso.

Stehr, N. (2002) *Knowledge and Economic Conduct. The Social Foundations of the Modern Economy*, Toronto: University of Toronto Press.

Stephens, J.D. (1979) *The Transition from Capitalism to Socialism*, Urbana and Chicago: University of Illinois Press.

Stonier, T. (1983) *The Wealth of Information. A Profile of the Post-industrial Economy*, London: Methuen.

Storrie, D. (2002) *Temporary Agency Work in the European Union*, Dublin: European Foundation for the Improvement of Living and Working Conditions.

Strandh, M. (2000) *Varying Unemployment Experiences? The Economy and Mental Well-being*, Umeå University: Department of Sociology.

Svallfors, S. (2004) *Klassamhällets kollektiva medvetande. Klass och attityder i jämförande perspektiv*, Umeå: Borea.

Sørensen, A.B. and A.L. Kalleberg (1981) 'An Outline of a Theory of the Matching of Persons to Jobs', 49–74, in I. Berg (ed.) *Sociological Perspectives on Labor Markets*, New York: Academic Press.

Therborn, G. (1976) *Science, Class and Society. On the Formation of Sociology and Historical Materialism*, London: Verso.

Therborn, G. (1980) *The Ideology of Power and the Power of Ideology*, London: Verso.

Thompson, P. and D. McHugh (1995) *Work Organisations. A Critical Introduction*, 2nd edn, Basingstoke and London: Macmillan.

Thurow, L.C. (1975) *Generating Inequality. Mechanisms of Distribution in the US Economy*, New York: Basic Books.

Tilly, C. (1978) *From Mobilization to Revolution*, Reading, MA: Addison-Wesley.

Tilly, C. and C. Tilly (1998) *Work under Capitalism*, Boulder, CO: Westview Press.

Toffler, A. (1980) *The Third Wave*, London: William Collins.

Touraine, A. (1971) *The Post-industrial Society. Tomorrow's Social History: Classes, Conflicts and Culture in the Programmed Society*, New York. Random House.

van den Berg, A. (1988) *The Immanent Utopia. From Marxism on the State to the State of Marxism*, Princeton, NJ: Princeton University Press.

van den Berg, A., B. Furåker and L. Johansson (1997) *Labour Market Regimes and Patterns of Flexibility. A Sweden – Canada Comparison*, Lund: Arkiv.

Van Parijs, P. (ed.) (1992) *Arguing for Basic Income: Ethical Foundations for a Radical Reform*, London: Verso.

Van Ruysseveldt, J. and J. Visser (1996) (eds) *Industrial Relations in Europe. Traditions and Transitions*, London: Sage Publications.

Visser, J. (1996). 'Traditions and Transitions in Industrial Relations: A European View', 1–41, in Van Ruysseveldt and Visser (1996).

Vogler. C. (1994) 'Segregation, Sexism, and Labour Supply', 39–79, in A.M. Scott (ed.) *Gender Segregation and Social Change. Men and Women in Changing Labour Markets*, Oxford: Oxford University Press.

Vroom, V. (1964) *Work and Motivation*, New York: Wiley.

Walker, P. (ed.) (1979) *Between Labour and Capital*, Brighton: Harvester Press.

Warner, W.L. (ed.) (1963) *Yankee City*, abridged edn, New Haven, CT: Yale University Press.

Webb, S. and B. Webb (1897) *Industrial Democracy*, Vols 1–2, London: Longmans, Green & Co.

Weber, M. (1930) *The Protestant Ethic and the Spirit of Capitalism*, London: Unwin University Books.

Weber, M. (1978) *Economy and Society. An Outline of Interpretive Sociology* (ed. by G. Roth and C. Wittich), two vols, Berkeley: University of California Press.

Webster, F. (2002) *Theories of the Information Society*, 2nd edn, London and New York: Routledge.

Weiss, L. (1998) *The Myth of the Powerless State. Governing the Economy in a Global Era*, Cambridge: Polity Press.

Western, B. (1998) 'Institutions and the Labor Market', 224–43, in M.C. Brinton and V. Nee (eds) *The New Institutionalism in Sociology*, New York: Russel Sage Foundation.

Whelan, B.J. and C.T. Whelan (1995) 'In What Sense Is Poverty Multidimensional?', 29–48, in G. Room (ed.) *Beyond the Threshold: The Measurement and Analysis of Social Exclusion*, Bristol: Policy Press.

Whitfield, D. (1992) *The Welfare State. Privatisation, Deregulation, Commercialisation of Public Services: Alternative Strategies for the 1990s*, London: Pluto Press.

Wilkinson, F. (ed.) (1981) *The Dynamics of Labour Market Segmentation*, London: Academic Press.

Wilson, S. (ed.) (2004) *The Struggle over Work. The 'End of Work' and Employment Options of Post-industrial Societies*, London: Routledge.

Wilson, W.J. (ed.) (1993) *The Ghetto Underclass. Social Science Perspectives*, Newbury Park, CA, and London: Sage Publications.

Witz, A. (1992) *Professions and Patriarchy*, London and New York: Routledge.

Womack, J.P., D.T. Jones and D. Roos (1990) *The Machine That Changed the World*, New York: Rawson Associates.

Wright, E.O. (1978) *Class, Crisis and the State*, London: New Left Books.

Wright, E.O. (1985) *Classes*, London: Verso.

Wright, E.O. (1989) 'Rethinking, Once Again, the Concept of Class Structure', 269–348, in E.O. Wright *et al.* (eds) *The Debate on Class*, London: Verso.

Wright, E.O. (1994) *Interrogating Inequality. Essays on Class Analysis, Socialism and Marxism*, London and New York: Verso.

Wright, E.O. (1997) *Class Counts. Comparative Studies in Class Analysis*, Cambridge: Cambridge University Press.

Zoll, R. (1996) 'Modernization, Trade Unions and Solidarity', 77–88, in P. Leisink, J. van Leemput and J. Vilrokx (eds) *The Challenges to Trade Unions in Europe. Innovation or Adaption*, Cheltenham: Edward Elgar.

Index